An Introduction to Statistics and Data Analysis Using Stata®

From Research Design to Final Report

To our parents, Betty, Joe, Ginny, and Steve

An Introduction to Statistics and Data Analysis Using Stata®

From Research Design to Final Report

Lisa Daniels
Washington College

Nicholas Minot
International Food Policy Research Institute

Los Angeles | London | New Delhi
Singapore | Washington DC | Melbourne

For Information:

SAGE Publications, Inc.
2455 Teller Road
Thousand Oaks, California 91320
E-mail: order@sagepub.com

SAGE Publications Ltd.
1 Oliver's Yard
55 City Road
London, EC1Y 1SP
United Kingdom

SAGE Publications India Pvt. Ltd.
B 1/I 1 Mohan Cooperative Industrial
Area
Mathura Road, New Delhi 110 044
India

SAGE Publications Asia-Pacific Pte. Ltd.
18 Cross Street #10-10/11/12
China Square Central
Singapore 048423

Acquisitions Editor: Leah Fargotstein
Editorial Assistant: Claire Laminen
Content Development Editor: Chelsea Neve
Production Editor: Karen Wiley
Copy Editor: QuADS Prepress Pvt. Ltd.
Typesetter: Integra
Proofreader: Scott Oney
Indexer: William Ragsdale
Cover Designer: Ginkhan Siam
Marketing Manager: Shari Countryman

Printed in the United States of America

Library of Congress Cataloging-in-Publication Data

Names: Daniels, Lisa, author.

Title: An introduction to statistics and data analysis using Stata : from research design to final report / Lisa Daniels, Washington College, Nicholas Minot, International Food Policy Research Institute, Washington, DC.

Description: First edition. | Thousand Oaks, California : SAGE, [2018] | Includes bibliographical references and index.

Identifiers: LCCN 2018035896 | ISBN 9781506371832 (Paperback : acid-free paper)

Subjects: LCSH: Stata. | Social sciences–Statistical methods–Computer programs. | Quantitative research–Computer programs.

Classification: LCC HA32 .D37 2018 | DDC 005.5/5–dc23 LC record available at https://lccn.loc.gov/2018035896

This book is printed on acid-free paper.

19 20 21 22 23 10 9 8 7 6 5 4 3 2 1

BRIEF CONTENTS

DETAILED CONTENTS

PREFACE

This book provides an introduction to statistics and data analysis using Stata, a statistical software package. It is intended to serve as a textbook for undergraduate courses in business, economics, sociology, political science, psychology, criminal justice, public health, and other fields that involve data analysis. However, it could also be useful in an introductory graduate course or for researchers interested in learning Stata.

The book was developed out of our experience in teaching statistics and data analysis to undergraduate students over 20 years, as well as giving training courses in Stata and survey methods in more than a dozen countries. Based on these experiences, we have included three features that we feel are an integral part of data analysis. First, the book provides an introduction to research design and data collection, including questionnaire design, sample selection, sampling weights, and data cleaning. These topics are an essential part of empirical research and provide students with the skills to conduct their own research and evaluate research carried out by others. Second, we emphasize the use of code or command files in Stata rather than the "point and click" menu features of the software. We believe that students should be taught to write programs that document their analysis, as this allows them to reproduce their work during follow-up analyses and facilitates collaborative work (we do, however, include brief instructions on the use of Stata menus for each command). Third, the book teaches students how to describe statistical results for technical and nontechnical audiences. Choosing the correct statistical tests and generating results is useless unless the researcher can explain the results to various audiences.

As mentioned above, this book uses Stata, a statistical software package, to implement the various statistical tests and analyses. Although SPSS is one of the most widely used statistical packages, the use of Stata is growing rapidly. Muenchen (2015) tracks the popularity of software using 11 measures and shows that the use of Stata and R are growing more rapidly than the use of SPSS and SAS. Both of us used SPSS for years but have since switched to Stata. While SPSS produces tables that are more publication-ready, Stata has a more powerful set of commands for statistical analysis (particularly regression analysis) as well as a growing library of user-written commands that are easily downloadable from within the Stata environment.

This book frames data analysis within the research process—identifying gaps in the literature, examining the theory, developing research questions, designing a questionnaire or using secondary data, analyzing the data, and writing the research paper. As such, it does not provide the same depth of treatment that books dedicated to research methods or statistical analysis might. However, we feel that providing an integrated approach to research methods, data analysis, and interpretation of results is a worthwhile trade-off, particularly for undergraduate students who might not otherwise get exposure to research methods. We also offer resources for students who are interested in exploring in greater depth any of the topics covered in this book.

FEATURES OF THE BOOK

The literature on teaching statistics emphasizes the challenges students face in learning how to apply statistics to solve problems, the difficulty in understanding published results, and the inability to communicate research results. We address these problems throughout the book, as illustrated by the features described below:

1. *Description of the research process in the first chapter*

   The first chapter is devoted to the steps in the research process. These steps include choosing a general area, identifying the gaps in the literature, examining the theory, developing a research question, designing a questionnaire or using secondary data, analyzing the data, and writing the research paper. By starting with the big picture, students have a frame of reference to guide them as they then learn in detail about these steps in the chapters that follow.

2. *Summary table at the start of each chapter that includes the research question, hypothesis, statistical procedure, and Stata code*

   Each chapter related to a statistical technique begins with a table that identifies the research question, the research hypothesis, the statistical procedure needed to test the hypothesis, the types of variables used, the assumptions of the test, and the relevant commands in Stata. This table serves as a quick reference guide and preview of what is to come in the chapter. It also reinforces the ability to apply statistics to solve problems.

3. *Box with news article related to a statistical procedure*

   Following the summary table described above, a portion of a newspaper article is included to illustrate the use of the statistical technique applied to real-world data. A brief discussion of the news article follows along with the necessary statistical method to test the hypothesis and a critique of potential flaws in the research design. This is designed to help students understand published results, judge their quality, and again apply statistics to real-world problems.

4. *Tables with real-world examples from six fields of study*

    Section 2 of each chapter related to a statistical technique covers the circumstances in which that particular technique is appropriate. This is done by giving examples of research questions from six fields along with the null hypothesis and types of variables needed for the test. This is intended to help students identify research questions and apply statistics to solve problems. It also illustrates that the skills related to statistical techniques are applicable across multiple disciplines.

5. *Application of statistical tests using relevant data*

    We demonstrate the application of statistical methods using data sets that are interesting and relevant to college students. For example, we use the data from the Admitted Student Questionnaire for 2014, which includes questions related to SAT scores, family incomes, and student opinions about the importance of college characteristics. We also use the data generated by the Education Trust at College Results Online, which covers all 4-year colleges in the United States and includes information on admissions statistics, student characteristics, and college characteristics. To examine violence and discipline in U.S. high schools, we use the 2015–2016 School Survey on Crime and Safety. We explore issues related to opioid abuse, other drugs, and alcohol using the National Survey on Drug Use and Health from 2015. Finally, we use the General Social Survey from 2016 to illustrate examples throughout the book and for the exercises.

6. *Exercises to practice techniques learned in each chapter*

    It is essential for students to practice data analysis on a regular basis in order to become proficient data analysts. This book contains more than 45 exercises that can be done in class or as homework problems. Instructors have access to the full answer key for each problem.

7. *Instructions using Stata commands and menus*

    As described earlier, the use of Stata code or command files allows students to document their work, reproduce the results, and collaborate with others during the research process. Menus are also illustrated for those professors who prefer to teach with the menus.

8. *Communicating the results*

   In each chapter related to a statistical test, we include a section called "Presenting the Results," in which we illustrate how to report the results for a nontechnical audience and for a scholarly journal with more technical language. In addition to these sections, the last chapter is devoted entirely to writing a research paper.

9. *Data collection project instructions*

   To facilitate the application of statistics to the real world, the book includes a week-by-week set of instructions to administer a group project in which students engage in a primary research project including questionnaire design, sample selection, analysis, and report writing. This is included as part of the instructor resources on the book's website, which is described below.

RESOURCES FOR INSTRUCTORS

The book has a companion website at https://study.sagepub.com/daniels1e. This website has the following resources available for instructors:

- Access to the data sets used throughout the book

- Two sets of answer keys to the homework problems: A full set with all answers and output and an abbreviated set for students to check their work as they complete their homework.

- Suggestions for managing the homework grading load

- Sample tests

- Week-by-week project instructions as described earlier

- Sample syllabus that includes a list of material covered in each class when taught by the authors.

- PowerPoint® slides to accompany each chapter

RESOURCES FOR STUDENTS

Students have access to the companion website at https://study.sagepub.com/danielsle. Student resources on the site include the following:

- Access to the data sets used throughout the book

- Electronic flash cards of definitions for all terms in the glossary

In addition to the resources on the website, Appendices 1, 2, 3, and 4 offer a reference guide to all Stata commands used throughout the book, a summary of the hypotheses and tests used in each chapter, a decision tree for using the right statistic, and decision rules for statistical significance, respectively.

STRUCTURE OF THE BOOK

As described above, Part One of the book is titled "The Research Process and Data Collection." In Chapter 1, we offer an overview of the research process by briefly describing the major steps involved at each stage. We then describe primary data collection in Chapter 2, including sampling frames, sample selection techniques, and sampling weights. In Chapter 3, we review the principles of questionnaire design along with ethical issues. In Part Two of the book, "Describing Data," we introduce Stata in Chapter 4, discuss methods for preparing and transforming data in Chapter 5, and cover descriptive statistics in Chapter 6. Part Three, "Testing Hypotheses," includes five chapters that cover the normal distribution followed by hypothesis testing related to a single mean, two means, analysis of variance, and the chi-square statistic. In Part Four, "Exploring Relationships," we cover correlation, linear regression, regression diagnostics, and logistic regression. Finally, in Part Five, a chapter is devoted to writing a research paper, including a detailed description of each section of a research paper with a special emphasis on reporting statistical results.

REFERENCES

Muenchen, R. (2015). *Stata's academic growth nearly as fast as R's*. Retrieved from https://r4stats.com/2015/05/11/statas-academic-growth/

ACKNOWLEDGMENTS

We are extremely grateful for the help that we received from numerous individuals while writing this book. Leah Fargotstein, our editor from Sage, was an absolute pleasure to work with throughout the process. She was encouraging, helpful, and knowledgeable. We also received help from other staff at Sage and QuADS Prepress Pvt. Ltd. Elizabeth Wells and Claire Laminen exchanged endless e-mails with us related to permissions needed for printing articles in the book. Shelly Gupta and Tori Mirsadjadi also provided guidance in our quest for permissions. We are grateful for the help from Chelsea Neve in developing the website for the book and extra resources for students, including PowerPoint slides and electronic flash cards. The marketing team at Sage, Susannah Goldes, Shari Countryman, Andrew Lee, and Heather Watters were crucial in helping with the launch of the book. Karen Wiley did an excellent job in overseeing the production of the book. We are also thankful for help with the cover design, indexing, typesetting, and proofreading from Ginkhan Siam, William Ragsdale, Integra, and Scott Oney. Finally, we are grateful to our copyeditors, Rajasree Ghosh and Rajeswari Krithivasan from QuADS, whose incredible attention to detail helped improve the quality of the book.

Staff and students from Washington College also deserve thanks. Jennifer Kaczmarczyk did the bulk of the work to get the permissions started, wading through e-mails, contracts, and phone calls to follow up. Benjamin Fizer, a Washington College student, spent more than 50 hours capturing every dialog box, figure, and output. He also read the entire book to help develop the glossary and changed all of the Stata code in the book to the correct format. Amanda Kramer, from the Miller Library, helped identify databases from the various fields covered in the book. We are also grateful to the students enrolled in the data analysis course who pointed out errors in the book.

We would also like to thank the administration at Washington College, which supported this project financially in a number of ways. The college funded travel to three conferences related to textbook writing and Stata, as well as two "research reassigned time" awards that allowed one of us (Lisa) to reduce her course load in two semesters along with funds to pay for a student assistant during those semesters.

Bill Rising from Stata Corporation deserves special thanks for going through the book and offering numerous suggestions to improve our Stata code and language related to statistics. Any remaining mistakes must have been introduced after Bill read the book since he did not miss anything!

We would also like to thank the people who reviewed the book over six rounds of revisions. Their attention to detail as well as the big picture helped us improve the book in countless ways.

Eileen M. Ahlin, *Penn State Harrisburg*
Rachel Allison, *Mississippi State University*
Matthew Burbank, *University of Utah*
Hwanseok Choi, *University of Southern Mississippi*
Mengyan Dai, *Old Dominion University*
Kimberlee Everson, *Western Kentucky University*
Wendy L. Hicks, *Ashford University*
Monica L. Mispireta, *Idaho State University*
Steven P. Nawara, *Lewis University*
Holona LeAnne Ochs, *Lehigh University*
Parina Patel, *Georgetown University*
John M. Shandra, *State University of New York at Stony Brook*
Janet P. Stamatel, *University of Kentucky*
Anna Yocom, *The Ohio State University*

Finally, we are grateful to our two children, Andrea and Alex, who patiently (and sometimes not-so-patiently) sat through numerous dinner discussions about statistics, Stata, and "the book." Although they appeared not to be listening, our secret hope is that it seeped into their subconscious and gave them the love of statistics and data analysis that we both have.

THE RESEARCH PROCESS AND DATA COLLECTION

PART ONE

THE RESEARCH PROCESS

Chapter Preview

Steps	Example
Choose a research area and read the literature	• Impact of social media on self-esteem and well-being among teens
Identify the gaps or ways to extend the literature	• Limited research on uses and consequences of social media use among adolescents • Lack of distinction between social and nonsocial Internet use
Examine the theory	• Human beings have a desire to protect and enhance their self-esteem. • Self-esteem is strongly related to well-being.
Develop your research questions and form hypotheses	• Does the frequency with which teens use networking sites have an impact on their self-esteem and well-being? • Does positive or negative feedback affect self-esteem?
Design a questionnaire or use secondary data to address your questions	• Online survey among adolescents between 10 and 19 years of age who have a profile on a social networking site
Analyze the data	• Descriptive statistics of frequency of usage and types of feedback received from peers • Regression analysis to determine impact on self-esteem

Write the research paper	• Introduction
	• Literature Review
	• Data and Methods
	• Results
	• Discussion
	• Conclusion

Source: Valkenburg, Peter, and Schouten (2006).

1.1 INTRODUCTION

Research is often described as the creation of knowledge. It begins with the construction of an argument that can be supported by evidence. As described by Greenlaw (2009), scholars then create a "conversation" in scholarly journals to discuss the argument. In many cases, scholars will identify gaps in the argument and offer alternate views or evidence. In other cases, scholars may forward or extend the argument by offering new insights or examine the same argument from a different angle. Another equally valid form of research is to replicate what others have done. This can be done by conducting the same research in a different region, in a different time period, over a longer time period, or with a different set of participants. All of these may validate the original argument or disprove it.

The process described above is known as the scientific method, which is defined in the *Oxford English Dictionary* as follows:

> A method or procedure that has characterized natural science since the 17th century, consisting in systematic observation, measurement, and experiment, and the formulation, testing, and modification of hypotheses.

In this chapter, we will provide an overview of the steps in the research process that are illustrated in the chapter preview—reading the literature, identifying the gaps, examining the theory, developing research questions, forming hypotheses, designing the questionnaire or using secondary data, analyzing the data, and writing the report. Although more detailed instructions for these steps are offered in later chapters, it is important to understand the process as a whole.

1.2 READ THE LITERATURE AND IDENTIFY GAPS OR WAYS TO EXTEND THE LITERATURE

Students typically think that research begins by simply creating a question without any prior reading or knowledge of the topic. It is possible to choose a general area that interests you such as poverty, pollution, sports, social media, criminal justice, and so on, without reading about the topic. Once the general area is chosen, however, you must begin reading the *literature*. The literature can be defined as a body of articles and books, written by experts and scholars, that has been *peer reviewed*. A peer review is when two to three scholars are asked to anonymously evaluate a manuscript's suitability for publication and either reject it or accept it, typically with revisions based on their recommendations.[1] Articles in the body of literature will cite other sources and will be written for an audience of fellow scholars. Nonscholarly materials, such as newspapers, trade and professional sources, letters to the editor, and opinion-based articles are not considered as part of the literature. They are sometimes used in a scholarly paper, but never as a sole source of information.

Most disciplines have their own databases with articles, book chapters, dissertations, and working papers from their field. Table 1.1 shows a list of the key databases in several fields.

TABLE 1.1 ● DATABASES OF SCHOLARLY LITERATURE FROM DIFFERENT FIELDS			
Field	**Database**	**Content**	**Website**
Criminal Justice	ProQuest Criminal Justice Database	A comprehensive database of U.S. and international criminal justice journals	www.proquest.com/products-services/pq_criminal_justice.html
	Criminal Justice Abstracts	Titles and abstracts for articles from most significant sources in the field	www.ebsco.com/products/research-databases/criminal-justice-abstracts
Economics	Econ Lit	Over 1,000 journals plus books, dissertations, working papers, and book reviews	www.aeaweb.org/econlit
Political Science	JSTOR	6,800 political science journals, books, and pamphlets	www.jstor.org/action/showJournals?discipline=43693417
	Academic Search Complete	340 full-text political science reference books and monographs and more than 44,000 full-text conference papers	www.ebscohost.com/academic/subjects/category/political-science

---

[1] The home page of a journal will indicate if and how articles are peer reviewed.

TABLE 1.1 ● (Continued)

Field	Database	Content	Website
Psychology	PsycINFO	Four million bibliographic records, including more than 2 million digital object identifiers to allow for direct linking to full-text psychology articles and literature. Indexing of more than 2,500 scholarly psychology journals	www.apa.org/psycinfo
Public Health	PubMed	Access to 12 million MEDLINE citations back to the 1950s	www.ncbi.nlm.nih.gov/pubmed
	PAIS	Political, social, and public policy issues	www.proquest.com
	Nexis Uni	15,000 news, business, and legal sources	www.lexisnexis.com
Sociology	Sociological Abstracts	Abstracts of sociology journal articles and citations to book reviews drawn from more than 1,800 serial publications and abstracts of books, book chapters, dissertations, and conference papers	http://proquest.libguides.com/SocAbs
	JSTOR	8,000 sociology journals, books, and pamphlets	www.jstor.org/action/showJournals?discipline=43693423
	Academic Search Complete	900 full-text sociology journals, abstracts for more than 1,500 "core" coverage journals, data from nearly 420 "priority" coverage journals and more than 2,900 "selective" coverage journals, and indexing for books/monographs, conference papers, and other nonperiodicals	www.ebscohost.com/academic/socindex

In all of these databases, you can type in keywords from areas that interest you. You can then peruse article titles and read abstracts to get a sense of the thought-provoking questions and research in your area of interest. Once you have found some key articles that zero in on your research interests, you can review earlier articles that were referenced by the key articles (backward citation searching) and search forward in time to see what other articles have cited your key articles since they were written. For example, if an article was written in 1995, you can find every article written since 1995 that has cited the original article. This can be done through Google Scholar, PubMed, Science Direct, Scopus, and Web of Science. As you find more articles related to your specific topic, you will find that the literature will indicate what has been done in your area of interest, what questions remain, and if there are gaps or contradictions in the literature. You can then identify your own research questions based on the contradictions or gaps in the literature or the need for forwarding or extending the argument. As mentioned earlier, you can also replicate what other authors have done by repeating the same study based on a different time period, a different region or country, or a different set of data.

For more information on how to identify gaps in the literature and write a literature review, refer to Chapter 15, "Writing a Research Paper," which offers guidelines on each section of a research paper along with examples from journal articles to illustrate these concepts.

1.3 EXAMINE THE THEORY

A *theory* can be defined as a set of statements used to explain phenomena. Darwin's theory of evolution, for example, is used to explain changes in species over time. Economists use demand theory to explain the relationship between the quantity demanded of a product and its price. Each field or discipline will have its own set of theories.

Theory plays an important role in developing your research questions and hypotheses. In the article used in the chapter preview, for example, Valkenburg et al. (2006) cite the theory that humans have a desire to protect their self-esteem and that self-esteem affects well-being. From this basic theory, they develop their research question related to how social media usage affects self-esteem and thus well-being.

Theory is also used to examine the results of your research. In other words, do your results conform to the stated theories? How do they differ? Why might they differ? These concepts are covered in more detail in Chapter 15, "Writing a Research Paper."

1.4 DEVELOP YOUR RESEARCH QUESTIONS AND HYPOTHESES

As described in the previous sections, you begin to form your research questions as you read the literature and examine the theory. Your questions may change in the early stages of the research as you continue to find more articles on the topic or new ways that scholars have examined or answered the questions in your research area.

In the example used in the chapter preview, the authors identify two research questions that are illustrated below in Figure 1.1. Each of these questions can then be restated as a *hypothesis* or an answer to the questions. As you begin your research, you won't know the answer to your research questions, but your hypotheses indicate what you expect to

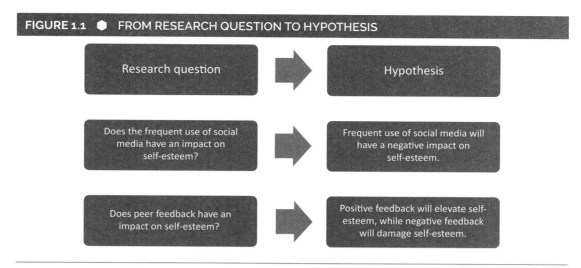

FIGURE 1.1 ● FROM RESEARCH QUESTION TO HYPOTHESIS

find based on theory. Your research may then find evidence to support or refute your hypothesis, which is a key feature of a hypothesis. It must be testable.

Developing the research questions is often the most difficult part of the research process and requires a lot of work up front before the questionnaire or study design can or should begin.

In addition to identifying the research question, it is also important to begin thinking about your key variables (self-esteem, social media usage, and feedback in this case) and how they relate to one another. In particular, self-esteem is the *dependent variable* because its value depends on the two independent variables, social media usage and feedback received. A dependent variable is defined in general as a variable whose variation is influenced by other variables. This is covered in more detail in later chapters.

1.5 DEVELOP YOUR RESEARCH METHOD

Once you have identified your research questions, your next step is to develop your research method. There are many types of research methods, such as qualitative research (narrative research, case studies, ethnographies), quantitative research (surveys and experiments with statistical analysis), and mixed methods that include both qualitative and quantitative approaches. Since this textbook focuses on quantitative analysis of primary data (data collected by the researcher) and secondary data (data that have been collected by someone else), the remaining chapters in this book will be devoted to sampling, questionnaire design, and data analysis with a final chapter on writing a research paper. For more complete works on the other types of research methods mentioned, see Leedy and Ormrod (2001) or Creswell and Creswell (2018).

1.6 ANALYZE THE DATA

The majority of the remainder of this book covers *data analysis*. It begins with descriptive statistics such as the mean, median, and standard deviation. We then cover testing of hypotheses and exploring relationships through advanced statistical techniques or inferential statistics. These will be discussed in detail in Chapters 6 through 14.

1.7 WRITE THE RESEARCH PAPER

Once all steps of the research process are completed, you begin to write your research paper. The typical sections in a research paper are the introduction, the literature review, the method section, the results, a discussion, and the conclusions. Each of these sections is described in Chapter 15 along with examples from published articles. We also review conventional guidelines and style guidelines for reporting statistical results.

EXERCISES

1. Read the article "Prevalence and Motives for Illicit Use of Prescription Stimulants in an Undergraduate Sample" by Teter, McCabe, Cranford, Boyd, and Guthrie (2005). As you read the article, answer the questions below, which are based on guidelines offered by Greenlaw (2009).

   a. What question or questions are the authors asking?

   b. Describe the theoretical approach that the authors use to develop their research question.

   c. What answers do the authors propose?

   d. In what ways does the current study improve over previous research according to the authors of the article? In other words, what gaps do the authors identify in the current literature?

   e. What method do the authors use to answer their questions?

   f. What limitations do the authors identify in their study?

   g. What suggestions do the authors have for follow-up research that should be done?

2. Choose a general area of research that interests you. This could be sports, cancer, poverty, social media usage, gaming, and so on. Use the techniques identified in Section 1.2 to narrow your focus as you begin perusing the literature and using forward and backward searching for articles of particular interest to you. Once you have done the initial reading, you should develop a tentative research question and identify five articles that are most closely related to your question. For each of the five articles, answer the following questions:

   a. What question or questions are the authors asking?

   b. Describe the theoretical approach that the authors use to develop their research question.

   c. What is the hypothesis that the authors propose?

   d. What answers do the authors propose?

   e. In what ways does the current study improve over previous research according to the authors of the article? In other words, what gaps do the authors identify in the current literature?

   f. What method do the authors use to answer their questions?

   g. What limitations do the authors identify in their study?

   h. What suggestions do the authors have for follow-up research that should be done?

REFERENCES

Creswell, J. W., & Creswell, J. D. (2018). *Research design: Qualitative, quantitative, and mixed methods approaches*. Thousand Oaks, CA: Sage.

Greenlaw, S. A. (2009). *Doing economics*. Mason, OH: South-Western Cengage Learning.

Leedy, P. D., & Ormrod, J. E. (2001). *Practical research: Planning and design*. Upper Saddle River, NJ: Merrill Prentice Hall.

Teter, C. J., McCabe, S. E., Cranford, J. A., Boyd, C. J., & Guthrie, S. K. (2005). Prevalence and motives for illicit use of prescription stimulants in an undergraduate student sample. *Journal of American College Health, 53*(6), 253–262.

Valkenburg, P. M., Peter, J., & Schouten, A. P. (2006). Friend networking sites and their relationship to adolescents' well-being and social self-esteem. *CyberPsychology & Behavior, 9*(5), 584–590. doi:10.1089/cpb.2006.9.584

SAMPLING TECHNIQUES

Chapter Preview

Unit of observation	Type of entity being studied, such as individuals, households, or businesses
Population	The complete set of units that is the topic of a study
Sample	A subset of the population, intended to represent the population, from which data will be collected
Nonprobability sampling	Selection of units based on the discretion of researchers such that it is not possible to calculate the probability of selecting each unit
Probability sampling	Selection of units using random numbers, such that it is possible to calculate the probability of selecting each unit
Simple random sample	Sample in which each unit in the population has the same probability of selection
Systematic random sample	Sample in which the selected units are evenly spaced across the population
Multilevel sampling	Sample in which aggregated units (e.g., towns) are selected, followed by the selection of more disaggregated units (e.g., households)
Stratification	Division of the population into different groups, each of which may be sampled differently
Sampling weights	Weights used to calculate population averages in a way that compensates for the effect of the sampling method

2.1 INTRODUCTION

Primary data refer to data collected directly by the researchers. This contrasts with secondary data, which are data collected by another researcher or an organization such as a government agency. In the social sciences, primary data are often collected through a sample survey, where the researcher interviews (or hires others to interview) a subset of the population on a topic of interest. The quality of the data depends heavily on selecting a good sample and asking the right questions. This was dramatically illustrated by the polling for the 1936 U.S. presidential elections.

As described in Article 2.1, the *Literary Digest* had run polls in four previous elections, successfully predicting the winner in each. In 1936, they carried out a poll of

ARTICLE 2.1

Five biggest political polling mistakes in U.S. history

October 2, 2012 by NCC Staff

Alf Landon beats FDR in a landslide

The mother of all botched political polls was a 1936 *Literary Digest* straw poll survey that said GOP challenger Alf Landon would win in a landslide over the incumbent, Franklin Delano Roosevelt, with 57 percent of the vote.

The *Literary Digest* used national straw polls in 1920, 1924, 1928 and 1932, and it guessed the winner of each presidential election.

In 1936, a young rival pollster, George Gallup, made his own prediction before the magazine issued its poll: He said *Literary Digest* would get it all wrong, despite the *Digest*'s decent track record in previous polls.

So who was right? The *Literary Digest* disaster helped establish Gallup as the nation's preeminent pollster. The *Digest* polled about 2 million people, most of whom were magazine readers, car owners or telephone customers—and had money during the Depression. It was not a representative sample.

Gallup used a random poll sample of 50,000 people.

President Roosevelt won the 1936 election easily, with 63 percent of the vote, and the *Literary Digest* was out of business the following year. If he had won, Landon could have been our wartime president.

Excerpt from the *Constitution Daily* btlog, National Constitution Center (2012).

2 million voters and predicted that the Republican candidate Alf Landon would beat Franklin Roosevelt, the Democratic candidate. In fact, Roosevelt won in a landslide, beating Landon in 46 of 48 states. On the other hand, George Gallup used a random sample of just 50,000 voters and correctly predicted that Roosevelt would win.

The problem was that the *Literary Digest* relied on lists of "magazine readers, car owners, and telephone subscribers." During the Great Depression, these lists had a disproportionate number of high-income households who opposed Roosevelt and his New Deal policies. In addition, the *Literary Digest* conducted the poll by sending postcards to 10 million voters and relying on respondents to mail back their responses. The response rate was higher among Republicans than Democrats, which also contributed to the incorrect result (Squire, 1988).

The *Literary Digest* was discredited by this high-profile failure and closed soon after. The success of Gallup's prediction established the national reputation of his firm, which grew to become one of the largest political polling companies. It also catalyzed the development of modern random-sample polling. The lesson for sampling methods is that it is much more important to have a representative sample than to have a large sample. In addition, this experience highlights the fact that a low response rate can distort the results of a survey. Indeed, this is one of the reasons that magazine subscriber polls and online polls are not considered scientific or reliable, no matter how many people respond to them.

This chapter provides an introduction to the basic concepts of sampling, discusses some of the more common sampling methods, and explains the calculation and use of sampling weights. However, it only scratches the surface of a large and complex topic. Readers interested in a more in-depth treatment of sampling methods may wish to consult Rea and Parker (2005), Scheaffer, Mendenhall, Ott, and Gerow (2011), or Daniel (2011).

2.2 SAMPLE DESIGN

As discussed in the previous chapter, any research must begin with a careful consideration of the objectives of the study. What are the research questions? What information is needed to answer those questions? What is the *unit of observation*, defined as the type of entity about which the study will collect information? In social science research, the unit of observation is often individuals, households, businesses, or other social institutions. Table 2.1 gives four examples of units of observation, depending on the research question and information needed.

In statistics, the *population* is the complete set of individuals, households, businesses, or other units that is the subject of the study. Table 2.2 gives some examples of populations corresponding to the studies listed in Table 2.1. Note that each population is defined in terms of the type of unit of observation, the geographic scope, and the period of time.

The *sample* is a subset of the population consisting of units from which data will be collected. *Sampling* is the process of selecting the sample in a way that ensures it will be representative of the population. One option, of course, is to collect data from every unit in the population, that is, to carry out a census. This might be feasible if the population is defined narrowly or if the budget is very large. For example, if the population is defined as all the banks in a given town, it would probably be feasible to carry out a census. Alternatively, the governments of many countries carry out a population census every 10 years. But for most purposes, it is more cost-effective

TABLE 2.1 ● EXAMPLES OF RESEARCH QUESTIONS AND UNITS OF OBSERVATION

Research Question	Information Needed	Unit of Observation
Which political candidate is favored by voters?	The opinions of voters regarding each candidate	Voters
What is the average yield of rice farmers?	The rice production and area under rice among rice farmers	Rice farmers
Why do students transfer from one university to another?	The reasons that students give for wanting to transfer out	College students
How do regulations affect small businesses?	The cost of complying with a set of business regulations	Small businesses

TABLE 2.2 ● EXAMPLES OF SURVEYS

Description of Survey	Population	Sample
A polling firm collects information from 1,500 likely voters to understand their political views.	All likely voters in the country, defined as those who voted in at least two of the past three elections	1,500 likely voters
A statistical agency gathers information from 2,000 rice farmers to estimate the average yield for farmers in a district.	All rice farmers in the district, defined as those growing rice in the previous year	2,000 rice farmers
A university carries out a survey of 200 students to explore options for reducing the number of students who transfer out.	All full-time undergraduate students at the university in a year	200 students
A state government agency carries out a survey of 5,000 small businesses in a state.	All businesses in the state that have 10 or fewer full-time workers	5,000 small businesses

to conduct a *sample survey*, defined as systematic collection of data from a limited number of units (e.g., households) to learn something about the population. Using the same examples in Table 2.1, the concepts of the population and sample are illustrated in Table 2.2.

All surveys face a trade-off between the objectives of reducing cost and increasing accuracy. If cost were no object, then one could carry out a census (covering all units), and it would not be necessary to worry about whether the selected units were representative of the whole group. Alternatively, if accuracy were not a concern, one could just sample a handful of units in one location, which would minimize costs. In practice, most surveys are in between these two extremes. A key challenge is to ensure that the sample is designed in such a way that the sample accurately reflects the characteristics of the whole group.

2.3 SELECTING A SAMPLE

2.3.1 Probability and Nonprobability Sampling

How does the researcher select a sample for the survey? One intuitive approach is for the researcher to simply choose a set of units based on availability or subjective judgment. This is called *nonprobability sampling* because it is not possible to calculate the probability of selecting each unit. Below is a partial list of some of the various types of nonprobability sampling:

- *Convenience sampling* involves selecting units from available but partial lists or selecting people who are passing by a location such as a supermarket.

- *Purposive sampling* means that the researcher uses knowledge of the field to select units to be studied.

- *Snowball sampling* refers to picking an initial set of units, then a second round of units that are nearby or have links to the first-round selections. There may be additional rounds.

Nonprobability sampling has the advantage of being quick and inexpensive to implement. It is often used with qualitative research focused on in-depth exploration of a topic on a relatively small number of observations. Qualitative research can complement quantitative surveys in several ways. It can be carried out before a random-sample survey to identify key issues, contributing to the design of the questionnaire. Or it can be conducted after a survey to help interpret the results or explain unexpected findings. For an in-depth discussion of qualitative research and mixed methods that combine qualitative and quantitative research, see Creswell and Creswell (2017).

The main disadvantage of nonprobability samples is that they are likely to be biased, meaning that the sampled units do not accurately reflect the characteristics of the population (the 1936 polling by the *Literary Digest* is an example). For this reason, it is not possible to infer characteristics of the population from the characteristics of the sample. For example, a nonprobability sample of businesses will probably include mostly large, well-known businesses; those that have more visible locations; and those that advertise. Car dealers, supermarkets, and restaurants will be overrepresented, while the one-person key-making shop and the home-based day care provider will be underrepresented or excluded.

For these reasons, almost all larger surveys carried out by researchers and professional polling companies use *probability sampling*, defined as sampling in which the probability of selection can be calculated because the selection is made randomly from a complete list of units (indeed, it is also known as random sampling). The researcher defines the population and the selection method but does not have any discretion in deciding which individual units will be included in the sample.

If a random sample is well-designed and large enough, it will be representative of the population. In other words, the characteristics of the sample will be similar to the characteristics of the population. In the example above, the average size of businesses in the sample will be similar to the average size of businesses in the town. In technical terms, the average business size in the sample will be an *unbiased estimate* of the business size in the population. This means that if you took repeated samples using the same method, the average across samples would converge toward the population average as the number of samples increased.

Another advantage of a random sample is that we can estimate the *sampling error* of our sample-based averages—that is, the error associated with selecting a sample rather than collecting data from every unit in the population. As described in more detail in Chapter 8, the sampling error of a variable is based on (a) the size of the sample, (b) how it was selected, and (c) the variability of the variable in question. If the sample is large or the variability is low, the sample error is likely to be small. One way to describe the sampling error is the *95% confidence interval*, defined such that there is a 95% probability that the true average lies between the two numbers. If a political poll reveals that 45% of voters approve of a state governor with a margin of error of 3 percentage points, this means that the 95% confidence interval is 45% ± 3% or 42% to 48%. In other words, there is a 95% probability that this confidence interval contains the true level of approval (if you polled every voter in the state).

Note that a sample does not have to represent a large percentage of the population to be precise. In national political polls, a sample of 800 to 1,200 is usually sufficient to reduce the margin of error to less than 5 percentage points, in spite of the fact that the sample is roughly 0.001% (or 1 in 100,000) of the total voting population in the United States. It is also useful to note that these calculations count only sampling error. They do not include other sources of error such as respondents who give false answers or misidentifying who will decide to vote.

In a large majority of surveys, it is worth the additional effort to select the units randomly. The remainder of this section describes the methods used for different types of random sampling.

2.3.2 Identifying a Sampling Frame

To select a random sample, a researcher needs a *sampling frame*—that is, a list of all the sampling units in the population from which to select the sample. Ideally, the sampling frame would be a complete list of the units in the population, but this is not always possible. Sometimes an available list is smaller than the target population. For example, a researcher may wish to define the population as all rice farmers in a region, but the available list may include only members of a cooperative of rice farmers, thus excluding rice farmers who are not members. It is important to either complement the list with additional sampling to capture information on nonmembers or recognize this gap in describing and interpreting the results.

Other times, an available list may include more units than the target population. For example, suppose you want to survey likely voters, but the only information available is a list of registered voters, including some who rarely vote. In this case, one option is to contact all voters, ask each respondent if they voted in two of the past three elections, and proceed with the interview only if the answer is yes. Alternatively, the researcher could collect voting patterns and opinions from all voters and then examine the patterns for different definitions of "likely voter" in the analysis.

In some situations, no sampling frame is available. This is particularly common when the sampling unit is a specific type of household or business. For example, if a researcher wants to conduct a survey of bicycle repair shops, fish farmers, or beekeepers in a developing country where these businesses are not registered, it may not be possible to obtain a complete list to serve as a sampling frame, even at the local level. In such a situation, the researcher must create a sampling frame.

One approach is to use area sampling. The researcher obtains a set of maps of local areas, such as counties or urban neighborhoods. Using maps of each area, the researcher divides it into smaller units of similar size. One common approach is to use a grid to divide the map into equal-sized squares. Another option (relevant for urban surveys) is to use city blocks as the smaller unit. In either case, the researcher selects a sample of the smaller units and then collects information from all the sampling units within the selected unit. Below are two examples:

- To carry out a survey of farmers with fishponds, a district is divided into an 8 × 8 grid and 10 of the 64 squares are selected. Within each square, the team locates all farmers with fishponds and interviews them.

- To implement a survey of small-scale food shops, the city is divided into 80 neighborhoods using a map, and 20 neighborhoods are selected. Each selected neighborhood is divided into blocks using a street map. The survey team then visits a randomly selected set of eight blocks in each neighborhood. Within each block, every small-scale food retailer is interviewed.

In the absence of maps and a sampling frame, it may be necessary to carry out a listing exercise, in which the survey team first prepares a list of the sampling units within a given area. The sampling units are then numbered, and a random selection is made for follow-up interviews. This can be a time-consuming process, so it is useful to define the area as small as possible given the information available.

2.3.3 Determining the Sample Size

How large should a survey sample be? Not surprisingly, it depends. To explain the factors that determine the minimum sample size, it is helpful to use an example. Suppose we are designing a survey to test whether there is a gender difference in the salaries of recent graduates from a college. Would it be enough to interview 70 graduates or do we need a sample of 700? To answer this question, we need five pieces of information:

1. How small a difference in salaries do we want to be able to measure? In our example, if we want to detect a male–female salary difference as small as 3%, the sample size will have to be relatively large. If, on the other hand, we are satisfied with only being able to detect salary differences that are 20% or more, a smaller sample will suffice.

2. How much variation is there in salaries? If all the graduates have similar salaries, then we can estimate the mean (average) salary of men and women fairly precisely, so a small sample would be sufficient. If, on the other hand, there is a wide variation in salaries, then we would need a larger sample to achieve the same level of precision in the estimate.

3. How small do we want to make the probability of incorrectly concluding that there *is* a difference between men and women? The larger the sample size, the smaller the risk of making this type of error.

4. How small do we want to make the probability of making a mistake when we state that there is *no* difference between men and women? Again, the larger the sample, the lower the risk.

5. How was the sample selected? The sample design influences the size of sample needed to reach a given level of precision.

If we have information (or at least educated assumptions) about the five factors above, we can estimate the number of graduates that need to be interviewed in the survey. We will not describe the methods here because they make use of concepts taught in later chapters. However, a brief survey of the methods can be found in Appendix 9.

2.3.4 Sample Selection Methods

This section describes four types of sampling methods: (1) simple random sampling, (2) systematic random sampling, (3) multistage (or cluster) sampling, and (4) stratified random sampling. The Stata code to implement each of these methods is shown in Appendix 7, though it requires a solid understanding of Stata. We recommend studying Chapters 4 to 7 before attempting to consider Appendix 7.

2.3.4.1 Simple Random Sampling

Once we have the sampling frame, how do we select the sample? One approach is to select a *simple random sample*, in which the entire sample is based on a draw from the sampling frame, where each sampling unit has an equal probability of being selected. The probability of selecting each unit is n/N, where n is the number of units to be selected and N is the total number of units in the sampling frame. One disadvantage of a simple random sample is that the selected units may be "clumped" together in the sample frame, resulting in a sample that is less representative than desired. To address this problem, researchers are more likely to use a systematic random sample, as discussed next.

2.3.4.2 Systematic Random Sampling

A *systematic random sample* is one in which there is a fixed interval between selected units. First, a unit is randomly selected from among the first N/n units in the sampling frame. Subsequently, units are selected every N/n units. For example, a systematic random sample of 20 households from a list of 200 households starts with a randomly selected unit from the first $N/n = 10$ units. Suppose the random selection picks unit 4. After that, we select every $N/n = 10$ units, that is 14, 24, 34, and so on up to 194. The main advantage is that it spreads out the selected units evenly across the sampling frame. If the sampling frame does not follow any order, this will not make a difference. But typically, the sampling frame is sorted by some characteristic, such as location or size. In this case, a systematic random sample will ensure that the selected units are balanced in terms of that characteristic. For example, if the sampling frame is sorted by location from north to south, then a simple random sample might include a disproportionate number of units in the north. However, a systematic random sample spreads out the sample so that the number of selected units in the north and south will be proportional to the actual number of units in the north and south.

2.3.4.3 Multistage Sampling

Multistage sampling refers to a selection process in which the selection occurs in two or more steps (this is also called cluster sampling). For example, suppose we are carrying out a national survey. The researcher may randomly select 10 of the 50 states, 5 counties in each state, and 100 households in each county, for a total sample of 5,000 households. This represents a three-stage random sample, corresponding to the three types of units: states, counties, and households.

There are several possible motivations for multistage sampling:

- First, it may be used to overcome limitations on the availability of a full sampling frame. Often, it is not possible to use single-stage sampling because there is no sampling frame that covers the entire population of interest. In the case above, suppose the household lists are available only from county officials. It would be very expensive and time-consuming to gather lists from every county in the country to prepare a national sampling frame for a simple random sample. In contrast, it would be much easier to randomly select a subset of counties in the first stage and then get the list for each selected county for second-stage selection of households.

- Second, it may be used to ensure that the sample is well distributed across certain categories. In the example above, the design ensures that the sample includes 10 states and 5 counties within each state.

- Third, multistage sampling may be used to ensure that the sample is clustered to reduce the cost of data collection. Even if a national sampling frame is available, visiting 5,000 randomly selected households would be much more costly than visiting households in 50 counties. For this reason, multistage sampling is sometimes called cluster sampling.

2.3.4.4 Stratified Random Sampling

Stratification refers to dividing the population into categories (or strata) and specifying the sample size for each one rather than allowing the distribution to be determined by chance. The strata must be nonoverlapping, and they must cover the entire population. For example, national household surveys are often stratified into rural and urban areas, with a separate selection of households in each area. National surveys are often stratified by region as well. Surveys of enterprises are often stratified by size, specifying the number of small, medium, and large firms that will be included.

There are three reasons to design a stratified sample. First, stratification may be used to ensure that the sample for each stratum is large enough to allow reliable estimates at the stratum level. For example, suppose a country has six administrative regions, but one of them only has 2% of the national population. In an unstratified random sample of 1,200 households, roughly 2% of the sample (24 households) would be selected from the small region. If the sample is stratified by region, the researcher can ensure that each region has 200 households, which may be enough to generate reliable results for each region. In this case, stratification would be used to oversample the small region, meaning that the percentage of households sampled in the small region is larger than its share in the overall population. The other five regions would be undersampled in this process.

Second, stratification can be used to ensure that each stratum is proportionally represented in the sample. In this sense, stratification fulfills the same function as systematic sampling where the sampling frame is organized by stratum. If the strata are internally more homogeneous than the population, stratification will improve the precision of estimates compared with a simple random sample.

A third reason for stratification is to adapt to differences in the variability of key indicators across strata. As discussed earlier and later in Chapter 8, the precision of survey-based estimates in measuring a variable of interest is partly determined by the variability of the variable of interest (in the extreme, if there were no variability and all units were the same, a sample of one would be sufficient!). For example, suppose a survey is designed to estimate national income. In general, the variability of income is greater in urban areas than in rural areas. Because of this, it is useful to oversample urban households, meaning that we select a larger share of urban households than rural households. Well-designed stratification can reduce the confidence interval in survey-based estimates without increasing the overall size of the sample.

2.4 SAMPLING WEIGHTS

Sampling weights are numbers used to estimate population parameters (e.g., means and percentages) from sample statistics, compensating for "distortions" that may be introduced by sampling. For example, suppose 90% of the population lives in rural areas, but the sample is stratified so that it is 50% urban and 50% rural. In this case, the average income in the sample will be disproportionately affected by urban households. If urban incomes are higher, the average income for the sample will be higher than the average income of the population. In other words, the average income from the sample is biased upward because it has a disproportionately large number of urban households. However, using sampling weights, we can calculate the weighted average, which will give greater weight to each rural household and lesser weight to each urban household, providing an unbiased estimate of national income.

2.4.1 Calculating Sampling Weights

Sampling weights are calculated as the inverse of the probability of selection. They can also be interpreted as the number of units in the population that each unit in the sample represents.

In the case of simple random sampling or one-stage systematic random sampling, the probability of selecting any one unit is n/N, where n is the size of the sample and N is the size of the population. Thus, the sampling weight (w) is calculated as the inverse:

$$w = \frac{N}{n} \tag{2.1}$$

Note that the sampling weight is the same for all units. Such a sample is considered "self-weighted" because the sample average is equal to the weighted average and represents an unbiased estimate of the population average. In this case, the main use of sampling weights is to extrapolate from sample totals to population totals. For example, suppose a survey of seniors at a university collects information on 100 out of 2,000 seniors. The weight is 2,000/100 = 20, so each senior in the sample represents 20 in the senior class. If you wanted to estimate the total spending on books by the senior class, you would just multiply the total for the sample by 20.

In the case of a single-stage stratified sample, we carry out the calculation for each stratum. The weight for stratum i (w_i) is as follows:

$$w_i = \frac{N_i}{n_i} \tag{2.2}$$

where N_i is the population of stratum i and n_i is the sample size for stratum i. Taking the example of urban–rural stratification, suppose there are 900,000 rural households and 100,000 urban households in the population, and the sample contains 4,000 households divided equally between urban and rural areas. Thus, the weight for rural households would be 900,000/2,000 = 450, and the weight for urban households would be 100,000/2,000 = 50. In other words, each rural household in the sample represents 450 households in the population, while each urban household in the sample stands for just 50 in the population. Calculating weighted averages would give more weight to rural households in the sample, thus compensating for the fact that they were undersampled in the survey.

For multistage sampling designs, the calculation of the sampling weights is a little more complicated, but it follows the same general rule: The sampling weight at each stage is the inverse of the probability of selection. There is a separate ratio for each stage in the sampling. Consider the example of a three-stage random sample:

- In the first stage, we select 10 of the 50 states.

- In the second stage, we select 5 counties in each of the 10 selected states.

- In the third stage, we select 100 households in each selected county.

The sampling weight for each county (w_c) is the product of three ratios, each representing the inverse of the probability of selection in that stage of selection:

$$w_c = \frac{50}{10} \frac{C_s}{5} \frac{H_c}{100} \tag{2.3}$$

where 50 is the total number of states, 10 is the number of states selected, C_s is the total number of counties in state s, 5 is the number of counties selected in each state, H_c is the total number of households in county c, and 100 is the number of households selected in each county.

This equation can be adapted to other multistage sample designs, keeping in mind the fact that the number of terms should be equal to the number of stages in the sampling. A simple way to double-check the calculation of the sample weights is to sum the sample weights over the units in the sample. The total should be roughly equal to the number of units in the population.

Up to this point, we have been discussing a type of weight called inverse probability sampling weights (IPSW). The other type of weight is relative sampling weights, defined as the IPSW for each unit divided by the average IPSW. As such, the average value of relative weights is always 1.0. For estimating weighted means and percentages of the population, relative weights and IPSW give the same results. However, relative weights cannot be used to estimate population totals, while IPSW can be used for this purpose.

2.4.2 Using Sampling Weights

How are the sampling weights used? Suppose our variable of interest in a national survey is household income. We can estimate national income as a weighted sum of household income across the sample using the following equation:

$$X = \sum_{i=1}^{n} x_i w_i \qquad (2.4)$$

where X is the estimate of the total for the population (e.g., national income), x_i is the value of the variable for household i (e.g., household income), and w_i is the IPSW for household i. As a reminder, $\sum$ is the summation sign, so the right side of the equation means that we should take the sum of $x_i w_i$, as i goes from 1 to n. In other words, $X = x_1 w_1 + x_2 w_2 + x_3 w_3 + \cdots + x_n w_n$.

Estimates of population means and percentages can be calculated as follows:

$$\bar{x} = \frac{\sum_{i=1}^{n} x_i w_i}{\sum_{i=1}^{n} w_i} \qquad (2.5)$$

The numerator is an estimate of the sum of x across the population, as shown in Equation 2.4. The denominator is the sum of the weights across the sample, which is an estimate of the size of the population. Thus, the overall expression is an estimate of the average value of x across the population. If x_i is a binary variable taking values of 0 or 1, such as gender, then this equation gives an estimate of the proportion of the population for which $x_i = 1$. In the case of categorical variables, such as region or marital status, the average has no meaning, but the variable can be broken up into a set of binary variables, one for each category. The equation above can be used to estimate the proportion of the population in each category.

However, statistical packages, such as Stata, will do these calculations for us. In Chapter 6, we show how sampling weights can be used to adjust the calculations of totals, means, and percentages in Stata.

EXERCISES

1. Suppose you have a sampling frame of 1,200 hardware stores in a state, numbered from 1 to 1,200. Describe how you would select a systematic random sample of 100 stores for a survey. Give an example of what the sample might look like, showing the store numbers of the first five selected stores.

2. Give three possible reasons why one might want to use a multistage random sample rather than a single-stage random sample.

3. You have been hired to design a survey of political opinions in 10 "swing" states, but you need to have a large enough sample (say, 400 respondents per state) to generate reliable results for each state. What type of sampling method do you need to use?

4. There are 20,000 people in the country of Wakanda. Most of the population (i.e., 17,500) live in urban areas and the rest live in rural areas. If you drew a stratified sample of 250 people from urban areas and 250 people from rural areas, what would be the sampling weights for urban and rural areas?

5. Suppose that we develop a multistage sampling design and choose five states (out of 50), three counties within each state, and 300 households in each county. In the state of Pennsylvania, where there are 67 counties, we randomly select the following three counties:

County	Population
Montgomery	819,000
Bucks	630,000
Allegheny	1,200,000

Assuming there are three people per household, what is the sampling weight for the selected households in each of these three counties?

REFERENCES

Creswell, J. W., & Creswell, J. D. (2017). *Research design: Qualitative, quantitative, and mixed methods approaches*. Thousand Oaks, CA: Sage.

Daniel, J. (2011). *Sampling essentials: Practical guidelines for making sampling choices*. Thousand Oaks, CA: Sage.

National Constitution Center. (2012). *The five biggest polling mistakes in U.S. history*. Philadelphia, PA: Author. Retrieved from https://perma.cc/5LFL-TSAK

Rea, L. M., & Parker, R. A. (2005). *Designing and conducting survey research: A comprehensive guide*. San Francisco, CA: Jossey-Bass.

Scheaffer, R. L., Mendenhall, W., III, Ott, R. L., & Gerow, K. G. (2011). *Elementary survey sampling*. Boston, MA: Brooks/Cole, Cengage Learning.

Squire, P. (1988). Why the 1936 *Literary Digest* poll failed. *Public Opinion Quarterly, 52*(1), 125–133.

QUESTIONNAIRE DESIGN

Chapter Preview

Structured questionnaire	Fixed set of questions phrased in a standardized way and given in the same order for every respondent
Semi-structured questionnaire	Some standardized questions, but some part of the questionnaire is informal and flexible. Topics may vary from one respondent to another.
Open-ended question	A question that allows the respondent to answer in any manner with the response being recorded in the form of a narrative text
Closed-ended question	A question for which the response can be expressed as a single number or categorical response
Question order	Order questions by topic. Move from general to specific questions. Place sensitive questions last.
Question phrasing	Be specific about who is referred to. Be specific about time frame. Be clear about definitions. Avoid leading questions.
Continuous responses	Responses that can take on any value Need to specify the unit of measure
Categorical responses	Responses represent categories
Skip patterns	Guidelines that indicate which questions should be skipped when questions don't apply to all respondents based on previous answers

3.1 INTRODUCTION

What questions should be included in the survey? How should the questions be phrased? And how should the responses be recorded? These are some of the important issues involved in designing the questionnaire, one of the most important and time-consuming steps in implementing a survey. If a key question is omitted from the questionnaire, important information will be lost. If too many questions are included in the questionnaire, respondents may tire and stop answering, leading again to the loss of information. And if a question is poorly phrased, the results may be difficult or impossible to interpret.

This chapter provides some guidelines for the design of questionnaires, including question order, phrasing, and response codes. For additional information on questionnaire design, Grosh and Glewwe (2000) have edited a volume with detailed information on questionnaire design for developing countries. Ekinci (2015) provides a more concise review, focused on business and management research. Rea and Parker (2005) provide another valuable reference on the issues of questionnaire design.

3.2 STRUCTURED AND SEMI-STRUCTURED QUESTIONNAIRES

An important distinction in questionnaire design is between structured and semi-structured questionnaires. A *structured questionnaire* has a fixed set of questions, phrased in a standardized way, and given in the same order for every respondent. Some questions may be skipped for certain types of respondents; for example, a question about the respondent's spouse would be skipped for respondents who are single. However, the same rules about skipping questions apply to all respondents. Furthermore, the questions in structured questionnaires are generally designed so that the responses are either a continuous variable or a categorical variable, rather than open-ended questions with narrative responses.

In a *semi-structured questionnaire*, some of the questions are standardized and asked in a specific order, but part of the questionnaire is more informal and flexible, with questions and topics of discussion that vary from one respondent to another. The unstructured section of the questionnaire may consist of a list of suggested questions or just topics of discussion. The questions in this section are often open-ended, and the order is flexible. This portion of the interview is more journalistic in nature, where new questions are formed in response to the answers to the previous questions.

The entire interview may be informal and unstructured. However, the list of suggested questions and topics for discussion is not normally considered a questionnaire, so it is outside the scope of this chapter.

The results of unstructured interviews (and the unstructured portion of semi-structured interviews) are difficult to analyze in a systematic way for several reasons. If the questions are not standardized across respondents, then the sample varies across questions making it difficult to summarize. Furthermore, interviewers may be less likely to ask sensitive or difficult questions, introducing some bias in the results. Responses to open-ended questions can be summarized qualitatively, but statistical analysis requires either time-consuming classification of responses or complex computer algorithms for analysis of text. For this reason, unstructured and semi-structured surveys generally use small samples.

On the other hand, unstructured interviews provide rich information on the perceptions, beliefs, and motivations of respondents. They may uncover issues or patterns that the researcher did not anticipate at the beginning of the study. Unstructured interviews can be used to identify key issues in preparation for the design of a structured questionnaire for a large-scale formal survey. In addition, unstructured interviews can be used after a formal survey to help interpret or explain the results of the survey. Because our main interest is generating data for analysis, this chapter focuses primarily on the design of structured questionnaires. Table 3.1 summarizes some of the characteristics of each type of survey.

TABLE 3.1 ● SUMMARY OF DIFFERENCES BETWEEN STRUCTURED, SEMI-STRUCTURED, AND UNSTRUCTURED SURVEYS			
	Structured Surveys	**Semi-Structured Surveys**	**Unstructured Surveys**
Types of questions	Mainly closed	Open and closed	Mainly open
Phrasing, order, and content of questions	Standardized for all respondents	Partly standardized	Varies across respondents
Sample size	Can be large	Usually small	Usually small
Type of results	Quantitative	Quantitative and qualitative	Qualitative
Strengths	Numerical results; can generate unbiased estimates of population parameters with confidence intervals	Mix of both	May reveal new issues or unexpected responses; questions adapt to earlier answers
Weaknesses	Questions and responses are fixed before the survey begins	Mix of both	Qualitative results, only practical for small sample

3.3 OPEN- AND CLOSED-ENDED QUESTIONS

Although we referred to open-ended questions above, it is useful to define the term more precisely. An *open-ended question* (or open question) is one that allows the respondent to answer in any manner, with the response being recorded in the form of narrative text or summary notes. Examples of open-ended questions include "What is your view of gun-control legislation?" or "Why do you think some people succeed and others don't?"

In contrast, a *closed-ended question* (sometimes called a closed question) is one for which the respondent either gives a number or selects from a set of predetermined responses. Closed questions can be divided into two categories depending on the type of response.

1. A closed question may generate a continuous variable, representing a measurement of a physical quantity such as weight, length, time duration, or frequency. Examples include "How old are you?" and "How many hours a week do you watch television?"

2. A closed question may generate a categorical variable. This includes yes/ no questions, such as "Are you married?" and "Do you own a car?" It also includes multiple-choice questions, such as "What is your education level?" and "What is your marital status?" where the respondent chooses between several options. In each case, the response is verbal, but it is coded in the database as a number.

As discussed above, most medium- and large-scale surveys use structured questionnaires with closed-ended questions. For this reason, we focus on this type of questionnaire for the remainder of the chapter.

3.4 GENERAL GUIDELINES FOR QUESTIONNAIRE DESIGN

Before we discuss the specifics of designing the questionnaire, it is useful to list a number of general guidelines to make the questionnaire clear and easy for the interviewer to use and for the respondent to understand.

- All questions should be written out in full to ensure that the question is asked in the same way to all respondents. This applies even when the questions are being organized in a table, such as when the survey is collecting information on each member of the household.

- Instructions to interviewers (also called enumerators) should be clearly distinguished from the questions themselves. This can be done by using a different font or putting the instructions in brackets.

- In the questionnaire, each categorical response option should be written out in full. This helps standardize the way the questions are asked. In addition, each categorical response should have a number code.

- In paper questionnaires, it is preferable for the enumerator to record the number code of the response rather than circling or marking the response on the list. In addition, it is a good idea to use boxes to indicate where each response code should be written. This will reduce the time and increase the accuracy of data entry by making it easy to find and enter the response code in the computer.

- For complex questionnaires, you could use a word processor such as Word, but it is generally easier to format a questionnaire using a spreadsheet such as Excel. Using a spreadsheet makes it easier to create boxes where response codes will be recorded. It is also easier to organize questions into columns or tables and adjust tables to fit on a single sheet of paper. In addition, merging cells and then inserting columns in a Word table sometimes creates havoc with table formatting, while Excel and other spreadsheets give better results.

- Computer-assisted personal interview (CAPI) methods are becoming widespread. CAPI software is available to program computers, tablets, or phones to record data in the field (e.g., ODK, SurveyCTO, and Surveybe). In addition to eliminating the time and errors associated with entering data into a computer from paper questionnaires, this approach allows the researcher to incorporate quality checks into the tablet program, flagging errors and allowing the enumerator to correct them during the interview.

- There are many software packages that will allow you to design an online questionnaire, and some of them are free. Survey Monkey, for example, is free for small-scale surveys, though there is a fee if the questionnaire or the sample is large. There are many similar packages that are easy to learn and have the ability to create many types of questions, including multiple choice, rank order, slider, and tables. These packages will also allow you to print a copy of the questionnaire if you plan to do an in-person interview where an enumerator fills in the questionnaire.

3.5 DESIGNING THE QUESTIONS

The research questions of the study help determine the range of questions to be included in the survey. The questions should of course address the central research questions, but they should also include questions to help explain the responses to the main questions. For example, political opinion polls naturally focus on respondents' support for different candidates, but they also ask questions about the respondents' age, sex, education, and party identification, since these characteristics often help "explain" political preferences. Similarly, a survey of college students regarding the time spent on sports could include questions about the student, including sex, age, scholarship status, high school experience with sports, and so on.

3.5.1 Question Order

The order of the questions should follow four general guidelines. First, the questions should follow an order determined by the topics, moving from one topic to the next. For example, group questions about education together before moving on to health. Whenever possible, the questionnaire should avoid returning to a topic covered earlier. This keeps the interview as close to a "natural" conversation as possible for in-person interviews. In addition, it probably reduces frustration among respondents that might be caused by going back to an earlier topic.

Second, within each topic the questionnaire should start with general questions before moving on to specific questions. The general questions will help determine which specific questions should be asked. For example, if a general question determines that the respondent does not drink alcohol, one can avoid specific questions about how much they drink. Similarly, a general question whether the respondent has children should precede questions about those children.

Third, it is better to start the interview with topics that are not sensitive, such as household composition. More sensitive topics, such as income level or use of contraception, should be asked toward the end of the interview for two reasons. First, the respondent will probably feel more comfortable discussing sensitive topics after spending some time with the enumerator. Second, if the sensitive topics cause the respondent to break off the interview or stop filling out the questionnaire, less information will be lost if these questions are toward the end of the interview.

Finally, it is preferable to have the questions most important for the intended analysis toward the beginning of the questionnaire. This way, if the interview cannot be completed, at least the essential questions will have been covered. Clearly, these guidelines may conflict with one another. This highlights the importance of testing the questionnaire one or more times before finalizing the wording, question order, and response options.

3.5.2 Phrasing the Questions

In designing the questions, it is important to make sure they are clear and unambiguous. This means avoiding research jargon or other vocabulary that might not be familiar to some of the respondents. The questions should also avoid abbreviations and acronyms unless they are universally understood. Finally, the questions need to be specific about *who* they refer to. In English, "you" can mean you (singular), referring to the respondent himself or herself, or it can mean you (plural), referring to the respondent's family. Take the following question:

"Have you taken out a loan?"

It is not clear *who* the question refers to, the respondent alone or anyone in the household. If the researcher is interested in access to credit by the household, a better phrasing would be as follows:

"Have you or anyone in your household taken out a loan?"

The questions also need to be explicit about *when*, that is, the time period referred to. In the question above, it is not clear if the respondent should include a loan received many years ago as a college student. Thus, the question above would be better phrased as follows:

"Have you or anyone in your household taken out a loan in the past 12 months?"

Note that "in the past year" is ambiguous because it could mean over the past 12 months or during the current calendar year. For this reason, "in the past 12 months" or "since this time last year" is better.

Finally, the questions should be explicit about *what* they are referring to. In the example above, what is the definition of a "loan"? Should it include $20 borrowed from a friend or is it limited to official bank loans? If the latter, do we include loans from credit cooperatives and other nonbank financial institutions? To remove the ambiguity, the question could be rephrased as follows:

"Have you or anyone in your household taken out a loan from a bank or other financial institution in the past 12 months?"

Another important factor in phrasing questions is to avoid making any assumption about the respondent that has not been verified in a previous question. Table 3.2 gives some examples of questions that make assumptions about the respondent that may or may not be true.

TABLE 3.2 ⬢ QUESTIONS WITH EMBEDDED ASSUMPTIONS	
Question	**Implicit Assumption**
How old is your oldest child?	The respondent has at least one child.
How much do you pay in rent?	The respondent rents his or her housing.
What is your favorite radio station?	The respondent listens to the radio.
Which state were you born in?	The respondent was born in the United States.

One way to address this problem would be to include a response option for the excluded answer, such as "I don't have a child," or "I don't pay rent." A better approach, however, is to add a prior question that determines whether this is a valid question. For example,

No.	Questions	Response Codes or Units	Response
A1	Do you have any children?	1. Yes 2. No	
			If no, skip to A3
A2	How many children do you have?	Number	

It is important to provide clear instructions of which questions to skip based on the response to earlier questions. The topic of skip patterns is discussed in Section 3.7.

It is also important to avoid "double-barreled" questions, meaning questions that may have two (or more) responses because the wording of the question combines two issues. Examples include the following:

- "Do you believe that supermarkets should sell cheaper and more nutritious food?"

- "Do you think the county government should spend less on salaries and more on roads?"

- "How often do you purchase gasoline and how much do you spend?"

Many (but not all) double-barreled questions can be identified by the fact that they contain two concepts linked with the word "and." The solution is to separate the individual queries into two or more questions, so that respondents are not forced to answer two questions with one response.

Finally, the researcher should also ensure that the questions are neutral and do not "lead" the respondent to answer in a certain way. Table 3.3 provides some examples

TABLE 3.3 ● EXAMPLES OF LEADING QUESTIONS		
Topic	**Leading Question Toward a "Yes" Response**	**Leading Question Biased Toward a "No" Response**
Welfare	Do you feel the government has a moral responsibility to assist families in need through no fault of their own?	Do you support the use of your hard-earned tax dollars to hand out welfare checks to people?
Infrastructure spending	Do you agree that the government should be investing more in our crumbling infrastructure to promote economic growth?	Do you think the government should indulge in runaway spending on pork-barrel projects that could worsen the fiscal deficit?
City health code	Do you support the new city law that would strengthen the health code and protect people from unsanitary conditions in restaurants?	Do you support the new city regulations on restaurants that impose unnecessary costs on family businesses and threaten food service jobs?

of questions that clearly express a point of view on the topic and "lead" respondents to adopt the same view. To nudge respondents one way or another, they use terms and concepts with positive associations (e.g., "family business" and "protect people") or ones with negative associations (e.g., "runaway spending" and "pork-barrel projects"). Some of them include reasons for supporting or opposing the statement within the question.

The above examples are heavily biased to demonstrate the effect, but in actual questionnaires, the bias may be less obvious. One method for testing for bias is to have someone read over the question and guess which response the researcher would give for that question. If the wording provides clues to the researcher's own views, the question should be revised.

Researchers designing questionnaires should also be aware of "social desirability bias," which refers to the tendency of respondents to give answers that are socially acceptable rather than accurate. Questions about whether the respondent has voted may overestimate the proportion of adults who vote because people may be reluctant to admit that they did not vote. Likewise, questions about domestic violence, illegal drug use, or cruelty to animals are likely to underestimate their prevalence. Questions should be phrased to make respondents comfortable enough to admit the truth. In addition, the results should be interpreted with a recognition that the responses may overestimate socially desirable responses.

3.6 RECORDING RESPONSES

As mentioned above, closed questions can yield two types of responses: (1) a continuous variable or (2) a categorical variable. The methods for capturing information from each type of question are described below.

3.6.1 Responses in the Form of Continuous Variables

A continuous variable describes a quantity of something and requires a unit, such as kilograms or years. Examples of questions leading to a continuous variable are as follows:

- How old are you (age at last birthday)?

- How tall is your child, expressed in centimeters?

- What is the area of your farm in hectares?

- How much gasoline do you purchase each week, expressed in gallons?

- How much do you spend per month on mobile phone service?

For continuous variables, it is necessary to gather information on the unit of measure (e.g., centimeters, hectares, or gallons). This can be done within the question itself, when it is appropriate to assume that all responses can be given in the same unit. For example,

No.	Questions	Response Codes or Units	Response
B1	How many times per month do you go out to the movies?	Times/month	

Note that this example includes a page header to help the enumerator stay organized. In other cases, respondents may use different units. In this case, it is better to calculate the conversion in data analysis than to ask enumerators to make the calculations. In this case, the unit of measure is entered as a separate variable.

B2	2	How frequently do you go out to the movies?	Times	per
			1 Week	
			2 Month	Time unit
			3 Year	

In addition, for any questions that involve flows, the unit of time should be specified or the respondent should be allowed to select the time unit. For example, income, spending, driving habits, and frequency of exercise all have a time dimension, which needs to be captured in the questionnaire.

3.6.2 Responses in the Form of Categorical Variables

For categorical questions, most large-scale formal surveys use precoded response options, meaning that the possible responses to each question are specified before implementing the survey. There are three advantages of precoding:

1. During the interview, the response can be recorded quickly by checking a box or writing a number, rather than writing the full response in words.

2. After the survey, there is no need to examine all the answers and classify them into groups, a time-consuming process.

3. Finally, it avoids the situation where a response is ambiguous or covers two different response options.

The disadvantage of precoding responses is that the response options must be carefully selected to cover all likely responses. It may be useful to include an "other" option and, in some cases, allow the respondent to specify in words a response that is not listed.

In preparing the response codes for categorical questions, it is important that the response options be mutually exclusive and exhaustive. The responses should be *mutually exclusive* (nonoverlapping). For example, a respondent might be both divorced and a widow. Either in the questionnaire for online surveys or in the training for in-person interviews, enumerators need to be instructed how to deal with difficult cases like this. For example, the enumerators could be instructed to select the first option that applies. Or the question could indicate that the respondent should "check all that apply."

In addition, the response options should be *exhaustive*, covering all or at least the vast majority of cases. The use of "other" ensures that the response options are exhaustive, but ideally "other" should represent only a small share of the responses, say, less than 5% of the total.

Closed questions can be used to collect information on opinions. One approach is to give a statement to the respondent and ask about the degree of agreement using a 5-point Likert-type scale. For example, political polls often use this type of question:

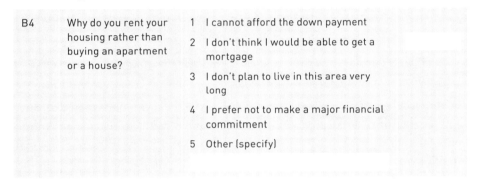

B3	3	My representative in Congress stands for the interests of people like me.	1 Strongly agree
			2 Agree
			3 Neither agree nor disagree
			4 Disagree
			5 Strongly disagree
			98 Do not know

Closed questions can even be used to address "why" questions if the researcher has a good idea of the most common responses. In this case, it may be useful to include "Other" as a response option. If "Other" is likely to be a common response, the researcher may wish to allow the respondent to specify what the "Other" response is. For example,

B4	Why do you rent your housing rather than buying an apartment or a house?	1	I cannot afford the down payment
		2	I don't think I would be able to get a mortgage
		3	I don't plan to live in this area very long
		4	I prefer not to make a major financial commitment
		5	Other (specify)

3.7 SKIP PATTERNS

Skip patterns are guidelines in the questionnaire to tell the enumerator which questions should be skipped over based on the responses to earlier questions. It is important that these be clearly specified in the questionnaire to ensure consistency in the way questions are asked from one respondent to the next. When asking about members of the household, many questions are age-specific. For example, questions about school attendance are not appropriate for infants, while questions about occupation and marital status only make sense for adults. Rather than basing the skip patterns on vague terms such as *infant* and *adult*, the questionnaire should specify the appropriate age range for each question.

Skip pattern instructions, like other instructions to the enumerator, should be distinguished from the wording of questions. For example, instructions to the enumerator may be put in italics or in brackets to distinguish them.

The skip patterns can get complicated, particularly if there are multiple branches that the interview could take. For example, a set of questions about housing can take three paths depending on the answers to the first and third questions.

B5	Do you own or rent your housing?	1. Own 2. Rent	
			If "Own," skip to B7
B6	How much do you spend on rent each month?	$/month	
			Skip to B9
B7	Do you have a mortgage?	1. Yes 2. No	
			If "No," Skip to B9
B8	How much do you pay per month for your mortgage?	$/month	

Clearly specifying the skip pattern is important whether the responses are being recorded on a paper questionnaire or on a tablet. With paper questionnaires, the skip pattern must be included in the questionnaire so that the enumerator can clearly see which questions should be asked next, based on the previous answer. This is a common source of error in implementing paper-based questionnaires, so it is worth emphasizing the skip patterns in training the enumerators.

With tablet-based questionnaires, the skip patterns need to be incorporated into the program with a series of if–then commands so that the enumerator is automatically guided to the correct question, depending on the responses to previous questions. One of the important advantages of tablet-based questionnaires is that, by incorporating the skip patterns into the program, data collection errors are greatly reduced.

The skip patterns have implications for the analysis of the data. Questions that are skipped over in the interview will be recorded as missing values in the data. In the earlier example, the respondents are first asked whether they have any children and, if the response is "yes," then asked how many. In this case, the variable for number of children will be missing (rather than zero) if there are no children. Calculating the average of this variable will give the average among those respondents with children. If the researcher wants the average number of children including the zeros, the missing values will need to be replaced with zeros.

3.8 ETHICAL ISSUES

The formal review of ethics in research was prompted by a number of cases of extreme abuse of research participants, most notably the Tuskegee Syphilis Study (1932–1972). Congress passed the National Research Act of 1974, which led to the Belmont Report, outlining issues and guidelines for the use of human subjects (National Commission for the Protection of Human Subjects of Biomedical and Behavioral Research, 1979). Subsequent regulations require the establishment of institutional review boards (IRBs) to review and approve (or reject) research plans to protect the rights and interests of human subjects. IRBs are certified and regulated by the Office for Human Research Protections of the Department of Health and Human Services. Almost all universities, hospitals, and research institutes in the United States have created IRBs.

Biomedical research is strictly controlled to ensure that the risks associated with testing new drugs and treatments are understood by the participants and that the potential benefits outweigh the risks. Medical researchers must apply for and obtain approval for each study from their IRB. The regulations are not as tight on surveys and other forms of social science research, but approval from an IRB is required if the research involves human subjects. Even without the risks associated with new drugs or treatments, respondents are offering their time to answer questions, some of which may be on sensitive topics.

IRB approval is based on three broad criteria. First, it is necessary that respondents or participants give informed consent to participate in the study. *Informed consent* means that the respondents must give prior approval for their participation after receiving information about the study and the nature of their involvement. This typically takes the form of a paragraph explaining to the respondents about who is carrying out the survey, the goals of the survey, and any risks or benefits of participation.

Second, participants must be assured of *confidentiality*, meaning that the results of the survey will be presented in aggregate form so that the responses of individuals cannot be identified. Furthermore, if the data are shared with other researchers, any variables that allow the identification of individual respondents (e.g., names, addresses, phone numbers, or GPS [Global Positioning System] coordinates) will be removed from the data set.

Third, the IRB approval depends on an assessment that the costs and risks to the participants are justified by some benefit to the public at large. Although somewhat subjective, this criterion ensures that the research is worthwhile, taking into account any cost or inconveniences to the participants. There are special protections for vulnerable groups, including racial minorities, very ill people, children, and prisoners.

Additional information on IRBs is available from Qiao (2018) and Protection of Human Subjects (2009).

EXERCISES

1. Which of the following questions generate responses that are continuous variable responses and which ones generate responses that are categorical variables?

    a. How old are you?

    b. What is the highest educational degree you have completed?

    c. How many years of education do you have?

    d. What state were you born in?

    e. Are both of your parents still alive?

    f. How many times per week do you exercise?

    g. What is your weight in pounds?

2. Identify the hidden assumption(s) or the flaw(s) in the following questions.

    a. How much do you earn at your job?

    b. What is the age of your oldest child?

    c. In light of his ineffectiveness, do you agree that the governor should not be reelected?

    d. How old (in years) is your car?

    e. How frequently do you go shopping?

    f. Do you think the town firefighters should be full-time workers and paid more?

3. What are skip patterns in a questionnaire and what purpose do they serve?

REFERENCES

Ekinci, Y. (2015). *Designing research questionnaires for business and management students*. Thousand Oaks, CA: Sage.

Grosh, M., & Glewwe, P. (2000). *Designing household survey questionnaires for developing countries: Lessons from 15 years of the Living Standard Measurement Study*. Washington, DC: World Bank. Retrieved from http://siteresources.worldbank.org/INTPOVRES/Resources/477227–1142020443961/2311843–1197996479165/part1_DesigningHHS.pdf

National Commission for the Protection of Human Subjects of Biomedical and Behavioral Research. (1979). *The Belmont Report: Ethical principles and guidelines for the protection of human subjects of research*. Retrieved from www.hhs.gov/ohrp/sites/default/files/the-belmont-report-508c_FINAL.pdf

Protection of Human Subjects. (2009). Code of Federal Regulations, Title 45, Part 46. Retrieved from www.hhs.gov/ohrp/regulations-and-policy/regulations/45-cfr-46/index.html

Qiao, H. (2018). A brief introduction to institutional review boards in the United States. *Pediatric Investigation, 2*(1), 46–51. Retrieved from https://onlinelibrary.wiley.com/doi/abs/10.1002/ped4.12023

Rea, L. M., & Parker, R. A. (2005). *Designing and conducting survey research: A comprehensive guide*. San Francisco, CA: Jossey-Bass.

DESCRIBING DATA

PART TWO

AN INTRODUCTION TO STATA

Chapter Preview

Opening Stata	Click on Start and search for Stata
	Double-click on any file generated with Stata
	Double-click on the Stata icon
Stata windows	Results
	Review
	Command
	Variables
	Properties
Working with existing data	Command window
	Menus
	Do-files
Entering your own data into Stata	Entering data
	Renaming variables
	Creating variable labels
	Creating value labels
Using log files and saving your work	Opening and closing a log file
	Copying output to a word processor
	Saving changes to your data

Getting help	Help command
	Search command
	Stata website
	UCLA's Institute for Digital Research and Education website
Stata command examples	**tab instagrm**
	rename var1 hand
	label define handlabel 1 "Right" 2 "Left"
	label value hand handlabel
	log using "c:\gunlaw", **text**
	save "c:\filename.dta"

4.1 INTRODUCTION

Stata is a powerful statistical software package that is relatively easy to learn. As described in the preface, it has been growing rapidly in popularity and is used almost exclusively in some fields. It is particularly popular in the fields of biomedicine, epidemiology, economics, political science, psychology, and sociology. Learning data analysis with Stata will provide you with a distinct, marketable skill.

In this chapter, we will learn the basics of Stata and move on to more advanced skills in later chapters, where we will use Stata to examine descriptive statistics and test hypotheses. By completing the examples and exercises in this book, you will have a basic knowledge of Stata that you can build on as you develop more advanced statistical skills through further study or use.

4.2 OPENING STATA AND STATA WINDOWS

You can open Stata by clicking on Start and then searching for the Stata program. If the Stata icon is on your desktop, you can click on the Stata icon. You can also click on any file created with Stata to open the package. We will begin by double-clicking on the GSS2016.dta file and examining Stata's five main windows.

Figure 4.1 shows the opening screen. Like most software packages, the top row offers a set of menus followed by a second row of icons for functions that are used most frequently. In addition to these standard features, there are five windows that appear: (1) the Results Window (which is the largest window in the center without a label), (2) the Review Window, (3) the Command Window, (4) the Variables Window, and (5) the Properties Window.

FIGURE 4.1 ● OPENING STATA SCREEN

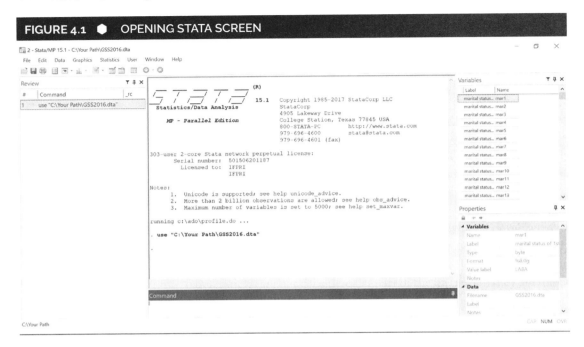

4.2.1 Results Window

Once you start using Stata to analyze data, all of your recent commands, output, and error messages will appear in the Results Window. The slide bar or scroll on the right side can be used to look at earlier results that are not on the screen. However, the Results Window does not keep all of the output generated. By default, it will keep about 500 lines of the most recent output and delete any earlier output. If you want to store output in a file, you must use a log file, which is described in more detail below.

4.2.2 Review Window

This window lists all of the recent commands. If you click on one of the commands, it will be copied to the Command Window, where it can be executed by pressing the "Enter" key. Or you can modify the command first and then run the command. If you double-click on the command, it will be directly re-executed by Stata.

4.2.3 Command Window

This window allows you to enter commands that will be executed as soon as you press the "Enter" key. You can also use recent commands again by using the "Page Up" key (to go to the previous command that appears in the Review Window) and "Page Down" key (to go to the next command). If you double-click on a variable in the Variables Window, it will appear in the Command Window.

4.2.4 Variables Window

This window lists all the variables in the data set that is open. You can increase the size of this window to see the full variable labels. If you create new variables, they will be added to the list of variables. If you delete variables, they will be removed from the list. You can insert a variable into the Command Window by double-clicking on it in the Variables Window.

4.2.5 Properties Window

The Properties Window provides information about the variables in the open data set. If you click once on any variable in the Variables Window, the Properties Window will give you information about that variable, such as the name, label, and type of variable, along with information about the data set.

4.3 WORKING WITH EXISTING DATA

Let's begin by using the General Social Survey data set from 2016 (GSS2016) that we already opened above. This is a data set that explores attitudes, behaviors, and demographic information about people living in the United States. It has been collected almost every year since 1972. Because we will use the survey from just one year, 2016, it is called a cross-section data set. This means it looks at a cross section of responses at one point in time. Every row represents the response of one individual, and all responses are from the same point in time. If instead, we followed the inflation rate, interest rates, and money supply in one country over 30 years, it would be a time-series data set, since it represents data or information over time. In that case, each row represents a different year. Finally, a panel data set combines both cross-section data and time-series data. For example, if you followed 100 patients after surgery for 10 years and measured their progress, you would be using cross-section data (100 patients in 1 year) and time-series data (each patient's results every year over 10 years). In this case, each row represents one cross-section unit (a patient) and one time period (a year).

Let's suppose that we want to find out what proportion of the population uses Instagram. This is called a categorical variable since it has two categories—yes, the respondent uses Instagram, and no, the respondent does not use Instagram. Continuous variables, on the other hand, are variables that take on a specific value such as someone's exact age or income. Types of variables and their measurement are discussed in more detail in Chapter 6.

There are three ways to obtain information on what proportion of the population uses Instagram using Stata: (1) the Command Window, (2) menus, and (3) do-files.

OUTPUT 4.1: FREQUENCY TABLE OF INSTAGRAM USE

```
. tab instagrm

      use
  instagrm  │     Freq.      Percent        Cum.
 ───────────┼───────────────────────────────────
       yes  │       423        30.83       30.83
        no  │       949        69.17      100.00
 ───────────┼───────────────────────────────────
     Total  │     1,372       100.00
```

In the Command Window at the bottom of the screen, we would type in **tab instagrm** and press "Enter." You can also type **tab ins** and then the "Tab" key. This will fill in the rest of the variable name automatically. The information in Output 4.1 would then appear in our Results Window. Notice that our command **tab instagrm** also appears in the Review Window located to the left of the Results Window. If we double-click on the command in the Review Window, the command will be executed again. If we click only once on the command in the Review Window, it will appear in the Command Window.

The second method with which to interact with Stata is by using menus. To generate the same output as in Output 4.1, we would click on the sequence listed below that would bring us to Dialog Box 4.1. In this box, we would select the variable "instagrm" in the drop-down menu under "categorical variable."

In the Results Window, you will notice that the command **tabulate instagrm** is shown above the output. When we typed the command into the Command Window, we shortened tabulate to **tab**. Stata accepts abbreviations for commands, but in some cases, such as the **table** and **tabulate** commands, **table** must be spelled out completely. Otherwise, **table** is mistaken for **tabulate**. If you are unsure, you can use the help file to look up a command, and it will underline that portion of the command that must be typed.

Finally, the third way to interact with Stata is through the use of "do-files." A do-file is a file where you type commands or code rather than using menus. By using do-files, you can save, revise, and rerun commands. This is particularly helpful if you have completed much of your analysis but then make changes to the data or if you add new observations to your data set. Instead of writing out new commands in

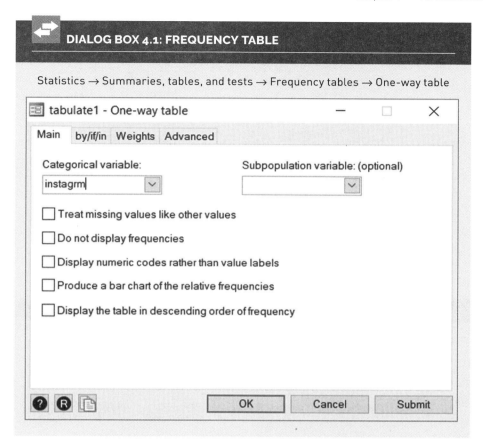

DIALOG BOX 4.1: FREQUENCY TABLE

Statistics → Summaries, tables, and tests → Frequency tables → One-way table

the Command Window or clicking on menus for each analysis, you would simply highlight the commands in your do-file and run them all at once. Do-files are also important since they document changes to your data set and allow you to collaborate with others. Most data analysis should be carried out using the do-file editor.

To use a do-file to generate a frequency table of Instagram users, we would open a do-file. The fastest way to open a new do-file is to click on the icon that shows a notepad with a pencil or by pressing "Ctrl 9." You could also use menus by clicking on "Window → Do-File Editor → New Do-File Editor." Once you have your do-file open, type in **tab instagrm** on the first line. Pressing on "Enter" will only take you to the second line and will not run the command. Instead, you can either put your cursor anywhere on the line and press "Ctrl d." If you have more than one line in your do-file, this will run all of the commands. If you only want to run one command, then you need to highlight at least one character on the line that you want to run before pressing "Ctrl d." Instead of "Ctrl d," you can also click on the icon that shows a paper with the corner folded down and an arrow.

4.4 ENTERING YOUR OWN DATA INTO STATA

To enter your own data into Stata, we would start by double-clicking on the Stata icon. We would then open the data editor by clicking on the icon that shows a spreadsheet with a pencil. We could also use the menus and click on "Data → Data Editor → Data Editor (Edit)."

With the data editor open, we can now type data into the cells. Suppose, for example, there are 10 students in a classroom. We would first fill in the first column with numbers 1 through 10 so that each student has an identification number or ID. We could then ask each student to indicate how many siblings the student has including himself or herself and record the response in the second column. Finally, we could ask each student if he or she is right-handed or left-handed. Right-handed would be recorded as "1" and left-handed would be recorded as "2." The data would appear as illustrated in Figure 4.2.

FIGURE 4.2 ●   ENTERING YOUR OWN DATA FOR TWO VARIABLES PLUS AN ID

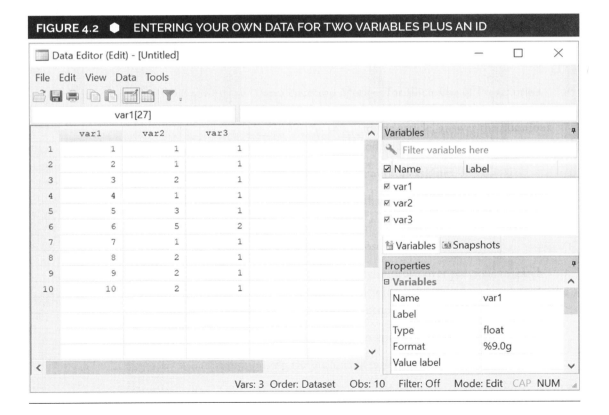

FIGURE 4.3 ● DO-FILE TO CREATE VARIABLE NAMES, VARIABLE LABELS, AND VALUE LABELS

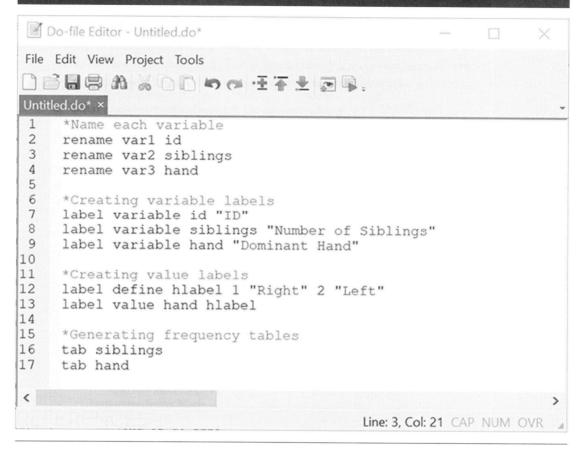

```
Do-file Editor - Untitled.do*

File  Edit  View  Project  Tools

Untitled.do* ×
 1     *Name each variable
 2     rename var1 id
 3     rename var2 siblings
 4     rename var3 hand
 5
 6     *Creating variable labels
 7     label variable id "ID"
 8     label variable siblings "Number of Siblings"
 9     label variable hand "Dominant Hand"
10
11     *Creating value labels
12     label define hlabel 1 "Right" 2 "Left"
13     label value hand hlabel
14
15     *Generating frequency tables
16     tab siblings
17     tab hand

                                          Line: 3, Col: 21  CAP  NUM  OVR
```

Next, we would want to give each variable a name, a variable label, and value labels for the question about dominant hand. To do this, we would open a do-file by putting the cursor on the main screen of Stata and clicking on the do-file icon. In our do-file, we would type the following commands as illustrated in Figure 4.3 and explained below.

First, note that we can write notes within the do-file to indicate what we are doing. If there is an asterisk at the beginning of a line, Stata will ignore the line. We can also skip lines to keep the do-file more organized.

The first four lines are used to rename the variables from "var1," "var2," and "var3" to "id," "siblings," and "hand," respectively. In Stata, variable names are case sensitive,

> **OUTPUT 4.2: FREQUENCY TABLES AFTER CREATING VARIABLE NAMES, VARIABLE LABELS, AND VALUE LABELS**

```
. tab siblings
```

Number of Siblings	Freq.	Percent	Cum.
1	4	40.00	40.00
2	4	40.00	80.00
3	1	10.00	90.00
5	1	10.00	100.00
Total	10	100.00	

```
. tab hand
```

Dominant Hand	Freq.	Percent	Cum.
Right	9	90.00	90.00
Left	1	10.00	100.00
Total	10	100.00	

meaning that "siblings," "Siblings," and "SIBLINGS" would be considered three separate variables. For each variable, you must be consistent with the capitalization.

Lines 6 through 9 are used to give each variable a label, which is often shown in the Stata output. This is useful when the variable name alone does not give enough information about the variable. In Lines 11 through 13, we are creating value labels, which indicate for the variable "hand" that each number represents right or left. Note that we first define a set of labels using **label define** hlabel 1 "Right" 2 "Left." The word "hlabel" can be any word that we choose. We then apply these labels in Line 13. Finally, we can generate two tables in Lines 16 and 17 that use the variable labels and value labels. The output from this do-file is shown in Output 4.2.

4.5 USING LOG FILES AND SAVING YOUR WORK

As mentioned earlier, the Results Window does not automatically keep all of the output that you generate. It only stores about 500 lines. When it is full, it begins to delete the old results as you add new results. You can increase the amount of memory allocated to the Results Window, but even the maximum amount of memory will not be enough for a long session with Stata. Thus, we need to use the **log** command to save our output in a "log file."

There are several ways to start a log file. You can use the icon that shows a notebook with a spiral binding, or you can click on File and then Log from the menus. You can also use a **log** command in the Command Window. Finally, you can use **log** commands in the do-file. Because it is so important to learn to use do-files for most of your work, we will focus on the use of **log** commands within do-files.

Let's use the GSS2016.dta file to work through an example about views on gun permits in the United States. After opening the file, we could type the following commands into a do-file as shown in Figure 4.4.

Line 1 tells Stata to change the directory to the location of the folder where you want to store the log file. We could indicate that location in Line 2 as part of the path in quotation marks. However, if we want to collaborate and allow others to use our do-file, it is better to use this technique. Each collaborator could then change the directory to their own path and run the rest of the do-file.

FIGURE 4.4 ● DO-FILE TO OPEN AND CLOSE A LOG FILE

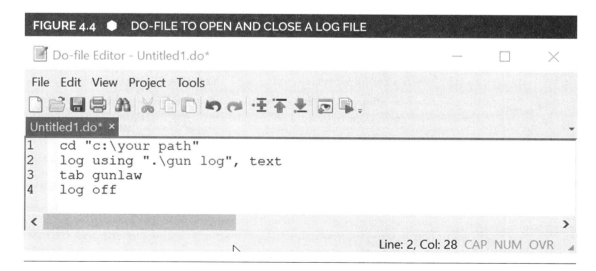

FIGURE 4.5 ●   LOG FILE IN TEXT FORMAT GENERATED BY STATA

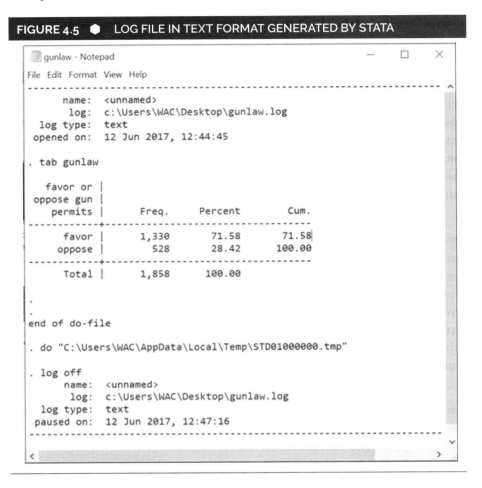

```
 gunlaw - Notepad                                          —      □      ×

File Edit Format View Help
- - - - - - - - - - - - - - - - - - - - - - - - - - - - - - - - - - - - - - - - - -
       name:  <unnamed>
        log:  c:\Users\WAC\Desktop\gunlaw.log
   log type:  text
  opened on:  12 Jun 2017, 12:44:45

. tab gunlaw

   favor or |
 oppose gun |
    permits |       Freq.      Percent         Cum.
- - - - - - - - - - - -+- - - - - - - - - - - - - - - - - - - - - - - - - - - -
      favor |       1,330        71.58        71.58
     oppose |         528        28.42       100.00
- - - - - - - - - - - -+- - - - - - - - - - - - - - - - - - - - - - - - - - - -
      Total |       1,858       100.00

.

.
end of do-file

. do "C:\Users\WAC\AppData\Local\Temp\STD01000000.tmp"

. log off
       name:  <unnamed>
        log:  c:\Users\WAC\Desktop\gunlaw.log
   log type:  text
  paused on:  12 Jun 2017, 12:47:16
- - - - - - - - - - - - - - - - - - - - - - - - - - - - - - - - - - - - - - - - - -
```

Line 2 tells Stata where you want to save the log file (your path) and the name of the log file. You could put it in any directory and folder. You can also give the log file any name. At the end of Line 2, we used the command **text** to let Stata know that we want the format to be a text file. If we didn't specify this, Stata would make this a Stata Markup and Control Language (smcl) file that could only be opened in Stata. A text file, on the other hand, can be opened in Word, Notepad, or any word processor.[1] Line 3 generates a frequency table on views about favoring or opposing

---

[1] Many students in a course related to Stata may not have Stata installed on their own computers. By converting the log to text, they can review their work on their own computers without Stata. If, however, you do have Stata on your computer, the smcl files within Stata are easier to read than text files outside of Stata.

gun permits. Finally, the last line closes the log file. Figure 4.5 shows the full contents of the log file that is generated.

Notice that the formatting for the table shows dotted lines instead of solid lines. Although you could cut and paste this table into a report, the dotted lines are not ideal. Instead, there are several ways to copy the table into a document. Within Stata, you can highlight a table and then use menus to click on "Edit" and "Copy as picture." If you prefer an image with a border, you could use the "Snipping Tool" that is included in all Windows operating systems. There are also several equivalent software tools for Mac such as Grab that is built into every operating system for a Mac computer.

In addition to the **log** commands that we illustrated above, there are several commands that you may want to use. For example, if you run the same do-file multiple times as you add to it or make changes, you must tell Stata to replace the existing log file with the newer version. Or if you want to add output to an existing file, you can do this with the **append** command. These are done as follows:

```
log using "c:\your file directory name\gunlaw", replace
log using "c:\your file directory name\gunlaw", append
```

Also, there is a difference between **log off** and **log close**. With the command **log off** that we used above, we can turn the log back on by running the command **log on**.[2]

If you use **log close**, you can only turn the log back on by running the command **log using**.

In addition to saving your commands in a do-file and your output in a log file, you may also want to save your data set if you made new variables or changes to any existing variables. It is good practice to always keep a copy of your original file. This allows you to start over if you make any mistakes as you modify the data. For this reason, when you do save your file, you should save it under a new name that is different from the original file name. If it is the first time you are saving your new file, you would use the first command below. If you are saving changes to the data set again later to a file that already exists, you would need to use the second line that includes the **replace** command. You could also use the "save file" icon in the tool bar at the top of the screen, but it is better to get in the habit of adding all commands to your do-file so that you can document your work and rerun the do-file as you continue your analysis.

---

[2] When using the **log on** and **log off** commands, Stata keeps the log file open and ready to use. If you then want to use a new log file in the do-file, you will get an error message.

```
save "c:\your file directory name\new file name.dta"
save "c:\your file directory name\same file name as above.dta",
replace
```

If for some reason you do want to save several versions of a data file, it is convenient to put the dates in the file name. Avoid using "new" or "old" in the file names as these labels are vague and will become outdated.

4.6 GETTING HELP

Documentation for earlier versions of Stata came with a set of books that took up an entire bookshelf—about 12,000 pages! Today, all documentation is built into the software. You may also find information on the Stata website or the UCLA (University of California, Los Angeles) website. These sources are described below.

4.6.1 Help Command

If you know the name of a Stata command, but need more information about how to use it, you can access the **help** command in two ways. First, you can type **help** into the Command Window along with the name of the command. For example, you could type **help tabulate**. This will open a screen that shows the **tabulate** command, various options that can be used with the command, how to access it from the menus, and some examples. You can also access the help files by clicking on "Help" in the menus and then "Stata command."

4.6.2 Search Command

The **search** command can also be accessed from the Command Window or by clicking on "Help" from the menus and then "Search." If we type **search tabulate** into the Command Window, this will open a screen with a long list of resources in addition to Stata's help files. For example, it will include web resources and information from other users.

4.6.3 Stata Website

At Stata's website, www.stata.com, you can find information on Stata products, training courses, technical support, and documentation. The training courses include online courses, video tutorials, and classroom training. Finally, you can join user groups from this site where you may post questions about Stata and receive responses from other users.

4.6.4 UCLA's Institute for Digital Research and Education Website

In addition to Stata's website, there are many other websites with information about Stata. One that may be particularly useful is UCLA's website, idre.ucla.edu/stata. This site offers learning modules and classes related to Stata.

4.7 SUMMARY OF COMMANDS USED IN THIS CHAPTER

In each chapter where we use Stata code, all of the commands used in the chapter will be summarized in this last section before the chapter exercises. In addition, all Stata code used throughout the book is summarized in Appendix 1.

Frequency table

```
tab instagrm
```

Variable names, variable labels, and value labels

```
rename var1 siblings
label variable siblings "Number of Siblings"
label define hlabel 1 "Right" 2 "Left"
label value hand hlabel
```

Log files

```
log using "c:\your file directory name\gunlaw", text
log using "c:\your file directory name\gunlaw", replace
log using "c:\your file directory name\gunlaw", append
log off (turn log back on using "log on")
log close (turn log back on by running "log using"
```

Save files

```
save "c:\your file directory name\new file name.dta"
save "c:\your file directory name\same file name as above.
dta", replace
```

Help commands

```
help tabulate
search tabulate
```

EXERCISES

1. Twenty-five college students were asked four questions about their TV and movie viewing habits:

   (1) Which TV service do you use most often to watch television shows and movies?

   (2) How many hours a week do you spend watching television or movies?

   (3) How often do you binge watch television (watching more than three episodes of the same show in a row)? They could choose from (a) not at all, (b) sometimes—one to three times per week, and (c) frequently— more than three times per week.

   (4) Gender

   Based on their responses that are in the table below, enter these data into Stata and then complete the following tasks that will allow you to practice labeling variables, developing value labels, saving your work, and generating frequency tables.

   a. Enter the data for each of the four variables. For the three categorical variables, create a numeric code for each response. For example, for TV Source, 1 = Amazon Prime, 2 = Cable, 3 = Hulu Plus, 4 = iTunes, and 5 = Netflix.

   b. Once you have entered the data, rename each variable.

   c. Give each variable a variable label.

   d. Give each numeric code a value label.

   e. Save your data file (you will use this again in a later chapter).

   f. What percentage of the sample identify as males and females?

   g. Which type of TV service is used most frequently?

   h. What percentage of students binge watch TV frequently?

Student Responses to Survey About TV and Movie Viewing Habits

Student	TV Source	Hours per Week	Binge Frequency	Gender
1	Hulu Plus	14	Not at all	Male
2	Amazon Prime	18	Sometimes	Female
3	Hulu Plus	20	Frequently	Female
4	Netflix	5	Frequently	Male
5	Netflix	12	Frequently	Male
6	iTunes	10	Not at all	Female
7	iTunes	8	Frequently	Female
8	iTunes	7	Sometimes	Male
9	Cable	24	Frequently	Male
10	Hulu Plus	30	Sometimes	Female
11	Netflix	10	Sometimes	Male
12	Netflix	15	Frequently	Female
13	iTunes	12	Sometimes	Male
14	iTunes	14	Sometimes	Female
15	Amazon Prime	2	Sometimes	Female
16	Netflix	8	Frequently	Male
17	iTunes	10	Frequently	Male
18	Cable	19	Sometimes	Female
19	Netflix	18	Sometimes	Female
20	iTunes	21	Frequently	Male
21	iTunes	22	Sometimes	Male
22	iTunes	23	Frequently	Female
23	Netflix	17	Frequently	Female
24	Netflix	14	Sometimes	Male
25	Amazon Prime	13	Sometimes	Female

2. To determine how many people in the United States use Facebook and Snapchat, use the GSS2016 data set to complete the following exercises. These exercises will also allow you to practice using the **log** commands.

   a. Open a do-file and then use it for all of your commands for this exercise.

   b. Open a log file and name it "gss log."

   c. Open the GSS2016 data set.

   d. Generate a frequency table of the variable "facebook."

   e. Stop your log file by using "**log off**."

   f. Turn your log file back on.

   g. Generate a frequency table of the variable "snapchat."

   h. Stop your log file by using "**log close**."

   i. Submit your log file as your answer to all parts of Question 2.

3. The Admitted Student Questionnaire (ASQ) is administered by colleges each year to its incoming first-year students. The 2014 ASQ data set contains the responses from all students who answered the questionnaire that year—more than 5,000. Use this data set to explore how many colleges students applied to in the 2014–2015 academic year and to practice copying the output for use in other documents.

   a. Generate a table that shows the number of colleges that each student applied to during the 2014–2015 academic year (Q65).

   b. Copy and paste that table into a Word document by highlighting the table, right clicking on the table, and then selecting "Copy as picture."

   c. Change the font size of the output to fit it all on the results screen in Stata. To do this, highlight the table, right click, and choose font. Then set the font to a smaller size (8 or 9) so that the whole table fits on the screen.

   d. Copy the table you resized by using Snipping Tool if you are using a Windows operating system. To do this, open the Snipping Tool software, click on "New," place the cursor in the upper-left corner of the table, and then drag the cursor to the lower-right corner while holding down the left button on the mouse. Then click on "Ctrl c" to copy the table and then "Ctrl v" to paste it into a Word document.

PREPARING AND TRANSFORMING YOUR DATA

Chapter Preview

Checking for outliers	Codebook
	Frequency tables
	Descriptive statistics
	Histograms
Creating new variables	Generate
	Using operators
	Recode
	Egen
Missing values	Missing
	Replace

5.1 INTRODUCTION

Whether you are using primary data that you collected yourself or secondary data, you will want to spend some time "cleaning" your data. This involves checking all variables for missing data, errors, or *outliers*. An outlier is an observation that lies extremely far from the mean or other values in a variable. For example, if someone records that he or she is 125 years old or that he or she earns 25 billion dollars, you will want to investigate these numbers and possibly make some changes to the data. Or if someone records that he or she watches 24 hours a day of television on average, you know there must be a mistake.

In addition to checking for missing data, errors, or outliers, you will also want to make new variables using the existing data. This could involve adding several variables together or transforming a variable, such as age, into categories or age ranges. You may also want to know how many people responded to several different variables combined.

All of these procedures are covered in this chapter along with documenting your work through the use of do-files. Do-files are particularly important when cleaning a data set since you will need to keep track of all changes that you make. In addition, before you begin cleaning your data, you should always make an original copy of the file that will not be changed. This allows you to start over if you make any mistakes as you modify the data.

5.2 CHECKING FOR OUTLIERS

As described in the Introduction, outliers occur when a true value is simply far outside of the range of other observations. Because these extreme values will affect most of the statistics that we will learn about later in this book, we need to identify outliers and then decide what to do with them.

One method with which to examine your variables and look for outliers is to use the command **codebook**. By typing this into the Command Window or in a do-file, Stata will generate information about every variable in your data set. Outputs 5.1 and 5.2 give examples of two types of variables from the GSS2016 data set—a continuous variable and a categorical variable, which are discussed in more detail in Chapter 6. In Output 5.1, you can easily see the age range of your respondents and the number of missing values. The **missing .: 0/2,867** tells you that there are zero missing values

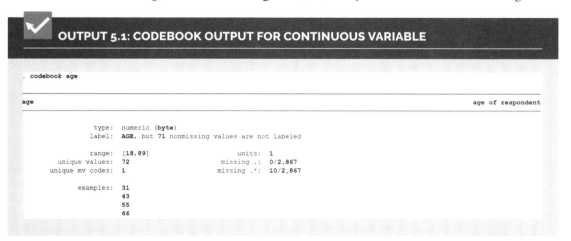

OUTPUT 5.1: CODEBOOK OUTPUT FOR CONTINUOUS VARIABLE

```
. codebook age

age                                                                    age of respondent

              type:  numeric (byte)
             label:  AGE, but 71 nonmissing values are not labeled

             range:  [18,89]              units:  1
     unique values:  72            missing .:  0/2,867
   unique mv codes:  1            missing .*:  10/2,867

          examples:  31
                     43
                     55
                     66
```

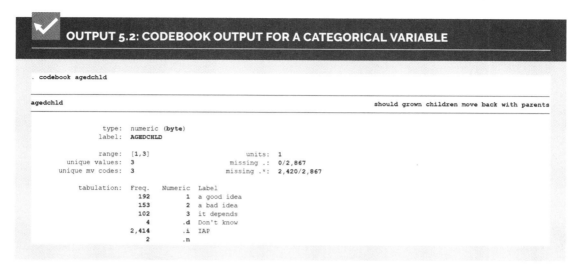

OUTPUT 5.2: CODEBOOK OUTPUT FOR A CATEGORICAL VARIABLE

```
. codebook agedchld

agedchld                                                         should grown children move back with parents

               type:  numeric (byte)
               label: AGEDCHLD

               range:  [1,3]                    units:  1
        unique values:  3                  missing .:  0/2,867
      unique mv codes:  3                 missing .*:  2,420/2,867

          tabulation:  Freq.   Numeric  Label
                         192         1  a good idea
                         153         2  a bad idea
                         102         3  it depends
                           4        .d  Don't know
                       2,414        .i  IAP
                           2        .n
```

with no explanation out of 2,867 observations. The **missing .*: 10/2,867** tells you that there are 10 answers that are missing with a code for why they are missing. If you then examine the variable with the command or **tab age, missing**, you can see that there are 10 respondents who have no recorded answer.

In Output 5.2, respondents are asked if grown children should move back in with their parents. In this case, you can see that there are three possible answers. In addition, there are three codes for missing values—don't know, inapplicable (IAP), and missing without a given reason (.n).

In addition to the codebook, it is also useful to generate frequency tables for categorical variables with a limited number of responses and descriptive statistics such as the mean and standard deviation for continuous variables. Histograms are also useful to identify patterns in your data. All of these methods are discussed further in Chapter 6.

Returning to the data set that we created in Chapter 4, where the respondents indicated the number of siblings they have and their dominant hand, let's suppose that we have one additional observation whereby the 11th person accidentally entered 20 for the number of siblings and "3" instead of "1" or "2" for right-handed and left-handed, respectively. Figure 5.1 shows the data editor screen for this data set. Because there are only 11 observations, we could easily identify these errors by simply looking at the raw data. With thousands of observations, however, we would need to examine the data using the codebook, frequency tables, descriptive statistics, and histograms.

FIGURE 5.1 ● DATA EDITOR SCREEN SHOWING ERRORS IN DATA

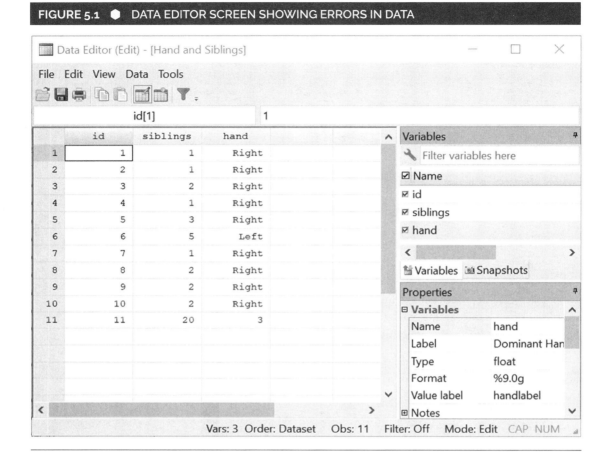

Once we have identified these errors, we would need to make changes to the data set. If we don't know what the respondent intended to write for the number of siblings, then we would have to delete the value. If we know that the respondent meant to type "2," we could legitimately change this in our do-file. The two commands would appear as follows:

```
replace siblings = . if id==11 (to change the value to
missing)
replace siblings = 2 if id==11 (to change the value to a 2)
```

In the first command, Stata changes the value in observation 11 to a "." indicating that the value is missing and to a "2" in the second command. Although we could do this directly in the data editor screen, it is better to record all changes in a do-file as mentioned earlier. In addition to documenting all changes, if we download a data set multiple times as new observations are added to an online questionnaire, for example, it will have the same errors each time. By writing a do-file, we can correct the errors each time by simply running the do-file.

Similarly, to change the number 3 in the 11th row to a 2 for the variable hand, we would write,

```
Replace hand = 2 if id==11
```

Although researchers are tempted to simply remove all outliers, there are some basic rules regarding when it is acceptable to drop an outlier and how it should be documented. If the outlier is a data entry error, such as watching 24 hours of TV a day, then you can remove this since you know it is a mistake. If, however, there is a legitimate outlier, such as 1 billion in a data set that asks for annual income, the researcher could remove the outlier and include a footnote to indicate that this one observation was removed.[1]

5.3 CREATING NEW VARIABLES

When you begin working with a data set, you will often want to create new variables. This can be done in a number of ways. In this section, we will cover the following methods:

- generate
- recode
- egen

5.3.1 Generate

The **generate** command is used to create a new variable. The Stata code for **generate** is as follows:

```
gen newvar = expression [if expression]
```

The command **gen** must be in lowercase, like all Stata commands, while "newvar" represents the new variable being created. As discussed in the previous chapter, Stata variable names are case sensitive, meaning that uppercase letters are considered different from lowercase letters. After defining the variable, you must use the same

---

[1] For a complete review of outliers and advanced methods for dealing with them, see Osborne (2012).

capitalization whenever you refer to it. The "expression" in the code above is mathematical such as "price*quantity" or "annual salary/260 days." If the expression is an equality or inequality, such as (age > 15), then the new variable will take the value of 0 if the expression is false and 1 if it is true. Finally, if you use an **if** command, the new variable will have missing values when the if statement is false. Table 5.1 shows some examples.

5.3.2 Using Operators

Operators are symbols used in equations as shown in Table 5.1 above. Most of the operators are obvious (e.g., + and –), but some are not. Table 5.2 lists the most commonly used operators. In Stata, you cannot use words such as "or," "and," "eq," or "gt." Instead, you must use operator symbols.

The most difficult rule to remember is when to use = (single equal symbol) and when to use == (double equal symbol).

- Use a single equal symbol (=) when defining a variable.

- Use a double equal symbol (==) when you are testing an equality, such as in an "if" statement and when creating a dummy variable, which are discussed in later chapters.

5.3.3 Recode

The **recode** command redefines the values of a variable according to rules that you specify. The command is as follows:

```
recode varlist (oldvalues = newvalue) (oldvalues = newvalue)
… [if exp] [in range]
```

TABLE 5.1 ● EXAMPLES OF THE GENERATE COMMAND

Command	Operation
gen pctoffers=totoffers/applications*100	Creates a new variable that shows the percentage of job offers someone receives as a proportion of their total applications submitted.
gen salaryintern=beginningsalary if internship==1 & beginningsalary !=.	Creates a new variable that shows the beginning salary for a first job after college if the student had an internship. If they did not, the value will be missing.
gen highprice = (price > 1000) & price !=.	Creates a variable equal to 1 to indicate that the price is greater than 1,000 and 0 to indicate that it is 1,000 or lower.

Source: Adapted from Minot (2012).

TABLE 5.2 ● KEY OPERATORS FOR WRITING EQUATIONS IN STATA		
Operator	**Meaning**	**Example**
+	Addition	**gen income = agincome + nonagincome**
–	Subtraction	**gen netrevenue = revenue – cost**
*	Multiplication	**gen value = price * quantity**
/	Division	**gen exppc = expenditure/hhsize**
^	Power	**gen agesquared = age^2**
>	Greater than	**gen aboveavg = 1 if income > avgincome**
>=	Greater than or equal to	**gen adult = 1 if age >= 18**
<	Less than	**gen belowavg = 1 if income < avgincome**
<=	Less than or equal to	**gen child = 1 if age <=10**
=	Assignment operator	**gen expend = foodexp + nonfoodexp**
==	Equal	**gen femhead = 1 if sexhead==2**
!=	Not equal	**gen error = 1 if value1 != value2**
|	Or	**gen age=. if age==999 | age=9999**
&	And	**gen sexhead = 1 if sex==1 & relation==1**

Source: Adapted from Minot (2012).

Table 5.3 lists some examples of the **recode** command.

TABLE 5.3 ● EXAMPLES OF THE RECODE COMMAND	
Command	**Operation**
recode x (1=2)	Within the *x* variable, all 1s become 2
recode x y z (1=2) (3=4)	In variables *x*, *y*, and *z*, changes 1 to 2 and 3 to 4
recode x (1=2) (2=1)	In the variable *x*, exchanges the values 1 and 2
recode x (1=2) (*=3)	In the variable *x*, changes 1 to 2 and all other values to 3
recode x 1/5=2	In the variable *x*, changes 1 through 5 to 2
recode x y (1 3 4 5 = 6)	In variables *x* and *y*, changes 1, 3, 4, and 5 to 6
recode x (.=9)	In the variable *x*, changes missing to 9
recode x (9=.)	In the variable *x*, changes 9 to missing

Source: Adapted from Minot (2012).

Notice that you can use some special symbols in the **recode** command:

- ***** means all other values

- **x/y** means all values from *x* to *y*

- **x y** means values *x* and *y*

Output 5.3 shows an example of creating a new variable using the **recode** command. Suppose that we are interested in knowing the happiness level of someone who is currently married and living with his or her partner versus someone who is not currently married nor living with his or her partner. Using the GSS2016 data sets, we would first check the marital status variable, mar1, using a **codebook mar1**. Notice that there are five categories: (1) married, (2) widowed, (3) divorced, (4) separated, and (5) never married. Although we would assume that the labels are given values in the order from 1 to 5, it is always important to check this to be sure before you recode. We would now generate a new variable, "maritalstat," that is identical to the original

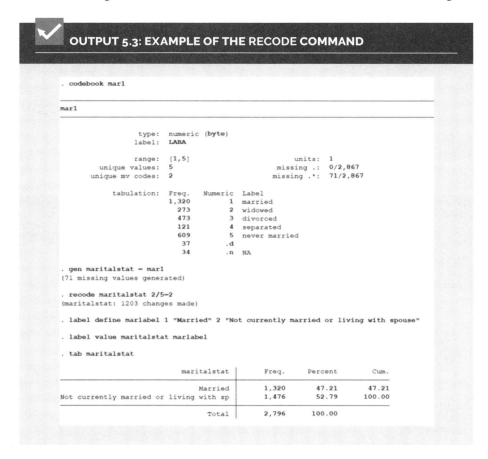

OUTPUT 5.3: EXAMPLE OF THE RECODE COMMAND

```
. codebook mar1

mar1

                    type:   numeric (byte)
                   label:   LABA

                   range:   [1,5]                      units:  1
           unique values:   5                      missing .:  0/2,867
         unique mv codes:   2                      missing .*: 71/2,867

              tabulation:   Freq.   Numeric  Label
                            1,320         1  married
                              273         2  widowed
                              473         3  divorced
                              121         4  separated
                              609         5  never married
                               37        .d
                               34        .n  NA

. gen maritalstat = mar1
(71 missing values generated)

. recode maritalstat 2/5=2
(maritalstat: 1203 changes made)

. label define marlabel 1 "Married" 2 "Not currently married or living with spouse"

. label value maritalstat marlabel

. tab maritalstat
```

maritalstat	Freq.	Percent	Cum.
Married	1,320	47.21	47.21
Not currently married or living with sp	1,476	52.79	100.00
Total	2,796	100.00	

variable mar1. Then, we begin the recoding process indicating that values 2 through 5 will all be equal to 2. Finally, we give new value labels to the variable showing that "1" is married and "2" is not currently married or living with a spouse.[2]

5.3.4 Egen

The **egen** command is an extended version of the **generate** command. It is used to create a new variable by aggregating the existing data. The command is as follows:

```
egen newvar = fcn(argument) [if exp] [in range], by(var)]
```

where

newvar is the new variable to be created

fcn is one of numerous functions such as

- count() max() min()
- mean() median() rank()
- sd() sum() rowtotal()

(See help **egen** for the full list.)

argument is normally just a variable or a variable list

var in the **by**() subcommand must be a *categorical* variable

Table 5.4 gives a few examples of the **egen** command using the mean, median, and sum and functions.

TABLE 5.4 ● EXAMPLES OF THE EGEN COMMAND	
Command	**Operation**
egen avgincome = mean(income)	Creates a variable of average income over the entire sample.
by region: egen regincome = median(income)	Creates a variable of median income by region.
by household: egen hhincome = sum(income)	Creates a variable of total income for each household.

Source: Adapted from Minot (2012).

---

[2] A less transparent but more streamlined approach to recode and generate the new variable maritalstat would be **recode mar1 2/5=2, generate(maritalstat)**.

Output 5.4 shows another example of the **egen** command. Using the 2014 Admitted Student Questionnaire data set (2014 ASQ Data), we may want to know how much emphasis students place on academics versus social life when choosing a college. Questions QA1, QA2, and QA3 ask students whether the quality of the faculty, majors of interest, and academic reputation are *very important* (= 1), *somewhat important* (= 2), or *not important* (= 3). Questions QA11, QA12, and QA14 ask about the importance of extracurricular opportunities, off-campus activities, and quality of social life using the same scale of *very, somewhat*, and *not important*. As shown in Output 5.4, we first generate two new variables using the **egen** command—academic and social. For the academic variable, **egen** counts the number of times variables QA1, QA2, and QA3 are given a value of "1" or *very important*.

OUTPUT 5.4: EXAMPLE OF THE EGEN COMMAND

```
. egen academic = anycount(QA1 QA2 QA3), values(1)

. egen social = anycount(QA11 QA12 QA14), values(1)

. egen academic_m = rowmiss(QA1 QA2 QA3)

. egen social_m = rowmiss(QA11 QA12 QA13)

. tab academic
```

QA1 QA2 QA3 == 1	Freq.	Percent	Cum.
0	95	1.63	1.63
1	548	9.43	11.06
2	1,893	32.56	43.62
3	3,278	56.38	100.00
Total	5,814	100.00	

```
. tab social
```

QA11 QA12 QA14 == 1	Freq.	Percent	Cum.
0	1,320	22.70	22.70
1	1,680	28.90	51.60
2	1,639	28.19	79.79
3	1,175	20.21	100.00
Total	5,814	100.00	

A frequency table of this variable shows that 3,278 students ranked all three questions as *very important*. Using the same method for the "social" variable, the frequency table for "social" shows that only 1,175 students ranked all three variables related to social activities as *very important*. Based on this sample, students do place more emphasis on academic reputation than on social life.

5.4 MISSING VALUES IN STATA

Missing values are represented as a "." or as ".a," ".b," ".c," … ".z" in Stata. As we saw earlier in the codebook, users can also specify multiple codes for missing such as "don't know," "not applicable," or "refused to answer." Most commands ignore missing values by default. Some commands, such as **tabulate**, have an option to display missing if you want to see how many observations are missing. This would be done using the code **tab mar1, missing**.

In some cases, you may use missing values in a way that you did not intend. For example, the **replace** command does not ignore missing values, so you must take them into account when you replace variables using a > (greater than) function as you may inadvertently replace missing values.

When there are missing values, statistical packages may eliminate that entire case (or row) from the data set. This is called a "listwise" deletion. In other cases, "pairwise deletion" is done, which eliminates a case only when it is missing a variable required for a particular analysis. In the case of Stata, the default is pairwise deletion.

Researchers will also use *imputation*, which is the practice of replacing missing data with other values. One common method is to substitute the mean value of a variable for any observation that is missing. This is a somewhat controversial procedure and is considered inappropriate by many researchers. For a more thorough discussion of how to deal with missing data, refer to Enders (2010), Little and Rubin (2014), or Sauro (2015).

5.5 SUMMARY OF COMMANDS USED IN THIS CHAPTER

As described in Chapter 4, this last section of each chapter summarizes all of the Stata code used in the chapter. In addition, all Stata code used throughout the book is summarized in Appendix 1.

Looking for outliers and missing data

```
codebook
```

```
tab age, missing
```

Replacing or removing data

```
replace siblings = .  if id==11
```
(to change the value to missing)

```
replace siblings = 2 if id==11
```
(to change the value to a 2)

Creating new variables

```
gen pctoffers=totoffers/applications*100
```

```
gen  salaryintern=beginningsalary  if  internship==1  &
beginingsalary !=.
```

```
gen highprice = (price>1000) & price !=.
```

```
gen income = agincome + nonagincome
```

```
gen netrevenue = revenue - cost
```

```
gen value = price * quantity
```

```
gen exppc = expenditure/hhsize
```

```
gen agesquared = age^2
```

```
gen aboveavg = 1 if income > avgincome
```

```
gen adult = 1 if age >= 18
```

```
gen belowavg = 1 if income < avgincome
```

```
gen child = 1 if age <=10
```

```
gen expend = foodexp + nonfoodexp
```

```
gen femhead = 1 if sexhead==2
```

```
gen error = 1 if value1 != value2
```

```
gen age=. if age==999 | age=9999
```

```
gen sexhead = 1 if sex==1 & relation==1
```

Recoding existing variables

```
recode x (1=2)
```

```
recode x y z (1=2) (3=4)
```

```
recode x (1=2) (2=1)
```

```
recode x (1=2) (*=3)

recode x 1/5=2

recode x y (1 3 4 5 = 6)

recode x (.=9)

recode x (9=.)

recode mar1 2/5=2, generate(maritalstat)
```

Working with labels

```
label define marlabel 1 "Married" 2 "Not currently mar-
ried or living with spouse"

label value maritalstata marlabel
```

Egen—aggregating existing data

```
by region: egen avgincome = mean(income)

by region: by household: egen regincome = median(income)

by household: egen hhincome = sum(income)
```

EXERCISES

1. To examine the age when someone first tried smokeless tobacco, use the National Survey on Drug Use and Health, 2015, data set to complete the following exercises.

   a. Generate a table of the age when someone first tried smokeless tobacco (smklsstry).

   b. Generate a new variable that is identical to smklsstry and call it smklssage.

   c. Recode smklssage so that the codes 994, 997, and 998 are blank.

   d. Recode smklssage so that you combine users into the following categories: never used smokeless tobacco, <10, 10 to 12, 13 to 15, 16 to 18, 19 to 21, and >21.

   e. Generate value labels for these age-groups and apply them to smklssage.

f. Generate a table of smklssage and notice the label that is in the left column of the table at the top.

g. Create a variable label "Age when first tried smokeless tobacco" and apply this to smklssage.

h. Generate a table of smklssage again and notice the change in the label above the left-hand column.

2. Use the GSS2016 data set to complete the following exercises that generate a categorical variable out of a continuous variable.

a. Generate a table of how many children a respondent has (childs).

b. Generate a new variable that is equal to 1 if the respondent has any children and 2 if the respondent has no children.

c. Create a variable label "Respondent has children" and apply it to your new variable.

d. Create value labels so that 1 is "Yes" and 2 is "No."

e. Generate a table of your new variable.

3. Use the GSS2016 data set to complete the following exercises related to regional income disparities in the United States.

a. Use the **egen** command to generate a variable that is the median value of real income (realinc) of all respondents in the data set.

b. Generate a new variable that is the difference between an individual's real income (realinc) and the median income of all individuals (the variable you created in Part "a").

c. Generate a new variable that is equal to 1 if an individual earns above the median income and 0 if the individual earns below the median income.

d. Define and apply value labels to the variable you created in Part "c."

e. Create a table that shows region of the United States in the rows and the variable you created in Part "c" in the columns. Have this table add across the rows and include no frequencies.

f. In a couple of sentences, describe the results and their meaning.

REFERENCES

Enders, C. K. (2010). *Applied missing data analysis: Methodology in the social sciences* (T. D. Little, Series Ed.). New York, NY: Guildford Press.

Little, R. J., & Rubin, D. B. (2014). *Statistical analysis with missing data* (2nd ed.). Hoboken, NJ: Wiley.

Minot, N. (2012). *Using Stata for data analysis*. Washington, DC: International Food Policy Research Institute.

Osborne, J. W. (2012). *Best practices in data cleaning: A complete guide to everything you need to do before and after collecting your data*. Thousand Oaks, CA: Sage.

Sauro, J. (2015, June 2). *7 Ways to handle missing data*. Retrieved from https://measuringu.com/handle-missing-data/

DESCRIPTIVE STATISTICS

Chapter Preview

What are descriptive statistics?	A summary or description of data
	Based on a sample or a population
	Used to describe a sample or population, to answer research questions, to check violation of assumptions, and to look for outliers
Types of variables and measurement	Categorical—nominal and ordinal
	Continuous—interval and ratio
Descriptive statistics for all variables	Frequency tables
	Mode
Descriptive statistics for ordinal, interval, and ratio scales	Median
	Percentile
Descriptive statistics for interval and ratio scales	Mean
	Variance
	Standard deviation
	Coefficient of variation
Descriptive statistics for nominal scales	Cross tabulation
Graphs to describe data	Bar
	Box plot
	Histogram
	Pie

6.1 INTRODUCTION

Descriptive statistics are used to describe or summarize data. For example, you may want to know the average age of the respondents in a study or the distribution of age. You may also want to know the percentage of respondents by gender. In some cases, you may have access to the data for an entire population, in which case descriptive statistics are used to describe the population. A census of the population, for example, is conducted every 10 years in many countries. Generally, however, descriptive statistics are based on a sample of a larger population. If you are conducting a survey of 300 students in a college where there are 1,500 students, for example, then descriptive statistics will describe that sample. They cannot be used to make generalizations or inferences about the population without further analysis or testing. We will learn how to test hypotheses and make inferences about the population in later chapters. In addition to describing data, descriptive statistics are used to answer research questions, to check for violations of assumptions, and to look for outliers. Before we cover descriptive statistics and how to use them, however, we need to know about the different types of variables and measures since this will affect which descriptive statistics can be used.

6.2 TYPES OF VARIABLES AND MEASUREMENT

In statistics, a *variable* is defined as a number or characteristic that can be measured and that varies over a sample or population. For example, age, income, gender, and political affiliation are variables that can be measured. Variables can be divided into two major categories: (1) categorical and (2) continuous. Within these two categories, there are different scales of measurement as illustrated in Table 6.1. These distinctions are important since they affect the type of analysis that can be done with each variable.

A *categorical variable* is a variable that has a limited number of possible values that fall into categories based on some qualitative property and quantitative ranges, such as 1 to 5, 6 to 10, and so on. It can be measured on a nominal or ordinal scale. A *nominal scale* is a measure with two or more categories that do not have a natural order. For example, gender, political affiliation, and first language are categorical variables measured on a nominal scale. An *ordinal scale* is a measure with two or more categories that can be ranked or ordered, but the distance between the categories can't be measured precisely. For example, education level could be measured as completion of grade school, some high school, high school, some graduate school, and so on. Although these can be ordered from the lowest to the highest level, the difference between each level is not precise or the same.

TABLE 6.1 ⬡ VARIABLE TYPES, SCALES OF MEASUREMENT, AND ANALYSES

Variable Type	Categorical		Continuous	
Scale of Measurement	**Nominal**	**Ordinal**	**Interval**	**Ratio**
Definition	A measure with two or more categories that do have not a natural order	A measure with two or more categories that can be ranked or ordered, but the distance between categories can't be measured precisely	A measure that has a numerical value and the magnitude between intervals is the same	A measure that is the same as an interval measure, but it also has a true zero value
Example	Gender Race First language	Military rank Education level (primary, some secondary, high school, etc.) Economic status (low-, middle-, or high-income)	Temperature in Fahrenheit Date Time of day	Income (exact dollar amount) Weight Sales
Frequencies	✓	✓	✓	✓
Mode	✓	✓	✓	✓
Median, percentiles		✓	✓	✓
Mean, variance, standard deviation			✓	✓
Cross tabulation	✓	✓		
Bar graph	✓	✓		
Box plot			✓	✓
Histogram			✓	✓
Pie chart	✓	✓		

A *continuous variable* is often described as a variable that can take on an infinite or large number of possible values such as temperature, age, and weight. It can be measured on an interval or ratio scale. An *interval scale* is a measure that has a numerical value and the magnitude between the intervals is the same. Temperature, date, and the time of day are examples of variables measured on an interval scale. A *ratio scale* is a measure that is the same as an interval measure, but it also has a true zero value or a complete absence of what is being measured. For example, when income or sales is zero, it means that there is no income or sales. For interval measures, however, you can't say that there is a zero time of day or a zero date.

Many questionnaires use a 5-point Likert-type scale with the categories of "strongly agree," "agree," "neutral," "disagree," and "strongly disagree." This is considered an ordinal scale since the responses can be ranked from the lowest to the highest. Researchers sometimes consider this an interval scale, which assumes that the distance is equal between each category. This practice is controversial since the distance between each category may not be identical, and it is subject to the interpretation of each respondent. Some statistical guides suggest that a higher number of categories (11 or more) would be sufficient to consider it an interval scale. The reason why this is important is because you can't calculate the mean or variance of an ordinal scale, but you can with an interval scale. If you can calculate the mean and the variance, it allows you to do more in-depth statistical tests.

The types of descriptive statistics that can be calculated for each type of variable are described in the following sections followed by a section on using graphs to describe data.

6.3 DESCRIPTIVE STATISTICS FOR ALL TYPES OF VARIABLES: FREQUENCY TABLES AND MODES

All variables, regardless of their scale of measurement, can be examined with a frequency table or the mode. Each of these is described below.

6.3.1 Frequency Tables

When using a new data set, researchers often begin by generating frequency tables to examine the distribution of each variable. Using the "College Results 2013" data set, we can generate a frequency table of the variable Sector3 to see how many colleges fall into the three categories of private not-for-profit, public, and private for-profit using the menus in Dialog Box 6.1 or the commands in Output 6.1.

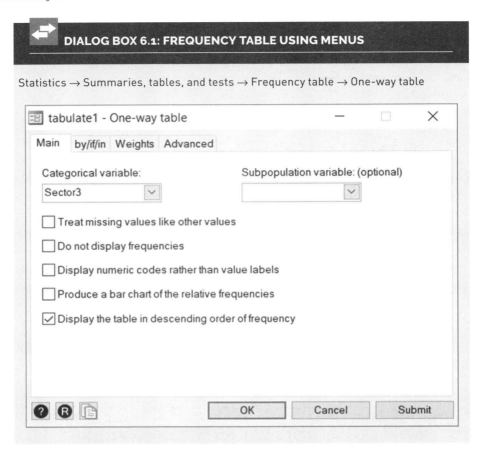

DIALOG BOX 6.1: FREQUENCY TABLE USING MENUS

Statistics → Summaries, tables, and tests → Frequency table → One-way table

OUTPUT 6.1: FREQUENCY TABLE OF COLLEGE TYPES

```
. tab Sector3, sort
```

Sector	Freq.	Percent	Cum.
Private notforprofit	1,235	54.55	54.55
Public	603	26.63	81.18
Private forprofit	426	18.82	100.00
Total	2,264	100.00	

The frequency and percent columns in Output 6.1 show the actual number and percentage of each type of college in the data set. The cumulative column adds up the percentages from the percent column, but for a nominal variable, this doesn't make any sense. For example, you can't report that 81.18% of colleges are public or less. If, on the other hand, we generated a frequency table for a continuous variable such as the number of students enrolled in colleges, we could report that 81% of colleges have 5,376 or fewer students.

If we wanted to generate frequency tables for multiple variables, we could use the Stata command **tab1** and then list the variables following the command as illustrated in Output 6.2. This eliminates the need to type tab multiple times on separate lines. This is not possible using menus.

OUTPUT 6.2: MULTIPLE FREQUENCY TABLES USING THE TAB1 COMMAND

```
. tab1 Sector3 atsp

-> tabulation of Sector3
```

Sector	Freq.	Percent	Cum.
Private forprofit	426	18.82	18.82
Private notforprofit	1,235	54.55	73.37
Public	603	26.63	100.00
Total	2,264	100.00	

```
-> tabulation of atsp
```

Admissions Test Scores Policy	Freq.	Percent	Cum.
Neither	262	14.65	14.65
Recommended	265	14.81	29.46
Required	1,262	70.54	100.00
Total	1,789	100.00	

Notice that in the table of admissions test score policies, the total number of colleges reporting their policy is 1,789 compared with 2,264 in the first table that lists the type of sector. If we wanted to include the number of missing values in the table, we could add ", missing" at the end of the command that generates a table. Generally, when a variable has missing data, it is important to identify patterns or reasons for the missing data. It could be due to respondents who refuse to answer a question or a skip pattern in a survey where only certain individuals are asked questions. For example, a survey may ask some questions only to individuals who work full time. There are many reasons why there might be missing observations and several ways to deal with missing data. A more advanced book on statistical analysis would cover these methods, and there are entire books written just about this problem. For a brief guide, Sauro (2015) suggests "7 ways to handle missing data." For a complete overview of missing data, refer to Enders (2010) and Little and Rubin (2014).

In the illustration above, we used a categorical variable with only three categories. If we generated a frequency table for a continuous variable, such as the number of students enrolled in colleges using the variable "Size" from the College results 2013 data set, there would be 2,264 lines in our frequency table or one for each unique value.

Finally, it is important to think about labeling tables with appropriate titles and sources. The title should indicate the statistic, the variable, and possibly the unit. A source should be listed at the bottom of the table if the table is taken from another article or if you want to cite the source of the data. One rule of thumb is that a table should be self-explanatory without any accompanying text.

6.3.2 Mode

The *mode* is the most common value in a variable. It can be used for both categorical and continuous variables. In some cases, there may not be a mode if all values appear once or the same number of times. In other cases, you could have a bimodal or multimodal distribution whereby there is more than one mode. Although the mode is sometimes called a "measure of central tendency," the mode could be at the low or high end of the distribution of a variable.

The easiest way to find a mode is to look at a frequency table and see which value appears most frequently. When a frequency table is too long to easily find a mode or multiple modes, however, you can use the Stata **egen** command that was covered in Chapter 5. In this case, the command would be as follows to find the mode of Size in the College results 2013 data set:

```
egen mode = mode(Size)
```

If we ran this command, it would warn us that there are multiple modes. We could then run the following commands to find each mode

```
egen mode1 = mode(Size), nummode(1)
egen mode2 = mode(Size), nummode(2)
egen mode3 = mode(Size), nummode(3)
egen mode4 = mode(Size), nummode(4)
egen mode5 = mode(Size), nummode(5)
```

The first line of the command tells Stata to create a new variable, mode1, which is the lowest mode of the variable Size. Similarly, the second line tells Stata to create a new variable, mode2, which is the second lowest value of the mode, and so on. When running the fifth line for the fifth lowest mode, Stata would tell us that there are only four modes. Finally, to see what these modes are, we would generate a frequency table of the four new variables—mode1, mode2, mode3, and mode4.

6.4 DESCRIPTIVE STATISTICS FOR VARIABLES MEASURED AS ORDINAL, INTERVAL, AND RATIO SCALES: MEDIAN AND PERCENTILES

6.4.1 Median

In addition to frequency tables and the mode described above, variables that are measured on an ordinal, interval, or ratio scale can be examined with the median and percentile values. A *median* is found by ranking a variable from its lowest to its highest value and then identifying the observation or number that falls exactly in the middle. If there is an odd number of observations for the variable, then there will be one number that represents the middle value. If there is an even number of observations, then you would use the average of the two middle values.

As described below in the section on means, it is often useful to calculate both the mean and the median, particularly when there are outliers. A mean or average will be skewed in one direction if there is a small number of unusually high or low values. A full example of this is given in Section 6.5 below.

6.4.2 Percentiles

A *percentile* is a value below which a percentage of the data fall within a variable. For example, if your Scholastic Aptitude Test (SAT) percentile was 85, then 85% of all students who took the test earned a lower score than you. Because the median is the exact middle value of a variable, the median is the 50th percentile.

To find the median and several percentiles for the size of a college in the 2013 College results data set, we would use the menus in Dialog Box 6.2 or the commands in Output 6.3.

The first two columns in Output 6.3 show the percentile and the value for each percentile. For example, the 90th percentile is 9,976 indicating that 90% of all colleges

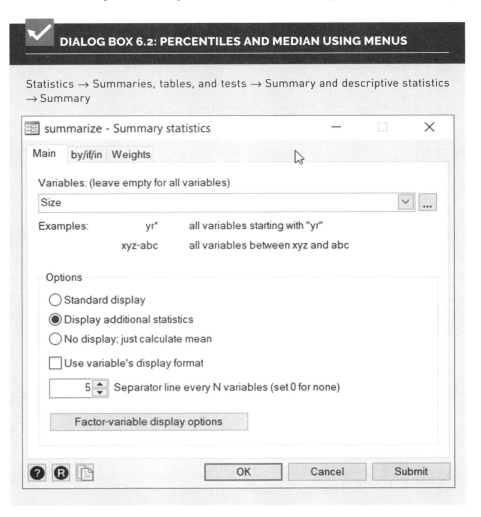

DIALOG BOX 6.2: PERCENTILES AND MEDIAN USING MENUS

Statistics → Summaries, tables, and tests → Summary and descriptive statistics → Summary

summarize - Summary statistics

Main   by/if/in   Weights

Variables: (leave empty for all variables)

Size

Examples: yr*   all variables starting with "yr"

                 xyz-abc   all variables between xyz and abc

Options
○ Standard display
◉ Display additional statistics
○ No display; just calculate mean

☐ Use variable's display format

5   Separator line every N variables (set 0 for none)

Factor-variable display options

OK   Cancel   Submit

OUTPUT 6.3: PERCENTILES AND MEDIAN

```
. sum Size, detail

                        Size (Undergrad FTE)

          Percentiles        Smallest
    1%           36              3
    5%          118              3
   10%          225             10        Obs              2,264
   25%         598.5            17        Sum of Wgt.      2,264

   50%        1538.5                      Mean          3782.575
                             Largest      Std. Dev.     7246.969
   75%        3877.5          41520
   90%          9976          53091       Variance       5.25e+07
   95%         17162          69351       Skewness      11.73627
   99%         28179         208742       Kurtosis      291.0279
```

> 25% of all colleges have fewer than 598.5 students.

have fewer than 9,976 students. The median or 50th percentile is 1,538.5. The third column shows the four smallest numbers in the variable and the four largest. Finally, the last column shows the number of observations and the mean along with other descriptive statistics that we will cover later.

Because there may be outliers in the data set, it is often common to consider the interquartile range, which is the range between the 25th and the 75th percentile. In Output 6.3, for example, we see that the four smaller values for size are unrealistic—a college with only three students? Similarly, the largest college reported 208,742 students! The interquartile range tells us that 50% of all colleges fall within 599 and 3,878 students, which helps eliminate the extreme outliers when examining school size..

6.5 DESCRIPTIVE STATISTICS FOR CONTINUOUS VARIABLES: MEAN, VARIANCE, STANDARD DEVIATION, AND COEFFICIENT OF VARIATION

In addition to frequency tables, modes, medians, and percentiles, continuous variables (those measured on the interval and ratio scale) can be examined using the mean, variance, standard deviation, and coefficient of variation. The methods to calculate these statistics are described below.

6.5.1 Mean

The calculation of the mean or average is expressed mathematically in Equation 6.1.

$$\overline{X} = \frac{\sum_{i=1}^{n} x_i}{n} \tag{6.1}$$

where x is the value of each individual observation of the variable and n is the number of observations or values of the variable.

For those of you not familiar with the summation sign, Σ, it is a symbol that indicates that you should add the values indicated by what lies to the right of the symbol. The symbols "$i = 1$" and "n" in the numerator indicate that you begin with the first observation of variable x and add each successive value together until you reach the last value or the nth unit. Finally, you divide this by "n" or the total number of observations. For example, if there are five values of x, Equation 6.2 shows the long form of the equation:

$$\overline{X} = \frac{\sum_{i=1}^{n} x_i}{n} = \frac{x_1 + x_2 + x_3 + x_4 + x_5}{5} \tag{6.2}$$

In this example, $\overline{X}$ represents a sample mean and is called a statistic. If we have information about each observation in a population, we would calculate the population mean and use the Greek letter mu, μ, to represent it. In this case, μ is a parameter since it describes the entire population.

Although an average is a commonly used statistic, it is often useful to calculate both the mean and the median, which was discussed in the previous section. The median is particularly useful when there are outliers or extreme values in a variable. Income is a classic example since a billionaire in the data set will skew the average to a higher value than is typical for a household. By calculating a median or middle value instead, it offers a much better picture of income for typical households in the middle of the income range.

To show the difference in the mean and median, suppose that we have a sample with five respondents and we ask their age. We receive the responses of 20, 25, 35, 40, and 95. Table 6.2 shows the results for the two measures. Although four of the five respondents are 40 years or younger, the mean indicates that the average age of the person in the sample is 43. The median, on the other hand, gives a better idea of someone in the middle of the group.

As shown in Output 6.3 earlier, the mean can be generated through Stata using the **summarize** command or using menus as shown in Dialog Box 6.2. Also, if you want to display less information than in the **summarize variable**, **detail** command, you can use the **summarize** command without the **detail** option. This is illustrated in Output 6.4.

There are many times when a researcher may want to examine the mean or the median for subgroups. For example, we can generate the average and median college tuition cost for three categories of college types in Output 6.5 by using the menus in Dialog Box 6.3 or the Stata commands in Output 6.5.

The three forward slashes "///" in the command are used in a do-file to let Stata know that the command continues on the next line and can only be used in do-files. The last command, format(%6.0fc), indicates that you want to format the numeric output so that there are six characters in total (including the comma) and zero numbers to the right of the decimal point. The "fc" stands for fixed numeric variable with commas. If you wanted to add two numbers to the right of the decimal place, the command would be **format(%9.2fc)**. Notice that the "6" changes to "9" to allow six characters to the left of the decimal place, the decimal point, and two digits to the right of the decimal place.

TABLE 6.2 ● CALCULATION OF CENTRAL TENDENCY

Measure	Calculation	Example	Result
Mean	Sum of all observations divided by the number of observations	$\frac{20+25+35+40+95}{5}$	43
Median	Observation that falls in the middle when ranked from low to high	20, 25, <u>35</u>, 40, 95	35

OUTPUT 6.4: MEAN OF COLLEGE SIZE

```
. sum Size

    Variable |      Obs       Mean    Std. Dev.      Min        Max
-------------+--------------------------------------------------------
        Size |    2,264   3782.575    7246.969        3     208742
```

DIALOG BOX 6.3: MEANS AND MEDIANS FOR SUBCATEGORIES USING MENUS

Statistics → Summaries, tables, and tests → Other tables → Flexible table of summary statistics

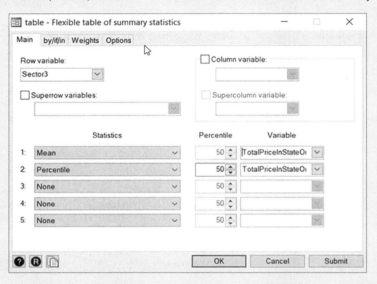

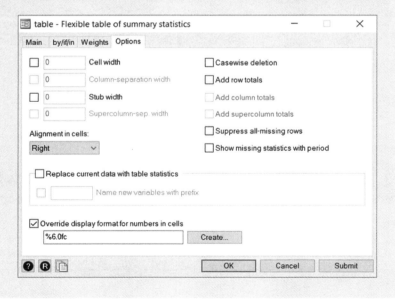

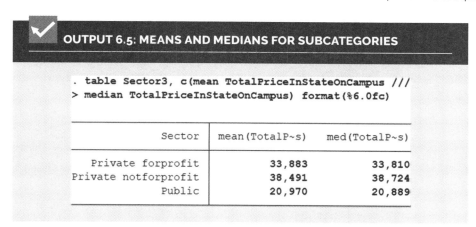

OUTPUT 6.5: MEANS AND MEDIANS FOR SUBCATEGORIES

```
. table Sector3, c(mean TotalPriceInStateOnCampus ///
> median TotalPriceInStateOnCampus) format(%6.0fc)
```

Sector	mean(TotalP~s)	med(TotalP~s)
Private forprofit	33,883	33,810
Private notforprofit	38,491	38,724
Public	20,970	20,889

Overall, the output shows that private nonprofit colleges have the highest average and median tuition costs.

6.5.2 Variance and Standard Deviation

Variance is a measure of how spread out the values of one variable are from their mean. Table 6.3 shows the formulas to calculate the variance for a population and the variance for a sample of a population.

In the numerator for both measures, the average is subtracted from each value in the variable. The differences are then squared and added together. In other words, it is measuring how far each value falls from the mean. Notice the difference in the denominators. For the population variance, the denominator is the number of units in the population. When you work with a sample, you are estimating the variation in the population. Because the sample will not be a perfect representation of the population, the measure adjusts for this difference by dividing by "$n - 1$." The *standard deviation* is simply the square root of the variance.

TABLE 6.3 ● POPULATION AND SAMPLE VARIANCE FORMULAS

Population Variance	Sample Variance
$$\sigma^2 = \frac{\sum_{i=1}^{N}(x_i - \mu)^2}{N}$$	$$s^2 = \frac{\sum_{i=1}^{n}(x_i - \bar{X})^2}{n-1}$$
where	where
N = number of units in the population	n = number of units in the sample
x = value of each individual observation of the variable	x = value of each individual observation of the variable
μ = the population mean	$\bar{X}$ = the sample mean

TABLE 6.4 ● CALCULATION OF VARIANCE AND STANDARD DEVIATION				
Variable	**Observations**	**Variance Calculation**	**Variance**	**Standard Deviation**
A	50, 50, 50	$\dfrac{(50-50)^2+(50-50)^2+(50-50)^2}{3-1}$	0	0
B	0, 50, 100	$\dfrac{(0-50)^2+(50-50)^2+(100-50)^2}{3-1}$	2,500	50

To show how the variance and standard deviation work, let's suppose that we have two variables with three observations that represent a sample of a population. Table 6.4 shows the three observations for each variable, the calculation of the variance, and the resulting variance and standard deviation. As you can see, the first variable is made of three observations that are identical: 50, 50, and 50. There is no variance in these numbers, and the resulting variance and standard deviation are zero. In variable B, however, there is a large variation in the three observations and thus a very large variance of 2,500 and a standard deviation of 50.

Using the "College Results 2013" data set, again we can examine college tuition with the Stata command below or the menus in Dialog Box 6.4. The results in Output 6.6 show the mean and standard deviation for colleges in the three categories of private for-profit, private not-for-profit, and public universities. As you can see from the output, the tuition at private not-for-profit universities has a higher standard deviation, but it also has a larger mean. To compare how much they vary relative to their mean, the coefficient of variation is often used.

6.5.3 Coefficient of Variation

The *coefficient of variation*, or CV, is calculated as the standard deviation divided by the absolute value of the mean and multiplied by 100 as shown in Equation 6.3. In other words, it tells us how much variation there is in a variable relative to its mean. Using the data from Output 6.6, the CVs would be 16, 32, and 21 for private for-profit, private not-for-profit, and public, respectively. Thus, we could say that the standard deviation for private not-for-profit colleges is 32% of its mean and has the largest variation among the three categories.

$$CV = \frac{s}{\overline{X}} * 100 \qquad (6.3)$$

In a recent news story about fantasy basketball, the CV of basketball players' performance (points per game) is compared to see which players are "safer." In other words, a low CV would imply that a player consistently scores close to his or her average,

DIALOG BOX 6.4: MEAN AND STANDARD DEVIATION

Statistics → Summaries, tables, and tests → Other tables → Flexible table of summary statistics

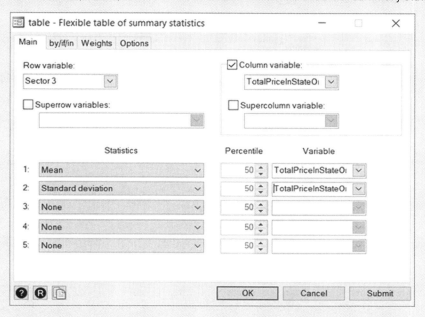

OUTPUT 6.6: MEAN AND STANDARD DEVIATION OF COLLEGE TUITION COSTS

```
. table Sector3, c(mean TotalPriceInStateOnCampus ///
> sd TotalPriceInStateOnCampus) format(%6.0fc)
```

Sector	mean(TotalP~s)	sd(TotalP~s)
Private forprofit	33,883	5,580
Private notforprofit	38,491	12,153
Public	20,970	4,420

whereas a high CV would suggest that the player's points per game vary widely (Daily Fantasy Sports Rankings, 2018).

In general, the CV is useful because the size of the standard deviation depends on the units used to measure a variable. For example, if a variable that asked for someone's age is measured both in years (e.g., 4 years and 2 months old) and in total months (50 months), the standard deviation will differ as illustrated in Table 6.5. Notice that the standard deviation for age in months is exactly 12 times the standard deviation for the age in years. If you just looked at the standard deviation, it would look like age in months has much greater variation than age in years. But the CVs show that they have the exact same variation relative to their mean. The CV is also useful since it allows you to compare two variables with different measurements such as years of education and income in dollars to determine which one has greater variation relative to their mean.

TABLE 6.5 ● A COMPARISON OF THE STANDARD DEVIATION AND COEFFICIENT OF VARIATION

	Age in Years	Age in Months
Observations	2	24
	4	48
	6	72
Mean	4	48
Standard deviation	2	24
Coefficient of variation	0.5	0.5

6.6 DESCRIPTIVE STATISTICS FOR CATEGORICAL VARIABLES MEASURED ON A NOMINAL OR ORDINAL SCALE: CROSS TABULATION

In addition to frequency tables and modes, categorical variables can be examined with cross tabulation, which is also referred to as a crosstab or a contingency table. This is defined and illustrated below.

A *cross tabulation* allows you to combine two categorical variables to learn more about their relationship or their joint distribution. For example, to show the percentage of colleges that require or recommend the SAT scores by each type of college, we would use the menus shown in Dialog Box 6.5 or the commands in Output 6.7.

DIALOG BOX 6.5: CROSS TABULATION

Statistics → Summaries, tables, and tests → Frequency table → Two-way table with measures of association

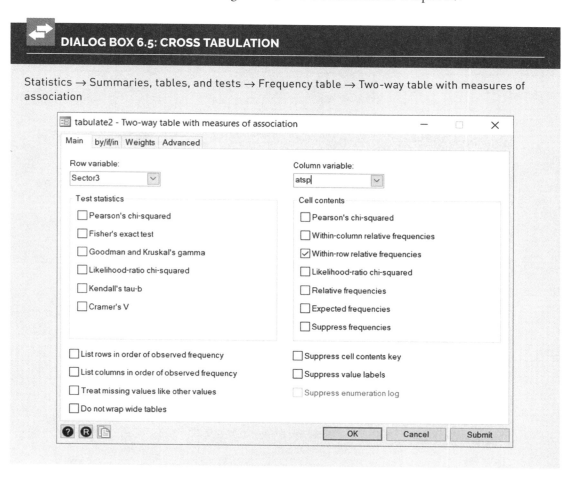

OUTPUT 6.7: COMBINING TWO CATEGORICAL VARIABLES USING THE TABULATE COMMAND

```
. tab Sector3 atsp, row
```

Key
frequency
row percentage

	Admissions Test Scores Policy			
Sector	Neither	Recommend	Required	Total
Private forprofit	104	72	9	185
	56.22	38.92	4.86	100.00
Private notforprofit	153	145	772	1,070
	14.30	13.55	72.15	100.00
Public	5	48	481	534
	0.94	8.99	90.07	100.00
Total	262	265	1,262	1,789
	14.65	14.81	70.54	100.00

Within each cell, the numbers on top are the actual number of colleges in that category and the number below is the percentage. By including the command **row** in the Stata command, the percentages add up across the rows to 100%. For example, we can see on the first row that 104 private for-profit colleges neither recommend nor require the SAT or ACT, which represents 56.22% of all private for-profit colleges.

If we changed Output 6.7 and wrote the Stata commands to add up over the columns, the output would not make sense, as shown in Output 6.8. In Output 6.8, the first column would be interpreted as follows. Among colleges that do not require or recommend the SAT, 58% are private not-for-profit colleges. Notice, however, that "private not-for-profit" colleges represent the largest percentage in all three columns. This is because they are the largest group. Instead, you would want to know what percentage of colleges within each type require or do not require the SAT.

OUTPUT 6.8: INCORRECTLY ADDING UP A CROSS TABULATION OVER THE WRONG VARIABLE

```
. tab Sector3 atsp, col
```

Key
frequency
column percentage

| | Admissions Test Scores Policy | | | |
Sector	Neither	Recommend	Required	Total
Private forprofit	104	72	9	185
	39.69	27.17	0.71	10.34
Private notforprofit	153	145	772	1,070
	58.40	54.72	61.17	59.81
Public	5	48	481	534
	1.91	18.11	38.11	29.85
Total	262	265	1,262	1,789
	100.00	100.00	100.00	100.00

These numbers only tell us private not-for-profit schools represent the largest group in the sample and nothing more.

When deciding whether to add up over rows or columns, the rule of thumb is that you always add up over the independent variable. As described in Chapter 1, an *independent variable* is defined as a variable whose variation is not influenced by other variables. In this case, the type of college is not influenced by their SAT policy, but the SAT policy might be determined by the type of college. Therefore, the type of college is the independent variable and the SAT policy is considered the dependent variable. A *dependent variable* is a variable whose variation is influenced by other variables.

A second rule of thumb that is sometimes followed is to place the dependent variable in the rows and the independent variable in the columns. If, however, there are far more categories in the independent variable and the table can't fit on a page without wrapping around, it is fine to switch the placement of the two types of variables but always add up over the independent variable.

One last word on cross tabulation is that you can use a continuous variable in a cross tabulation if you transform it into categories using the **recode** command discussed in Chapter 5. For example, if one of your continuous variables is income in exact dollar amounts, you could change this into a categorical variable by making the categories of below 50,000, 50,000 to 99,999.99, 100,000 and above, and so on.

6.7 APPLYING SAMPLING WEIGHTS

In Chapter 2, we described how sampling weights are used to extrapolate from the sample to the population. If a random sample is drawn, then sample weights serve to estimate totals in the population from sample data. If the sample is stratified and/or a multistage sample, then some types of units will be overrepresented and others underrepresented in the sample. Returning to the example from Chapter 2, suppose that the population is 10% urban and 90% rural, but the sample is split 50–50 between urban and rural households. This means that urban households are overrepresented in the sample, so any statistics calculated from the sample will be disproportionately affected by the urban households. Sampling weights compensate for the distortions introduced by sampling, allowing us to calculate means and percentages from the sample that are unbiased estimates of the population statistics.

Sampling weights can be used with many commands in Stata that generate tables. Suppose that the variable "wgt" contains the sampling weights. We can apply sampling weights to the tables created by Stata commands as shown below, where "**aw**" refers to "analytical weights."

We demonstrate the use of sampling weights with data from the 2016 General Social Survey (GSS). The GSS asks a wide range of questions to assess the opinions of adults in the United States. We can use the GSS to see whether having taken any science classes at a university (colsci) is associated with one's view of astrology (astrosci). Below are the commands to show this relationship and the output of this command. The **nof** command indicates "no frequencies" or only percentages.

The table in Output 6.9 indicates that people who have taken a college-level science course are less likely to believe that astrology is "sort of scientific" or "very scientific." But the GSS database comes with a sampling weight variable (wtss), which can be used to compensate for possible distortions caused by the sampling design of the GSS. Below, we generate the same table but applying sampling weights. The weights option must appear in brackets and must appear before the comma.

Comparing Outputs 6.9 and 6.10, it is clear that, in this case, the sampling weights do not make much of a difference. This suggests that any over- or undersampling of different groups in the United States, such as people from New England, was relatively minor. Nonetheless, if you are generating descriptive statistics from a survey for which sample weights are available, you should make use of those weights.

OUTPUT 6.9: RELATIONSHIP BETWEEN COLLEGE SCIENCE CLASSES AND BELIEFS ABOUT ASTROLOGY WITHOUT SAMPLING WEIGHTS

```
. tab astrosci colsci, col nof
```

astrology is scientific	r has taken any college-level sci course		Total
	yes	no	
very scientific	4.57	10.68	8.10
sort of scientific	23.55	34.62	29.94
not at all scientific	71.88	54.70	61.96
Total	100.00	100.00	100.00

OUTPUT 6.10: RELATIONSHIP BETWEEN COLLEGE SCIENCE CLASSES AND BELIEFS ABOUT ASTROLOGY WITH SAMPLING WEIGHTS

```
. tab astrosci colsci [aw=wtss], col nof
```

astrology is scientific	r has taken any college-level sci course		Total
	yes	no	
very scientific	4.88	10.88	8.31
sort of scientific	22.83	35.27	29.93
not at all scientific	72.28	53.85	61.76
Total	100.00	100.00	100.00

6.8 FORMATTING OUTPUT FOR USE IN A DOCUMENT (WORD, GOOGLE DOCS, ETC.)

As you will notice in the output in the previous sections, the formatting of the tables is not always ideal. The labels start with lowercase letters, some labels are too long, other labels have abbreviations that might not be clear to the reader, and so on. For this reason, you may want to edit the table before placing it in a Word or Google document. In addition, if you are publishing your work in a journal, many journals prefer only horizontal lines. All of this editing can be done by highlighting the table in the Stata results screen and then clicking edit/ copy table. You can then copy this into an Excel file where you could format each part of the table as needed. Finally, the Excel table can be copied into Word or a Google Doc. To do this, you need to select the table, right-click, and then select "copy table."

6.9 GRAPHS TO DESCRIBE DATA

In addition to tables with data, charts or graphs are often useful to display information. In some cases, it is easier to see a pattern with a graph. Although there are many types of graphs, we illustrate four of the most common—bar graphs, box plots, histograms, and pie charts.

6.9.1 Bar Graphs

Using the same data from the previous sections, "College Results 2013," we can generate a bar graph of the average tuition rate by the type of university (Figure 6.1) using the Stata command below or the menus in Dialog Box 6.6. Notice that the Stata command asks for a bar graph of the mean value of the continuous variable spread out "over" the sector or type of institution.

```
graph bar (mean) TotalPriceInStateOnCampus, over(Sector3)
```

6.9.2 Box Plots

We can also use a box plot for the same data displayed in the bar graph (Figure 6.2). With a box plot, in addition to comparing means, we can see the dispersion of a variable. The Stata command to create a box plot and the output are illustrated below followed by the menus in Dialog Box 6.7.

```
graph box TotalPriceInStateOnCa mpus, over(Sector3)
```

DIALOG BOX 6.6: BAR GRAPH

Graphics → Bar chart → Other tables → Flexible table of summary statistics

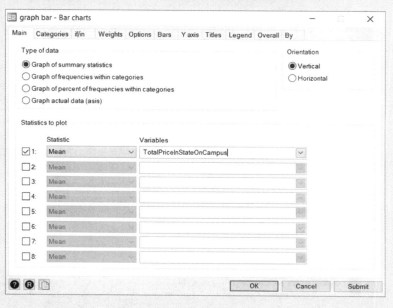

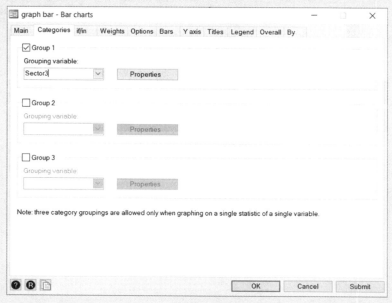

FIGURE 6.1 ● BAR GRAPH OF AVERAGE TUITION BY TYPE OF COLLEGE

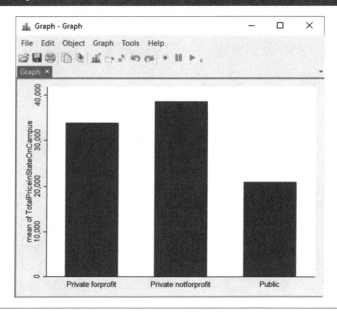

DIALOG BOX 6.7: BOX PLOT

Graphics → Box plot

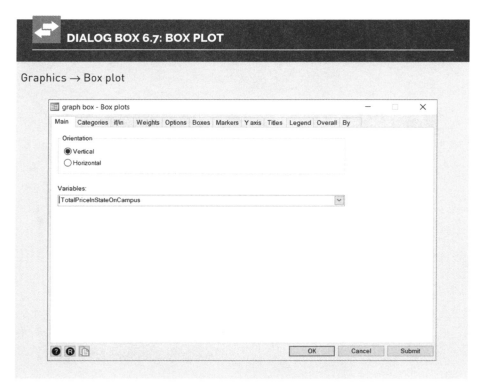

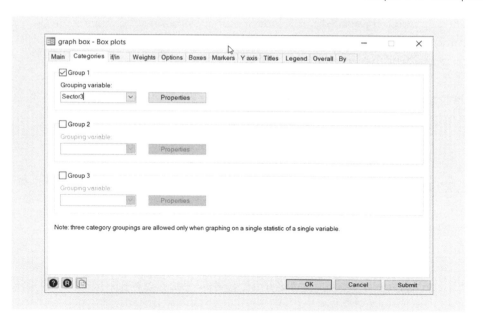

FIGURE 6.2 ● BOX PLOT OF AVERAGE TUITION BY TYPE OF INSTITUTION

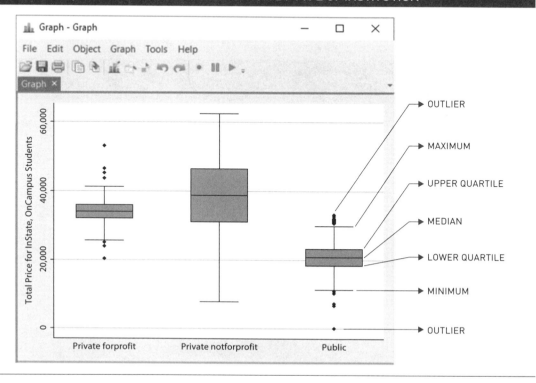

The line inside the shaded box represents the median value. The upper and lower borders of the box represent the upper and lower quartiles. In other words, the upper border is the 75th percentile and the lower border is the 25th percentile so that 50% of the observations fall within the range represented by the box. The "whiskers" or horizontal lines at the top and bottom of the graph extend out to the last value that is less than or equal to 1.5 times the interquartile range value.

From the box plot, it is easy to see that the private for-profit institutions have the highest median value and the greatest dispersion.

6.9.3 Histograms

While a bar graph or box plot is useful for a limited number of categories as in Figures 6.1 and 6.2, a histogram is a better choice for a continuous variable with numerous values. For example, college tuition, which is a continuous variable, can be illustrated as a histogram (Figure 6.3). The Stata command to generate a histogram is below, or this can be done using the menus in Dialog Box 6.8. The command asks Stata to generate a histogram of the continuous variable. The **bin(10)** command lets Stata know to use 10 bars, and the term **frequency** indicates that the vertical axis should show the number of times or frequency that the range of values represented by the bar appears.

```
hist TotalPriceInStateOnCampus, bin(10) frequency
```

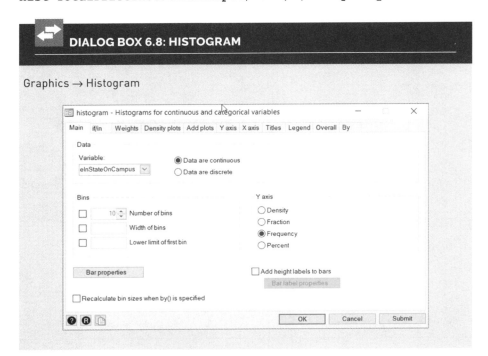

FIGURE 6.3   ⬡   HISTOGRAM OF TUITION OF COLLEGES IN THE UNITED STATES

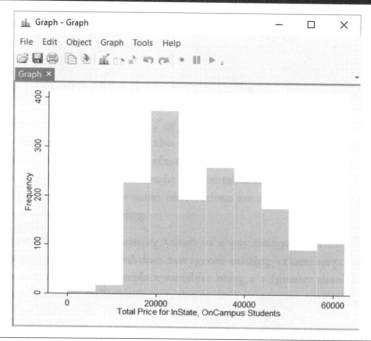

The frequency on the vertical axis shows the number colleges. Then, looking at the height of the bars, you can see how many colleges fall into each range. For example, slightly more than 100 colleges fall in the highest range of roughly $55,000 to $65,000.

6.9.4 Pie Charts

A pie chart is useful for a categorical variable with a limited number of categories where only one category can be selected by the respondent. For example, using the type of college from the previous examples, we can make a pie chart (Figure 6.4) that gives a visual example of the percentage of colleges in each category. If we choose a variable with 40 possible responses (e.g., a student's major), then each slice of the pie would be too small.

To generate a pie chart, we would run the Stata command below or use the menus in Dialog Box 6.9. The command **p_label(_all percent)** indicates that Stata should include the percentage inside of each pie slice.

```
graph pie, over(Sector3) plabel( _ all percent)
```

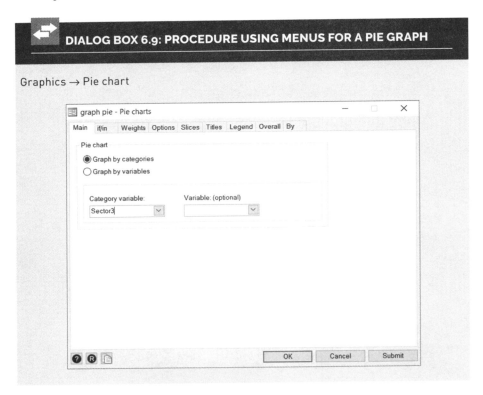

DIALOG BOX 6.9: PROCEDURE USING MENUS FOR A PIE GRAPH

Graphics → Pie chart

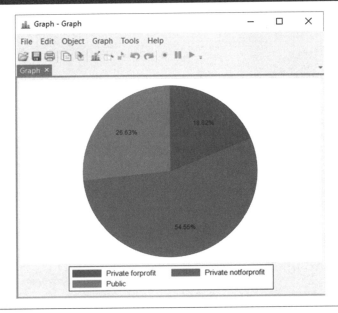

FIGURE 6.4 ● PIE CHART OF COLLEGE TYPES

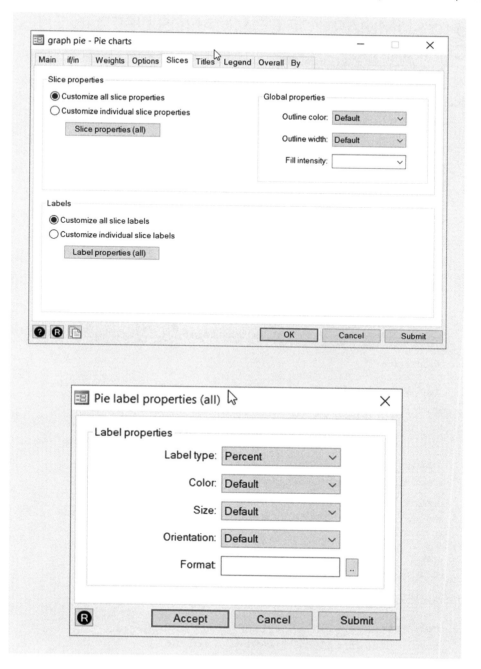

6.10 SUMMARY OF COMMANDS USED IN THIS CHAPTER

As described in Chapter 4, this last section of each chapter summarizes all of the Stata code used in the chapter. In addition, all Stata code used throughout the book is summarized in Appendix 1.

Frequency table

```
tab Sector3, sort
tab1 Sector3 atsp
```

Mode

```
egen mode = mode(Size)
egen mode1 = mode(Size), nummode(1)
egen mode2 = mode(Size), nummode(2)
egen mode3 = mode(Size), nummode(3)
egen mode4 = mode(Size), nummode(4)
egen mode5 = mode(Size), nummode(5)
```

Summary table

```
sum Size
sum Size, detail
```

Tables with mean, median, and standard deviation

```
table Sector3, c(mean TotalPriceInStateOnCampus ///
median TotalPriceInStateOnCampus) format (%6.0fc)
table Sector3, c(mean TotalPriceInStateOnCampus ///
sd TotalPriceInStateOnCampus) format(%6.0fc)
```

Table with row percentages

```
tab Sector3 atsp, row
```

Tables with and without sample weights

```
tab astrosci colsci, col nof
tab astrosci colsci [aw=wtss], col nof
```

Bar graphs, box plots, histograms, and pie charts

```
graph bar (mean) TotalPriceInStateOnCampus, over(Sector3)
graph box TotalPriceInStateOnCampus, over(Sector3)
hist TotalPriceInStateOnCampus, bin(10) frequency
graph pie, over(Sector3) plabel( _ all percent)
```

EXERCISES

1. For each of the following variables, indicate the type of variable (categorical or continuous) and its level of measurement (nominal, ordinal, interval, or ratio).

    a. Favorite type of cereal

    b. Car prices

    c. Total profits

    d. Level of happiness

    e. Birth date

    f. Time of birth

    g. Gender

2. Using the data set that you created from Exercise 1 in Chapter 4 (about binge watching television), follow the instructions below.

    a. Identify both the variable type and scale of measurement for each of the four variables (TV Source, Hours per week, Binge frequency, and Sex) in your data set.

    b. What is the mode for "Binge frequency"? Show your Stata command and output as part of this and for all following answers.

    c. What is the 25th percentile value for "Hours per week"? Explain what this means in words.

    d. What is the variance for "Hours per week"?

   e. Make a table that shows "Sex" in the rows and the mean and median of "Hours per week" in the columns. Format the table so that there are no numbers to the right of the decimal point. In other words, use only whole numbers.

   f. Calculate the coefficient of variation for "Hours per week" (use a calculator for this after obtaining the numbers that you need).

   g. Generate a cross tabulation of "Sex" and "Binge frequency." Be sure to think about whether the rows or columns should add up to 100%. Based on your table, what percentage of women binge watch frequently and what percentage of men binge watch frequently?

   h. Generate a bar chart that shows the average "Hours per week" that men and women binge watch TV.

   i. Generate a histogram of "Hours per week."

   j. Generate a pie chart of "Binge frequency." Label each slice of the pie with the percentage value.

3. Suppose there is a population of five people with height in inches as follows: 58, 62, 63, 70, and 77.

   a. Calculate the population variance using a calculator. Show your work to derive the final answer.

   b. Now suppose that you take a sample of three of these people who are 62, 63, and 77 inches tall. Calculate the sample variance using a calculator. Show your work to derive the final answer.

4. Using the GSS2016.dta file, answer the following questions related to discrimination at work.

   a. Generate a table without weights that shows the gender in the rows (sex) and whether the respondent experienced discrimination at work in the past 5 years (discwk5). Show only the percentages and decide whether to use row or column percentages.

   b. Generate the same table as in Part "a," but apply the weights (wtss) to the table.

REFERENCES

Daily Fantasy Sports Rankings. (2018, February 20). *Daily fantasy NBA: Consistency, scoring and fun facts from the first half of the season*. Retrieved from www.dailyfantasysportsrankings.com/2018/02/20/consistency-scoring-and-fun-facts-from-the-first-half-of-the-season/

Enders, C. K. (2010). *Applied missing data analysis: Methodology in the social sciences* (T. D. Little, Series Ed.). New York, NY: Guildford Press.

Little, R. J., & Rubin, D. B. (2014). *Statistical analysis with missing data* (2nd ed.). Hoboken, NJ: Wiley.

Sauro, J. (2015, June 2). *7 Ways to handle missing data*. Retrieved from https://measuringu.com/handle-missing-data/

TESTING HYPOTHESES

PART THREE

THE NORMAL DISTRIBUTION

Chapter Preview

Research question	Did students who took an SAT preparatory course earn significantly higher scores on math SAT tests compared with the other students at the same high school?
Null hypothesis	There is no difference in SAT scores among those students who took a preparatory course and those who did not.
Test	Standard score or z score
When to use	Comparing a sample mean with a population mean. The population standard deviation is known.
Calculate the standard error of the mean	$\sigma_{\bar{x}} = \dfrac{\sigma_x}{\sqrt{n}}$
Calculate the standard or z score	$Z = \dfrac{(X_i - \mu)}{\sigma_{\bar{x}}}$
Compare the p-value to the p critical	Use a "z score to percentile" calculator or z table.

7.1 INTRODUCTION

ARTICLE 7.1

New Data Links 20 Hours of Personalized Official SAT Practice on Khan Academy to 115-Point Average Score Gains on Redesigned SAT

05/08/17

Score improvements consistent across gender, family income, race, and ethnicity

NEW YORK and MOUNTAIN VIEW, CA — New data show studying for the SAT® for 20 hours on free Official SAT Practice on Khan Academy is associated with an average score gain of 115 points, nearly double the average score gain compared to students who don't use Khan Academy. Out of nearly 250,000 test takers studied, more than 16,000 gained 200 points or more between the PSAT/NMSQT® and SAT.

Khan Academy and the College Board announced the new findings today based on data from the first full year of the new SAT.

"On the new SAT, it's easier than ever for students to show their best work. Official SAT Practice on Khan Academy is free and personalized, and we see students achieving substantial score gains," said College Board President David Coleman. "The SAT has now become an invitation for students to practice and grow."

In addition to the 115-point average score increase associated with 20 hours of practice, shorter practice periods also correlate with meaningful score gains. For example, 6–8 hours of practice on Official SAT Practice is associated with an average 90-point increase.

Source: *New Data Links 20 Hours of Personalized Official SAT Practice on Khan Academy to 115-Point Average Score Gains on Redesigned SAT,* The College Board. ©2017, Reproduced with permission, https://www.collegeboard.org/releases/2017/average-score-gains-on-redesigned-sat

Many high school students in the United States take the Scholastic Aptitude Test (SAT) as part of the college admissions process. In addition to their individual score on a scale of 400 to 1,600, students are told their percentile or rank that allows them to compare their score with other test takers. High schools also use the SAT scores to compare their own students with national standards. In fact, a whole industry has evolved to help students improve their scores, with one example in Article 7.1. Some organizations offer free online courses, while others offer in-class preparation. But do they make a difference? And how much of a difference?

In this chapter, we will learn how to determine when something is unusually different or statistically significant. We will start by looking at exam scores and learn how a student can determine his or her rank within a class. We will then learn about sampling distributions and the standard error of the mean. Finally, we will use these concepts to test whether the average SAT scores among students who took a preparatory course are significantly different from the scores of students who did not take a preparatory course. Rather than using descriptive statistics as we did in Chapter 6, we are now turning to "inferential" statistics, whereby we are making inferences about a population based on a sample.

7.2 THE NORMAL DISTRIBUTION AND STANDARD SCORES

Suppose you receive an exam score of 60. You may be disappointed until you learn that you earned the highest score. Alternatively, you may earn an 85 and be quite satisfied until you learn that the average was a 95. If the professor announces the average score, you only know how you did relative to the average. If, however, the professor tells you the standard deviation, you can learn what percentage of students did just as well or better. We will use the exam.dta[1] data set and the normal distribution to learn how to determine this information.

The exam.dta data set shows the exam scores for 50 students in a statistics course. The mean score for the exam is 80 and the standard deviation is 5. Figure 7.1 shows a histogram of the variable "grade," which we learned how to generate in Chapter 6 using the command **hist**. We also learned in Chapter 6 that a histogram shows ranges of values on the horizontal axis and the number of times they appear or the proportion of each set of values on the vertical axis. In this case, the shape of the histogram looks like a bell curve. Many continuous random variables exhibit this shape with most values clustering around the mean and fewer observations in the extremes or in the tails of the bell curve. This is known as a *normal distribution*, and it is one of the most important concepts in statistics. It is important because not only do so many variables follow this distribution, but also we use the normal distribution to draw conclusions

---

[1] The exam.dta data set is a simulated data set. It does not represent actual grades of any students.

FIGURE 7.1 ● HISTOGRAM OF TEST SCORES

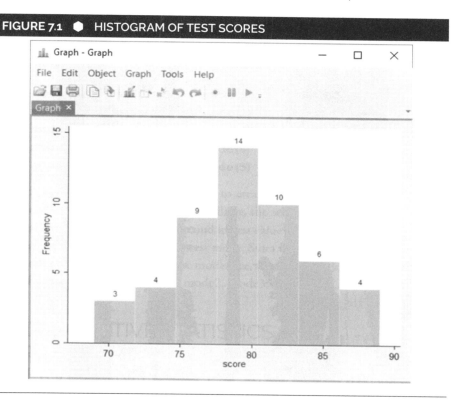

about the characteristics of a population based on a sample even when the underlying distribution is not normal (see Section 7.8 on the Central Limit Theorem).

Figure 7.2 shows the normal distribution, which exhibits perfect symmetry. Exactly half of the area under the curve falls on each side of the mean value. As illustrated, we can also see what percentage of the area falls with 1, 2, and 3 standard deviations of the mean. Using our data from the exam data set, the second line of numbers shows 80 as the mean score and increments of 5 on either side since the standard deviation is 5. In other words, we can say that 68% of students scored between 75 and 85 or within 1 standard deviation of the mean, 95% scored within 2 standard deviations (70–90), and 99% scored within 3 standard deviations (65–95) of the mean.

We can convert each number in our data set to a standard score, which is also known as a *z score*. Essentially, every student's grade can be expressed as the number of standard deviations that it deviates from the mean. The standard score is expressed in Equation 7.1.

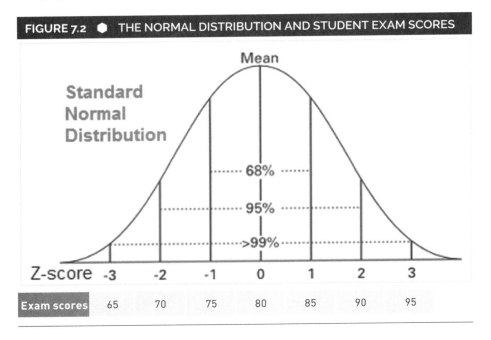

FIGURE 7.2 ● THE NORMAL DISTRIBUTION AND STUDENT EXAM SCORES

$$\text{Standard score or } Z \text{ score} = \frac{(X_i - \bar{X})}{\sigma_X} \tag{7.1}$$

where

X_i = the value of one individual's score

$\bar{X}$ = the average value of the variable X

σ_X = the standard deviation of the variable X

The numerator shows the difference between one student's score and the mean of all scores. If you earned an 85 and the class average was 80, for example, the numerator would be 5 points above the class average. The denominator is the value 1 standard deviation. Dividing how much your score differed from the mean by the standard deviation tells you how many standard deviations your score is above or below the mean. In this case, positive 5 divided by a standard deviation of 5 says that you are 1 standard deviation above the mean.

The next step to determine how many students did just as well or better is to find out how much of the area under the normal curve is to the right of 1 standard deviation. As we saw in Figure 7.2, 68% of the area under a normal curve lies within 1 standard deviation (–1 to +1) of the mean or 34% lies between the mean and 1 standard deviation on either side of the mean. Since 50% of the area under the curve lies to the right of the mean, we can subtract 34% from 50% to determine that 16% falls to the right of 1 standard deviation. We can then say that 16% of students earned 85 or higher scores and 84% earned lower scores. Since 16% of 50 students is 8 students, we know that 8 students earned equal or higher scores. Because the actual distribution isn't a perfect bell curve, this can be a rough estimate. If we use the **tab** command to generate a frequency table as we learned in Chapter 6, Output 7.1 shows that 3 students earned an 85, and 5 students earned higher than 85.

OUTPUT 7.1: FREQUENCY DISTRIBUTION OF EXAM SCORES

. tab score

score	Freq.	Percent	Cum.
69	1	2.00	2.00
70	1	2.00	4.00
71	1	2.00	6.00
73	2	4.00	10.00
74	2	4.00	14.00
75	2	4.00	18.00
76	4	8.00	26.00
77	3	6.00	32.00
78	6	12.00	44.00
79	3	6.00	50.00
80	5	10.00	60.00
81	3	6.00	66.00
82	2	4.00	70.00
83	5	10.00	80.00
84	2	4.00	84.00
85	3	6.00	90.00
86	1	2.00	92.00
87	1	2.00	94.00
88	2	4.00	98.00
89	1	2.00	100.00
Total	50	100.00	

There are many online calculators that will compute the area to the right or left of a standard score. If we use the calculator at "Measuring U" at www.measuringu.com/pcalcz.php, we will see the image in Figure 7.3.

Alternatively, we could use a z-score table, which is illustrated in Table 7.1 and included in Appendix 5. When using the table, you would look for your z score in the table, which is +1 in this case. Across from the +1, we see the areas for a one-tailed and a two-tailed probability. Because we only want to know how much area is above +1 and below +1, we would use the one-tailed probability. (In later chapters, we will want to know how much area is above +1 and below −1 or how much area is in the two tails rather than in one tail.) Looking at the image above the table for the one-tailed test, you can see a z with the area shaded to the right of the z. The one-tailed probability for +1 of 0.15866 represents the area that is shaded or roughly 16% of the area. Since the entire area under the curve represents 100% of the area, 100 minus 16 tells us that 84% of the area lies to the left of a z score of +1.

If the z score is negative, we can still use the table since a normal distribution is perfectly symmetric. For example, if the student scored a 75, his or her z score would be −1. We can see from the table that the area to the right of +1 is 0.15866, and therefore, we know that the area to the left of −1 is also 0.15866. Since the total area is equal to 1, 1 minus 0.15866 is 0.84134. In this case, roughly 16% of the students earned lower scores and 84% earned equal or better scores.

FIGURE 7.3 ● AREA UNDER THE NORMAL CURVE FOR A Z SCORE OF +1

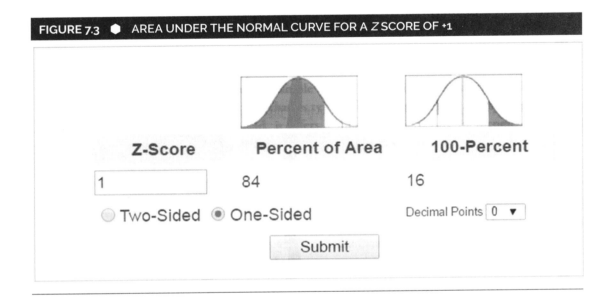

TABLE 7.1 ● AREAS UNDER THE NORMAL CURVE (Z SCORE)

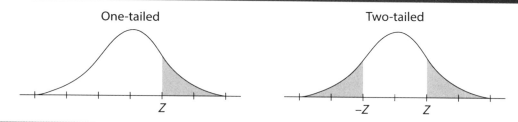

One-tailed   Two-tailed

Z Scores	Probability	
	One-tailed	Two-tailed
0	0.50000	1.00000
0.1	0.46017	0.92034
0.2	0.42074	0.84148
0.3	0.38209	0.76418
0.4	0.34458	0.68916
0.5	0.30854	0.61708
0.6	0.27425	0.54851
0.7	0.24196	0.48393
0.8	0.21186	0.42371
0.9	0.18406	0.36812
1	0.15866	0.31731
1.1	0.13567	0.27133
1.2	0.11507	0.23014
1.3	0.09680	0.19360
1.4	0.08076	0.16151
1.5	0.06681	0.13361
1.6	0.05480	0.10960
1.7	0.04457	0.08913
1.8	0.03593	0.07186
1.9	0.02872	0.05743
2	0.02275	0.04550
2.1	0.01786	0.03573

(Continued)

TABLE 7.1 ● (Continued)

2.2	0.01390	0.02781
2.3	0.01072	0.02145
2.4	0.00820	0.01640
2.5	0.00621	0.01242
2.6	0.00466	0.00932
2.7	0.00347	0.00693
2.8	0.00256	0.00511
2.9	0.00187	0.00373
3	0.00135	0.00270
3.1	0.00097	0.00194
3.2	0.00069	0.00137
3.3	0.00048	0.00097
3.4	0.00034	0.00067
3.5	0.00023	0.00047
3.6	0.00016	0.00032
3.7	0.00011	0.00022
3.8	0.00007	0.00014
3.9	0.00005	0.00010

Now let's suppose that the standard deviation for the class is 10 instead of 5. In that case, a student who earned an 85 when the average was 80 would have a standard score as follows:

$$Z \text{ score or Standard score} = \frac{85-80}{10} = 0.5$$

Using the z-score table, we can see that the area to the right of 0.5 is 0.30854 or roughly 31%. Therefore, 31% of students earned an equal or higher score compared with only 16% when the standard deviation was 5.

You can also use this same information to determine your percentile rank. If, for example, 16% earned an equal or higher score in Case A, then 84% earned a lower score. You would then be at the 84th percentile. In Case B, you would be at the 69th percentile. Table 7.2 shows the results from the two examples above.

TABLE 7.2 ● STANDARD SCORE EXAMPLES WITH EXAM GRADES

	Case A	Case B
Class mean	80	80
Standard deviation	5	10
One student's test score	85	85
Standard score or z score	1	0.5
One-tail probability	0.16	0.31
Number of students in class	50	50
Number of students who earned a higher score	8	16
Percentile rank	84th percentile	69th percentile

Although Stata doesn't calculate z scores, a user-written program is available in Stata to do this. In the Command Window, you would type in **help zscore** and scroll down until you see "Web resources from Stata and other Users." Then click on "zscore" and then on the link provided. Finally, click on "Click here to install." Once it is installed, type in the command **zscore varname**, and Stata will create a new variable called z_varname in your data set. Then, if you summarize the new variable, you will see that the mean is 0 and the standard deviation is 1.

7.3 SAMPLING DISTRIBUTIONS AND STANDARD ERRORS

In the previous section, we examined one student's score compared with the rest of the class. Using the normal distribution, we were able to see the percentile rank of the student. We can also use the normal distribution to examine how one sample compares with a population. To do this, we will first need to learn about sampling distributions and standard errors. We will define these terms below as we develop an example.

Although universities can have hundreds or thousands of students, let's suppose that only five students attend a university. The amount of money that they spend on eating out per week is shown in Table 7.3 along with the overall mean of $67 and a standard deviation of $19.60.

Survey designers rarely have the resources to gather information from the entire population. Instead, they take a sample to estimate the population characteristics. In this case, let's assume that we only have resources to sample two students. Table 7.4 shows all possible combinations of two students and the average amount spent for each sample of two. Although we typically would not sample the same person twice, we have included it here to illustrate the principle of the standard error of the mean.

TABLE 7.3 ● WEEKLY EXPENDITURE ON EATING OUT BY FIVE COLLEGE STUDENTS	
Student	**Weekly Amount Spent on Eating Out in Dollars**
A	55
B	45
C	90
D	85
E	60
Mean	67
Standard deviation	19.6

TABLE 7.4 ● SAMPLING DISTRIBUTION OF ALL POSSIBLE SAMPLES OF TWO STUDENTS			
All Possible Samples of Two Students	**Average Expenditure of Two Students**	**Sample Mean Minus Population Mean**	**Estimated Standard Error of the Mean**
AA	55	−12	0
AB	50	−17	5
AC	72.5	5.5	17.5
AD	70	3	15.6
AE	57.5	−9.5	2.5
BB	45	−22	0
BC	67.5	0.5	22.5
BD	65	−2	20
BE	52.5	−14.5	7.5
CC	90	23	0
CD	87.5	20.5	2.5
CE	75	8	15
DD	85	18	0
DE	72.5	5.5	12.5
EE	60	−7	0
Mean	67		
Standard error of the mean	13.83		

We know that the true mean of the population is $67. From all possible combinations of two students, we can see that the average of some samples is very close to the true mean and others are much farther from the true mean. With larger sample sizes, we would see less variability in the sample means. Similarly, lower variation in the population values would lead to less variability in the sample means.

The distribution of all possible values for a statistic (in this case, the mean) is called a sampling distribution. When we take the standard deviation of all possible sample means, it is called the standard error of the mean, which is used extensively in statistics. Fortunately, we don't need to take all possible samples of a population to determine the standard error of the mean. Instead, we can calculate it by dividing the standard deviation of the population by the square root of the number of cases in our sample as shown in Equation 7.2.

$$\text{Standard error of the mean} = \frac{\sigma_X}{\sqrt{n}} = \frac{19.55671}{\sqrt{2}} = 13.83 \qquad (7.2)$$

where

σ_X = standard deviation of the population

n = sample size

Notice that the answer to the calculation in Equation 7.2 gives us the same answer that we calculated by using the standard deviation of all possible means.

We can now use this information about the standard error of the mean to test a hypothesis, which we will show below in the next section.

7.4 EXAMINING THE THEORY AND IDENTIFYING THE RESEARCH QUESTION AND HYPOTHESIS

With the large numbers of students who take the SAT test each year, there is an entire industry built around raising SAT scores through preparation. Many studies have shown that taking a preparatory course will raise a student's score. But are these tests biased? Are they taken by children from wealthier families or children enrolled in schools with higher achievement levels?

In this section, we will assume that the average math SAT score at High School X was 511 with a standard deviation of 120. To determine if the students could raise their scores significantly, the school randomly assigned 50 students within the high school to take a preparatory course prior to the test. The average score among the 50 students who took the course was 535. We now want to find out if the preparatory course worked or if their average score of 535 is significantly different from 511.

In Chapter 1, we learned that part of the scientific method or the research process is to examine the theory, identify a research question, and form a hypothesis. Theory suggests that preparation for exams will lead to higher scores. In this case, our specific research question can be stated as follows: "Did students at High School X who took a preparatory course earn higher average scores on math SAT tests compared with the population of students at High School X?" As described in Chapter 1, we can then state a hypothesis, which is the answer to the question. The hypothesis could be positive or negative. For example, we could state that the students who took the preparatory course earned a higher or a lower score. When using statistical tests, however, we would define a null hypothesis, which is a testable statement indicating that there is no difference or no change. In this case, for example, the null hypothesis would be that students at High School X who took the course earned the same score as the rest of the high school population. The researcher would then use statistical techniques to test the hypothesis.

7.5 TESTING FOR STATISTICAL SIGNIFICANCE

Now that we have identified our research question and stated our null hypothesis, we can test whether there is a statistically significant difference between the average score of the 50 students who took the preparatory course and the students who did not take the course.

Procedures

1. Calculate the standard error of the mean.

    Instead of looking at the standard deviation of the sample of 50 students, we must calculate the standard error of the mean since we are considering the distribution of possible means.

    $$\text{Standard error of the mean} = \sigma_{\bar{X}} = \frac{\sigma_X}{\sqrt{n}} = \frac{120}{\sqrt{50}} = 16.97$$

2. Calculate the standard score using the sample mean and the population mean in the numerator.

    In this step, our numerator shows the difference between the average score of the 50 students who took the course and the population of students at the school. When we divide by the standard error of the mean, we are essentially looking at how many standard deviation units the difference is above or below the population mean.

$$\text{Standard score} = \frac{(\bar{X} - \mu)}{\sigma_{\bar{X}}} = \frac{(535 - 511)}{16.97} = 1.41$$

3. Look up the area under the normal curve for a standard score of 1.41.

In the example in Section 7.2, we were looking at one individual's score and comparing it with the class average to determine that student's percentile rank. In this case, we are examining the scores of 50 students to determine if their score is unusual compared with the population average. Rather than looking at the area to the right of the standard score, we often want to examine both the extreme upper and lower values. It could be the case, for example, that students who take the course will earn a lower score. For this reason, we often test whether something is "different" rather than just higher or lower. In particular, we want to see how often we would see a score that is 535 or greater (24 points above the population average) or 487 or less (24 points below the population average).

If we use the calculator at "Measuring U," (www.measuringu.com/pcalcz.php), we can plug in our standard score of 1.41 and see the image in Figure 7.4.

Alternatively, we could use the areas under the normal curve in Table 7.1. Using our z score of 1.41 and the two-tailed probability, we can see that the area in the two tails is equal to 0.16151 or roughly 16% as shown by the online calculator. Using this information, we can now determine if 535 is statistically significant.

FIGURE 7.4 ● AREA UNDER THE NORMAL CURVE FOR A TWO-SIDED STANDARD SCORE OF 1.41

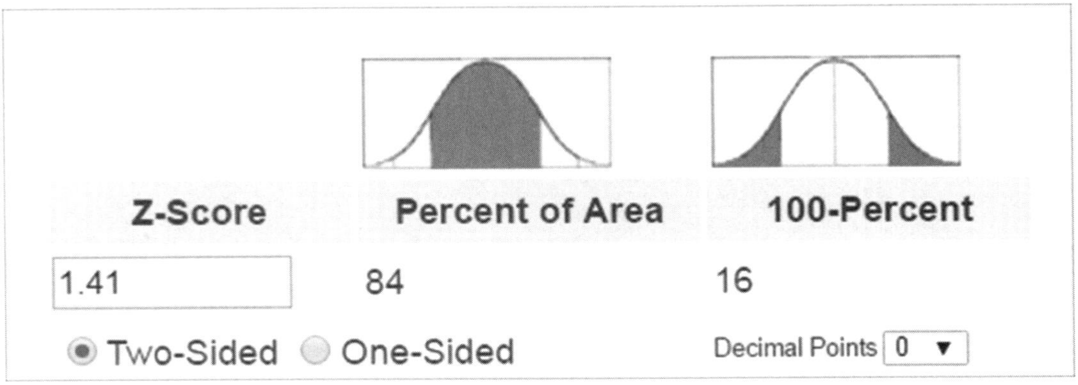

7.6 REJECTING OR NOT REJECTING THE NULL HYPOTHESIS

Before interpreting statistical tests, scientists or researchers set an alpha level, which is also referred to as p (critical). The alpha level is the probability of rejecting the null hypothesis when it is true, or a Type I error. It is typically set at 0.05, but researchers also use 0.01, 0.001, and sometimes 0.1. The larger the alpha level, the more likely you are to find statistically significant results.

Although probability is a number between 0 and 1, it is often expressed in percentage terms. For example, you could say that the probability of committing a Type I error is 0.05, or there is a 5% chance of committing a Type I error.

Using an alpha level of 0.05, we would say that the average SAT score of 535 is statistically significant if the probability of observing this value or greater (or ≤487, the opposite extreme) is 0.05.

In our example above, 16% of the samples fell in the two extremes. Our p-value is then 0.16. The official definition of a p-value from the American Statistical Association is given as follows: "Informally, a p-value is the probability under a specified statistical model that a statistical summary of the data (e.g., the sample mean difference between two compared groups) would be equal to or more extreme than its observed value" (Wasserstein & Lazar, 2016, p. 131).

We can now compare our p-value to the alpha level to determine whether our results are unusual or statistically significant. The rule along with our example is shown in Figure 7.5.

FIGURE 7.5 ● RULE FOR REJECTING OR NOT REJECTING THE NULL HYPOTHESIS

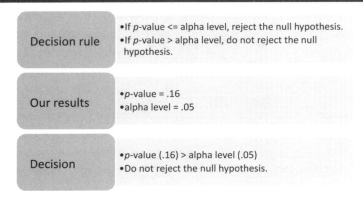

Decision rule
- If p-value <= alpha level, reject the null hypothesis.
- If p-value > alpha level, do not reject the null hypothesis.

Our results
- p-value = .16
- alpha level = .05

Decision
- p-value (.16) > alpha level (.05)
- Do not reject the null hypothesis.

In other words, you would expect to see scores of 535 or greater or 487 or lower in 16% of all samples. Since this is fairly high (much higher than 5%), we would say that it is not that unusual to see this score.

It is important to note that we would never say "we accept" the null hypothesis since there is always some chance that our samples did not accurately reflect the population. In fact, the alpha level tells us the probability of rejecting the null hypothesis when it is true. This is referred to as a Type I error as described earlier. A Type II error occurs when we do not reject the null hypothesis when it is false. Appendix 4 offers a summary of the decision rules for statistical significance described in this chapter.

Recently, the American Statistical Association released a statement on statistical significance and p-values to correct some of the many misuses of the concept. As they emphasize, the p-value does not indicate if a hypothesis is true or if the data were produced by random chance. Furthermore, they emphasize that researchers should consider other factors besides the p-values such as the "design of a study, the quality of the measurements, the external evidence for the phenomenon under study, and the validity of assumptions that underlie the data analysis." Finally, they suggest other methods in addition to p-values to test hypotheses, such as confidence intervals, which are discussed in later chapters (Wasserstein & Lazar, 2016).

7.7 INTERPRETING THE RESULTS

The results in Figure 7.4 show us that the probability of observing a standard score (or z score) that is greater than 1.41 or less than −1.41 is less than 0.16. As we discussed earlier, typically a p critical or alpha level is set at 0.05. We then compare our p-value of 0.16 with the alpha level of 0.05. Because our p-value is greater than 0.05, we do not reject the null hypothesis. In other words, there is not enough evidence to conclude that the students who took the preparatory course earned significantly higher or lower scores than the student population at High School X.

In Parts Three and Four of the book, each chapter involves a research question, a null hypothesis, and a statistical test. A summary of these for each chapter is offered in Appendix 2. This summary should help you to quickly identify what type of statistical procedure or test should be used and the procedures to implement the test.

7.8 CENTRAL LIMIT THEOREM

In the previous sections, we used the normal distribution to determine one student's percentile rank and to examine the scores of 50 students who took an SAT preparatory course compared with the population of students at that high school. As we mentioned earlier, the normal distribution is one of the most important concepts in statistics. It is used to draw conclusions about the characteristics of a population based on a sample. What is particularly unique is that the central limit theorem tells us that even if the population distribution is not normal, the sampling distribution of means from a population will approach a normal distribution as the sampling size increases. In other words, we can still use the area under the normal curve to determine the probability of observing an equal or more extreme value of the mean observed in our sample even when the population is not normal. We use an example below to illustrate this point.

Let's suppose that there are 1,000 students at High School X. Their math SAT scores range from 200 to 800, but they are not normally distributed. Instead, as you see in Figure 7.6, there appears to be a bimodal distribution or a distribution clustered around two different values of roughly 400 and 600.

According to the central limit theorem, if we draw many samples of 50 students, the means of each sample would form a normal distribution. Figure 7.7 shows the mean values of 1,000 samples of 50 students from the student population. As illustrated, the means form an almost perfect bell shape, which allows us to use the normal distribution to test hypotheses.

FIGURE 7.6 ◆ BIMODAL DISTRIBUTION OF SAT SCORES AT HIGH SCHOOL X

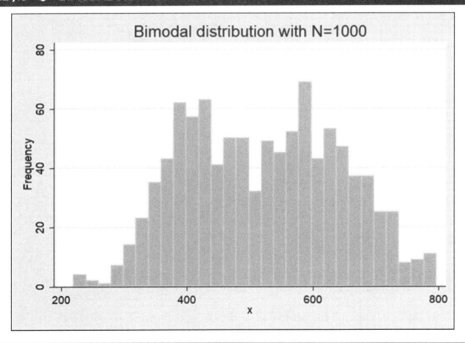

FIGURE 7.7 ● MEANS OF 1,000 SAMPLES OF MATH SAT SCORES FROM 50 STUDENTS

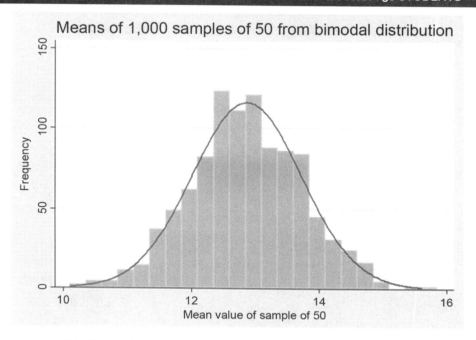

7.9 PRESENTING THE RESULTS

In addition to learning how to test hypotheses using statistics, it is important to learn how to convey the results. In particular, there may be times when you are reporting your results for a newspaper or a government report that is aimed at a nontechnical audience. You may also want to publish your results in an academic journal, which would require more details related to the statistical tests. Chapter 15, "Writing a Research Paper," offers guidelines on each type of test and how to report the results. We will also offer specific examples in each of the remaining chapters on how to address the two types of audiences based on the example used in the chapter.

Presenting the Results for a Nontechnical Audience

To present the results of the test to a nontechnical audience, we could submit the following statement:

> High School X randomly chose 50 students to take part in an SAT preparatory course. They then compared their math SAT score with the rest of the high school population. Students who took the course earned 535 on average,

which was higher than the high school average of 511, but it was not a statistically significant difference.

Presenting the Results in a Scholarly Journal

In a peer-reviewed journal, we would include more information. These results could be explained as follows:

> Using a standard score or *z* score, we compared the math SAT scores of 50 students, who were selected randomly to take a preparatory course, with the math scores of the rest of the population at High School X. Students who took the course earned 535 on average (*SD* = 90.25) compared with the high school average of 511 (*SD* = 120.00). This was not a statistically significant difference, $z = 1.41$, $p = 0.16$.

7.10 SUMMARY OF COMMANDS USED IN THIS CHAPTER

As described in Chapter 4, this last section of each chapter summarizes all of the Stata code used in the chapter. In addition, all Stata code used throughout the book is summarized in Appendix 1.

Histogram

```
hist grade
```

Frequency table

```
tab score
```

Z score

```
help zscore
zscore varname
```

EXERCISES

1. Your resting heart rate is 62. The average resting heart rate for the class is 72 and the variance is 25.

    a. What percentage of the class has a lower resting heart rate (round to the nearest whole number)?

b. If there are 85 students in the class, how many students (the actual number, not the percentage) have a higher resting heart rate? (round to the nearest whole number)

2. Many studies have confirmed that in the population, the flu lasts 21 days on average with a standard deviation of 7. The manufacturers of Tamiflu want to show that their product reduces the length of the flu. They choose a sample of 25 people for their experiment and give them Tamiflu at the start of their flu. The average length of the flu among the 25 people taking Tamiflu was 18 days.

   a. If you ran a test to determine if Tamiflu does reduce the length of a flu, what is the null hypothesis?

   b. Using an alpha level or p critical of 0.05, use statistics to show if there is a statistically significant difference in the average length of time with and without taking Tamiflu. Show all of your work to prove this and indicate if you would reject your null hypothesis and why or why not.

   c. Write a paragraph to explain your results to a nontechnical audience.

   d. Write a paragraph to explain your results in a scholarly journal.

3. Suppose that you have a population of three individuals and the number of times that they exercise per week is shown in the table below.

Individual	Exercise Times per Week
A	2
B	0
C	7
Mean	3
Standard deviation	3.60555128

   a. Write out all combinations of two individuals from the three (including drawing the same person twice) and show the mean of each pair.

   b. Calculate the standard error of the mean using the information from Part "a," using N-1 in the denominator of the formula for the variance.

   c. Generate the standard error of the mean using the formula rather than the information in your table.

REFERENCES

College Board. (Ed.). (2017, August 10). *New data links 20 hours of personalized official SAT practice on Khan Academy to 115-point average score gains on redesigned SAT.* Retrieved from www.collegeboard.org/releases/2017/average-score-gains-on-redesigned-sat

Wasserstein, R. L., & Lazar, N. A. (2016). The ASA's statement on *p*-values: Context, process, and purpose. *American Statistician, 70*(2), 129–133. doi:10.1080/00031305.2016.1154108

TESTING A HYPOTHESIS ABOUT A SINGLE MEAN

Chapter Preview

Research question	Do first-year college students gain 15 pounds?
Null hypothesis	First-year students gain 15 pounds in their first year of college.
Test	One-sample *t* test
Types of variables	One continuous variable (weightgain)
When to use	Comparing a sample mean with an established mean from a population The population standard deviation is not known.
Assumptions	1. The population is approximately normally distributed. 2. Sample observations are random.
Stata code: Generic	**ttest continuousvar==X** where "X" is some predetermined mean.
Stata code: Example	**ttest weightgain==15**

8.1 INTRODUCTION

ARTICLE 8.1

THE CONVERSATION
Academic rigor, journalistic flair

Arts + Culture   Economy + Business   Education   Environment + Energy   Ethics + Religion   Health + Medicine   Politics + Society   Science

How to beat the 'freshman five' weight gain

August 23, 2018 6.18pm EDT

Regular exercise can go a long way towards keeping off the weight gain at college and you don't have to be a serious athlete to participate. (Shutterstock)

■ Email
■ Twitter   5
■ Facebook   26
■ LinkedIn
■ Print

There is a widespread belief that a young adult's college years are accompanied by weight gain — the so called "freshman five."

This is not just an urban myth. <u>Research shows that approximately 85 per cent of overweight adults were not overweight as youth</u>. And, by studying changes in fat mass during the period between 18 and 28 years of age, we have found that the weight gain does occur in this early adult time period.

Indeed, the "freshman five" may only be the tip of the iceberg. Fat mass increases beyond the years of college into the late 20s, even in those who were normal weight in high school.

Source: Barbour-Tuck (2018).

Most college students have heard of "The Freshman 5," "The Freshmen 10," and sometimes the "Freshmen 15." It refers to the amount of weight that freshmen gain in their first year of college (Article 8.1). Originally known in the 1980s as the "Freshman 10" for a 10-pound weight gain, the number has increased to 15 over time in the United States and Canada. Outside of the United States and Canada, other countries have similar terms such as "first-year fatties," "the fresher five," and "the fresher spread." But is it true? Do first-year college students gain 15 pounds on average? In fact, studies have shown that it is not true. Instead, freshmen gain 2 to 6 pounds according to many studies. Some studies also show that only 10% of college freshmen gain 15 pounds or more.

In this chapter, we will learn how to test a sample mean to determine if it is significantly different from some specified value. For example, we can use data from a sample of freshmen at one college and compare their average weight gain over the first year with the value of 15 pounds. We can then determine if there is a statistically significant difference between the average weight gain and the mythical 15 pounds.

8.2 WHEN TO USE THE ONE-SAMPLE *t* TEST

Table 8.1 shows examples from different fields where the one-sample *t* test can be used. In each case, there is an assumed population average, but the population standard deviation is unknown. Each of these can be tested using the one-sample *t* test.

Figure 8.1 illustrates a decision tree that helps you decide which statistical test is appropriate for each type of analysis. As you can see, it will depend whether you are

TABLE 8.1 ● EXAMPLES OF THE ONE-SAMPLE *t* TEST			
Field	**Research Question**	**Null Hypothesis**	**Continuous Variable**
Criminal Justice	Does a judge in one district give harsher prison sentences to women convicted of child abuse?	There is no difference in the average sentence length by the judge compared with the national average.	Sentence time in months of women convicted of child abuse
Economics	Do Americans work a 40-hour workweek?	Americans work 40 hours per week.	Hours worked per week among those Americans who work full time
Political Science	What is the average age of pro-life supporters?	The average age of pro-life supporters is 53.	Age of pro-life supporters
Public Health	Do smokers gain weight within the first year after they stop smoking?	The average weight gain after 1 year without smoking is 0.	Weight gain after 1 year without cigarettes
Psychology	Is postpartum depression more common among mothers who do not have immediate family members living nearby than for mothers that do?	The average depression score on the "Quick Depression Assessment" test is 4.	Quick Depression Assessment test score
Sociology	What is the average age that children own their first cell phone?	Children own their first phone at the age of 9.	Ownership age of first phone

FIGURE 8.1 ◆ DECISION TREE FOR CHOOSING THE RIGHT STATISTIC

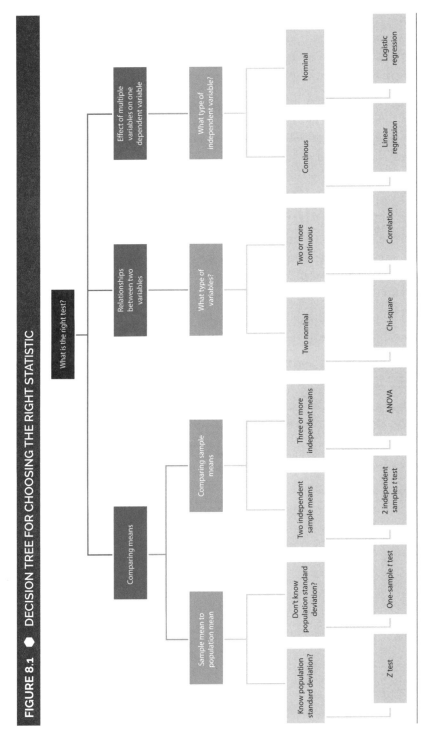

comparing means or relationships between variables. In this chapter, we will be looking at a sample mean (weight gained among freshmen at one college) and comparing it with an assumed population mean of 15; so we would follow the tree on the left-hand side from "comparing means" to "sample mean to population mean." Because we do not know the population standard deviation, we would follow the path to the one-sample *t* test.

8.3 CALCULATING THE ONE-SAMPLE *t* TEST

In Chapter 7, we learned about using the normal distribution and we tested if the math SAT scores of 50 students who took a preparatory SAT course to the average scores of the population of students at the same high school. In that case, we knew the population mean and the population standard deviation. In most cases, however, we will not know the population standard deviation. In fact, it is typical that we do not know anything about a population and therefore draw a sample to learn about the population.

In this chapter, we will assume that we know the population mean or some hypothesized value of the population mean (e.g., the Freshmen 15), but we do not know the population standard deviation. We will therefore use the sample standard deviation when calculating a *t* statistic, which is similar to the *z* score or standard score that we used in Chapter 7. The difference, however, is that the sample standard deviation could be larger or smaller than the population standard deviation, which introduces some uncertainty. In particular, the distribution of standard scores is no longer normal. To account for this, we use a *t* distribution, which looks like a normal distribution but has more areas in the tails to account for the error introduced. Furthermore, its shape depends on the sample size. A larger sample size will produce a *t* distribution that is closer to the normal distribution and eventually, with a large enough sample, the area under the *t* distribution is close to the normal distribution and either test can be used. Figure 8.2 shows the *t* distribution with two sample sizes and the normal distribution. The normal distribution is higher in the middle with less area in the tails. The two *t* distributions represent very small sample sizes (four and two) to emphasize the differences in the distribution. Notice that when the sample size is four, the distribution is much closer to the normal distribution than when the sample size is two.

To calculate the *t* statistic, we use the same formula that we used in the previous chapter when we calculated the standard score. In this case, however, we substitute

FIGURE 8.2 ● NORMAL AND *t* DISTRIBUTION FOR TWO SAMPLE SIZES

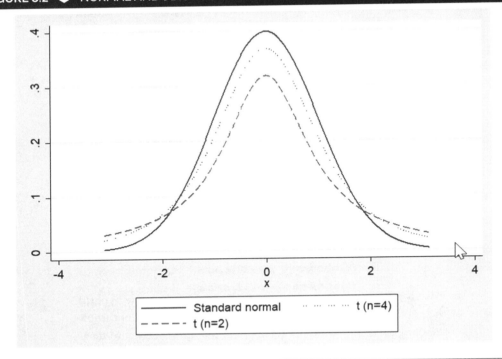

the sample standard deviation for the population standard deviation as shown in Equation 8.1.

$$t = \frac{(\bar{X} - \mu)}{\dfrac{s}{\sqrt{n}}} \qquad (8.1)$$

where

$\bar{X}$ = sample mean
μ = population mean
s = sample standard deviation
n = sample size

The numerator shows us the difference between the sample mean and the population mean. A larger difference will lead to a larger *t* statistic and a greater likelihood that there is a statistically significant difference. The denominator is the standard error of the mean, which is the estimated standard deviation of the sample means from all possible samples drawn from the population. Combined, the numerator and denominator tell you how many standard deviation units the observed sample mean is above or below the population mean.

8.4 CONDUCTING A ONE-SAMPLE *t* TEST

The Freshmen15 data set is a fictitious sample of 30 college students. It contains only one variable, weightgain, which indicates how many pounds each student gained after 1 year at college.

Research question

Do freshmen gain 15 pounds of weight on average after their first year of college?

Hypothesis

Freshmen gain less than 15 pounds.

Null hypothesis

Freshmen gain 15 pounds after 1 year of college.

Variables

Continuous variable—the number of pounds gained (weightgain)

Assumptions

In addition to using one continuous variable and one population mean, we make two assumptions to generate valid results:

1. *Normal distribution:* The continuous variable, weight gain in this example, should be approximately normally distributed within each category. It only needs to be approximately normally distributed since minor violations of normality do not affect the results.

2. *Sample observations are random:* Sample data must be selected randomly (refer to Chapter 2 on sample selection techniques).

Procedures using commands

Using a do-file, we would run the commands below:

```
ttest weightgain==15
```

Procedures using menus

Using menus in Stata, we would click on the sequence listed below that would bring us to Dialog Box 8.1. In the dialog box, we would select the variable "weightgain" and click on "One-sample." We would also fill in "15" for the hypothesized mean as displayed.

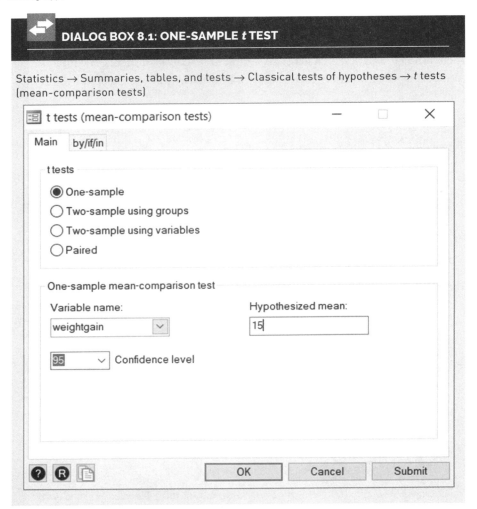

DIALOG BOX 8.1: ONE-SAMPLE *t* TEST

Statistics → Summaries, tables, and tests → Classical tests of hypotheses → *t* tests (mean-comparison tests)

8.5 INTERPRETING THE OUTPUT

Output 8.1 illustrates the results of our one-sample *t* test. We can see from the table that the average weight gain in our sample of 30 students is 10.7 pounds with a standard deviation of 6.8 pounds. When comparing these results with the hypothesized mean of 15 pounds, we turn to the *t* statistic of –3.46 and the hypotheses on the last two lines of output. The first hypothesis on the left (Ha: mean < 15) is that the mean or average weight gain is less than 15 pounds. The second hypothesis (Ha: mean != 15) is that the mean does not equal 15 pounds, and the third hypothesis (Ha: mean > 15) is that the mean is greater than 15. Since we typically want to consider the extreme values on either side of the average, we use the hypothesis that the mean is not equal

✓ **OUTPUT 8.1: STATA OUTPUT FOR THE ONE-SAMPLE *t* TEST**

```
. ttest weightgain==15

One-sample t test
```

Variable	Obs	Mean	Std. Err.	Std. Dev.	[95% Conf. Interval]	
weight~n	30	10.7	1.242125	6.803397	8.15957	13.24043

```
     mean = mean(weightgain)                                         t =  -3.4618
Ho: mean = 15                                    degrees of freedom =        29

    Ha: mean < 15                Ha: mean != 15                 Ha: mean > 15
 Pr(T < t) = 0.0008         Pr(|T| > |t|) = 0.0017          Pr(T > t) = 0.9992
```

to 15. Using that information, we see that when the null hypothesis is true (that the average weight gain is 15 pounds), the probability of observing a *t* statistic greater than 3.46 or less than −3.46 is less than .0017. Because this is less than 0.05, our alpha level, we reject the null hypothesis that the average weight gain is 15 pounds.

We can also examine the confidence interval in Output 8.1. In Chapter 7, we learned that 95% of all sample means should fall within roughly two standard errors of the mean. The exact number is 1.96 standard errors of the mean. To obtain the 95% confidence interval for the population mean, we would then multiply 1.96 by the standard error of the mean and add this to the sample mean to get the upper end of the confidence interval. For the lower end, we would then multiply −1.96 by the standard error of the mean and add this to the sample mean. In this chapter, however, we don't know the population standard deviation. We therefore have to use the *t* distribution. With a sample size of 30, we first calculate the "degrees of freedom" as the sample size minus 1 or 29 degrees of freedom. Degrees of freedom is a statistical term that indicates the number of observations that are free to vary. In other words, we could change 29 of the values in the sample and still get the same mean of 10.7 as long as we control or set the last value so that the mean is 10.7.

We can then use Appendix 6, which shows the critical values of the *t* distribution, to find the exact *t* statistic that would provide the area under the curve that represents 95% of all observations. With 29 degrees of freedom and the area under the two tails adding up to .05, we see a *t* value of 2.05. This would mean that 95% of all observations fall between −2.05 and +2.05 standard errors of the mean on either side of the sample mean. The confidence interval would then be calculated as follows:

Lower end $= 10.7 + (-2.05 \times 1.24) = 8.16$
Upper end $= 10.7 + (2.05 \times 1.24) = 13.24$

With this information, we can say that we are 95% confident that the true value of the average weight gain is in the range of 8.16 pounds to 13.24 pounds. The confidence interval can be used in place of a *p*-value to test a hypothesis. In other words, if the confidence interval does not contain the null hypothesis value (15 in this case), then we can say that the results are statistically significant.

8.6 PRESENTING THE RESULTS

Presenting the results for a nontechnical audience

To present these results to a lay audience who may not be familiar with statistical tests, we could write the following:

> Based on our sample of 30 students, we found that the average weight gain among college freshmen was 10.7 pounds. There was a statistically significant difference between our results and the hypothesized 15-pound weight gain portrayed in popular media.

Presenting the results in a scholarly journal

In a peer-reviewed journal, we would include more information. These results could be explained as follows:

> Using a one-sample *t* test, we examined the average weight gain of 30 college freshmen following their first year at college. Our results showed a 10.7-pound average weight gain (*SD* = 6.80). There was a statistically significant difference between our result and the hypothesized 15-pound weight gain found in popular media, $t(29) = -3.46$, $p = 0.00$.

8.7 SUMMARY OF COMMANDS USED IN THIS CHAPTER

As described in Chapter 4, this last section of each chapter summarizes all of the Stata code used in the chapter. In addition, all Stata code used throughout the book is summarized in Appendix 1.

One-sample t test

```
ttest weightgain==15
```

EXERCISES

1. Your local take-out restaurant claims that their food is delivered in 20 minutes. You decide to test their claim and order food from them 36 times over the next 3 months. On average, the food is delivered in 23 minutes with a standard deviation of 5 minutes.

   a. What is the null hypothesis?

   b. Would you reject or not reject the null hypothesis? Show your work to support your decision.

2. Based on your answer to Question 1, construct a 95% confidence interval for the true value of the delivery time.

3. The legal drinking age in the United States is 21 years. Many people, however, try alcohol before they turn 21. Use the National Survey on Drug Use and Health from 2015 to test whether the age when Americans first try alcohol (alctry) is 21 years. Before you run the test using Stata, use the command **tab alctry**. Notice that there are categories related to missing data—985 bad data, 991 never used alcohol, 994 don't know, 997 refused, or 998 blank. Next run the command **sum alctry**. You will notice that the mean age for first trying alcohol is 292 years, which doesn't make sense. You should also notice that the maximum value is 998. To remove these missing data from your test, include the command **if alctry < 72** at the end of your command since 71 was the oldest age reported.

   a. What is your null hypothesis?

   b. Would you reject or not reject your null hypothesis? Explain your decision using your output.

   c. Explain the 95% confidence interval in your output.

4. Based on your results to Question 3, write a few sentences that would explain your results to a nontechnical audience. Then write a few sentences to present your results in a scholarly journal.

REFERENCES

Barbour-Tuck, E. (2018, August 23). *How to beat the "freshman five" weight gain.* Retrieved from https://theconversation.com/how-to-beat-the-freshman-five-weight-gain-100718

TESTING A HYPOTHESIS ABOUT TWO INDEPENDENT MEANS

Chapter Preview

Research question	Do women do more housework than men in the United States?
Null hypothesis	There is no difference in the hours of housework done by men and women in the United States.
Test	Two independent-samples t test
Types of variables	One continuous variable: hour of household work (rhhwork)
	One categorical variable with two categories: 1 "male," 2 "female" (sex)
When to use	Two samples
	Two populations
	Population standard deviation is unknown
Assumptions	Independence of observations
	Normal distribution
	Homogeneity of variances
Additional tests needed	Equality of variances
Stata code: generic	**ttest continuousvar, by(categoricalvar)**
Stata code: example	**ttest rhhwork, by(sex)**

9.1 INTRODUCTION

ARTICLE 9.1

  Women in the U.S. Still Do Way More Housework Than Men

Women in the U.S. Still Do Way More Housework Than Men

The latest data from the Bureau of Labor Statistics reveal how little has changed

by   Sheelah Kolhatkar
🐦 sheelahk

June 26, 2015 – 10:53 AM EDT

Countless panels, conferences, studies, task forces, and books (see Anne Marie Slaughter's forthcoming blockbuster) pop up every year to address a seemingly intractable problem: why there are so few women CEOs, senators, law firm partners, venture capitalists, and hedge fund moguls, not to mention female executives lower down the chain. Once you attain the highest levels of powerful institutions in America, ample evidence shows, the scenery becomes overwhelmingly male.

For all the resources dedicated to untangling why this is, though, the answer may be relatively simple. Newly released data remind us that a large part of the answer lies at home.

According to Article 9.1, women have been doing more housework than men have since the Bureau of Labor Statistics began its annual Time Use Survey in 2003. A higher percentage of women engage in housework and they work longer hours. As we learned in Chapter 2 on questionnaire design, we should ask how they defined "housework." Does that include only cleaning and cooking in the home or does it include errands outside of the home such as grocery shopping? Is child care part of housework? As we also learned in Chapter 2, we would want to know more about the data. How large was the sample size? How were participants selected? Finally, we would want to know if there is a statistically significant difference in the mean score between the two groups.

In this chapter, we will learn how to test for a statistically significant difference between two independent-sample means drawn from two populations. This type of test is called the two independent-samples t test. It is used with one continuous variable (hours of housework in the example above) and one categorical variable with two categories (men and women). Although we don't have access to the time-use survey, we will use the General Social Survey to examine the number of hours of housework that men and women do each week on average. Other examples along with a review of assumptions, procedures, and interpretation of the output are included below.

9.2 WHEN TO USE A TWO INDEPENDENT-SAMPLES *t* TEST

There are many situations when we may want to compare two means. In this chapter, we only consider cases where there are two independent samples. This means that individuals or objects are assigned to one of two groups. Table 9.1 offers examples from different fields and identifies the continuous variable and the categorical variable with two groups.

We can also consult the decision tree in Figure 8.1 and Appendix 3 when we are unsure about which test to use. Since we are comparing the means, we would follow the path on the left to "comparing means." Next, we would choose "comparing sample means" since we now have two sample means in this case—the average number of hours worked by men and those worked by women. Underneath the "two independent sample means" is the two independent-samples t test.

TABLE 9.1 ● EXAMPLES OF TWO INDEPENDENT-SAMPLES *t* TEST

Field	Research Question	Null Hypothesis	Continuous Variable	Categorical Variable
Criminal Justice	Are men more likely to commit delinquent offenses than women?	There is no difference in the number of delinquent offenses committed by men and by women.	Number of offenses committed	1. Men 2. Women
Economics	Do men earn more than women in the same job with the same set of skills?	There is no difference between salaries of men and women in the same job with the same skill level.	Annual salary	1. Men 2. Women
Political Science	Are Democratic voters younger than Republican voters?	There is no difference in the average age of Democrats and Republicans.	Age	1. Democrats 2. Republicans
Psychology	Does multitasking while studying for an exam have an impact on the final score?	There is no difference in the final scores among students who multitask and those who do not.	Exam score	1. Those who multitask 2. Those who do not multitask
Public Health	Do women who smoke give birth to infants with a lower birth weight?	There is no difference in birth weight of children of pregnant mothers who smoke and those who do not.	Birth weight	1. Pregnant mothers who smoke 2. Pregnant mothers who do not smoke
Sociology	Do Catholics or Protestants spend more time volunteering for community work?	There is no difference in the number of hours per week that Catholics and Protestants spend volunteering.	Hours per week volunteering	1. Catholics 2. Protestants

9.3 CALCULATING THE *t* STATISTIC

To test for a significant difference between the two means, we must calculate a *t* statistic. Although Stata will calculate the *t* statistic in the example that follows in this section, it is important to understand how it is calculated in order to interpret its meaning. It is expressed in Equation 9.1 below.

$$t = \frac{(\bar{X}_1 - \bar{X}_2) - 0}{S_{\bar{X}_1 - \bar{X}_2}} \tag{9.1}$$

The numerator is simply the observed difference between the two means and how much greater it is than zero, which is the hypothesized difference. The denominator is the standard error of the mean difference. This is calculated as follows:

$$S_{\bar{X}_1 - \bar{X}_2} = \sqrt{\frac{S_1^2}{n_1} + \frac{S_2^2}{n_2}} \tag{9.2}$$

where

S_1^2 is the variance for the first sample
S_2^2 is the variance for the second sample
n_1 is the sample size for the first sample
n_2 is the sample size for the second sample

Combined, the full formula tells us how many standard error units the observed difference is from zero. As described in Chapter 7, this indicates how unusual our results are if the true difference is zero.

9.4 CONDUCTING A *t* TEST

Using the 2012 General Social Survey, we will examine the number of hours that men and women spend on housework each week.[1] We can begin by generating a summary of these values using the commands (or menus) that we learned in Chapter 6 as illustrated in Output 9.1.

Based on these results, we can see that on average women spend more time on housework than do men, but they have a much larger standard deviation. We now want to

---

[1]For simplicity's sake, we will ignore the sampling weights.

OUTPUT 9.1: AVERAGE AND STANDARD DEVIATION OF HOURS SPENT ON HOUSEHOLD CHORES BY MEN AND WOMEN IN THE UNITED STATES

```
. table sex, c(mean rhhwork sd rhhwork) format(%3.2fc)
```

Sex	mean(rhhwork)	sd(rhhwork)
Male	8.32	9.43
Female	11.86	12.70

use the data to test whether this is a statistically significant difference beginning with our research question below.

Research question

Do men and women spend the same number of hours on housework each week?

Null hypothesis

Men and women spend the same number of hours on housework each week.

Variables

Continuous variable—hours per week spent on housework (rhhwork)

Categorical variable—sex (*male* = 1, *female* = 2)

Assumptions

As described earlier, to use the two independent-samples *t* test, you must have one continuous variable and one categorical variable with two categories. We also make the following assumptions to generate valid results.

1. *Independence of observations:* Each individual can appear in only one of the two groups. In addition, they can only appear once in each group.

2. *Normal distribution:* The dependent variable, hours of housework in this example, should be approximately normally distributed within each category. It only needs to be approximately normally distributed since minor violations of normality do not affect the results. Normality can be tested with the Shapiro–Wilk test.

3. *Homogeneity of variances:* The variances of the two groups must be equal. This is tested with Levene's test. If the variances are not equal, Stata will generate output to show the results with unequal variances assumed with the command **unequal**.

Stata code for doing a t test

Using a do-file, we would run the commands below.

```
robvar rhhwork, by(sex)
ttest rhhwork, by(sex) unequal
esize twosample rhhwork, by(sex) cohensd unequal
```

Menus for doing a t test

Using menus in Stata, we would click on the sequence listed below that would bring us to Dialog Box 9.1. In the dialog box, we would select the variables "rhhwork" and "sex" in the two drop-down menus as displayed.

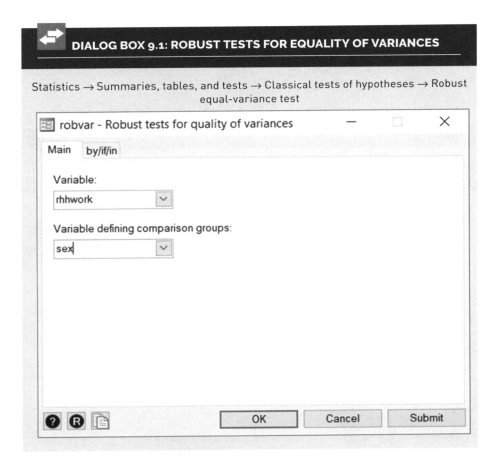

We would then click on the following sequence to bring us to Dialog Box 9.2. Depending on the results from the equality of variance test, we would leave the box "unequal variances" either checked or unchecked. This is explained further in Section 9.4 on interpreting the output.

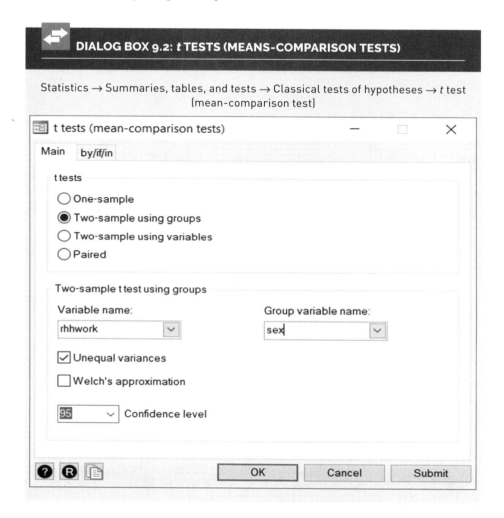

DIALOG BOX 9.2: *t* TESTS (MEANS-COMPARISON TESTS)

Statistics → Summaries, tables, and tests → Classical tests of hypotheses → *t* test (mean-comparison test)

Finally, we could click on the sequence below and fill in the variable names in the drop boxes as shown in Dialog Box 9.3.

DIALOG BOX 9.3: EFFECT SIZE BASED ON MEAN COMPARISON

Statistics → Summaries, tables, and tests → Classical tests of hypotheses → Effect size based on means comparison

esize - Effect size based on mean comparison   —   □   ✕

Main   by/if/in

Effect sizes
◉ Two-sample using groups
◯ Two-sample using variables

Two independent samples using groups

Variable name: Group variable name:
[rhhwork   ▽]   [sex   ▽]

Options
☑ Report Cohen's d
☐ Report Hedges's g
☐ Report Glass's Delta using each group's standard deviation
☐ Report point-biserial correlation coefficient
☐ Report all estimates of effect size
☑ Unequal variances
☐ Welch's approximation
[95   ▽] Confidence level

[OK]   [Cancel]   [Submit]

9.5 INTERPRETING THE OUTPUT

The first step to determine if there is a significant difference in the number of hours is to check for equality of variances. As we saw in the preview to the chapter, "homogeneity of variances" is one of the assumptions for this test. If the variances are not equal, this will increase the likelihood of rejecting the null hypothesis when it is true. We, therefore, first test the assumption and then make a correction if the variances are unequal.

To test for equality of variances, we run the robust equal-variance test with the null hypothesis that the two variances are the same. Output 9.2 shows the results. In this example, we only need to interpret the p-value (labeled as Pr) at the end of the row labeled W0. Because the value is less than 0.05, we reject the null hypothesis that the variances are equal.

Once we have determined that the variances are equal or unequal, we then run the t test. In this example, we specify unequal variance either in the commands or in the dialog box if we are using menus. The results are illustrated in Output 9.3. In the first column, we see the average number of hours for men (8.3) and women (11.9) and the overall average number of hours (10.2). The difference in the average hours worked by men and women is listed as "diff" at the bottom of the "Mean" column. To test

✔ OUTPUT 9.2: STATA OUTPUT FOR VARIANCE RATIO TEST

```
. robvar rhhwork, by(sex)

                   Summary of how many hours a week
                        does r spend on hh work
          Sex            Mean      Std. Dev.          Freq.

         Male       8.3207547     9.4333454            583
       Female      11.861472     12.702049            693

        Total      10.24373      11.458679           1,276

 W0  =   31.424330    df(1, 1274)       Pr > F = 0.00000003

 W50 =   21.521522    df(1, 1274)       Pr > F = 0.00000386

 W10 =   23.090941    df(1, 1274)       Pr > F = 0.00000173
```

When the null hypothesis is true (that the variances are equal), the probability of observing an F value at least as large as 31.42 is less than 0.05.

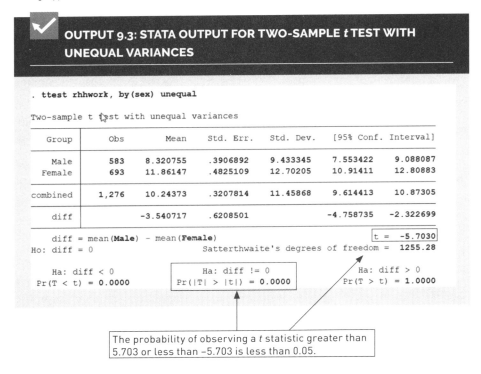

**OUTPUT 9.3: STATA OUTPUT FOR TWO-SAMPLE *t* TEST WITH
UNEQUAL VARIANCES**

```
. ttest rhhwork, by(sex) unequal

Two-sample t test with unequal variances
```

Group	Obs	Mean	Std. Err.	Std. Dev.	[95% Conf. Interval]	
Male	583	8.320755	.3906892	9.433345	7.553422	9.088087
Female	693	11.86147	.4825109	12.70205	10.91411	12.80883
combined	1,276	10.24373	.3207814	11.45868	9.614413	10.87305
diff		-3.540717	.6208501		-4.758735	-2.322699

```
    diff = mean(Male) - mean(Female)                    t =   -5.7030
Ho: diff = 0                    Satterthwaite's degrees of freedom =  1255.28

   Ha: diff < 0                   Ha: diff != 0                  Ha: diff > 0
 Pr(T < t) = 0.0000         Pr(|T| > |t|) = 0.0000          Pr(T > t) = 1.0000
```

The probability of observing a *t* statistic greater than
5.703 or less than –5.703 is less than 0.05.

whether this difference is statistically significant, we examine the *t* value and the significance level. According to the output, the probability of observing a *t* value greater than 5.7 or less than –5.7 is less than 5%. We therefore reject the null hypothesis and say that there is a statistically significant difference in the average hours spent on housework by men and women.

We can also examine the confidence interval from Output 9.3, which we learned how to generate in Chapter 8. Notice that the 95% confidence interval for the mean difference is from –4.76 to –2.32. This suggests that we are 95% confident that the true value of the difference is within that range.

In addition to examining the significance level of the difference in the two means, we may also want to examine the "effect size" or the magnitude of the difference between the two groups. Although there are several measures that can estimate the effect size, Cohen's *d* is commonly used. It is calculated as the difference between two means divided by the pooled standard deviation for the two independent samples. The results are illustrated in Output 9.4. According to Cohen (1988), effect sizes are defined as small when $d = 0.2$, medium when $d = 0.5$, and large if $d = 0.8$. Since the absolute value of Cohen's *d* in Output 9.4 is 0.3, it is between a small and medium effect.

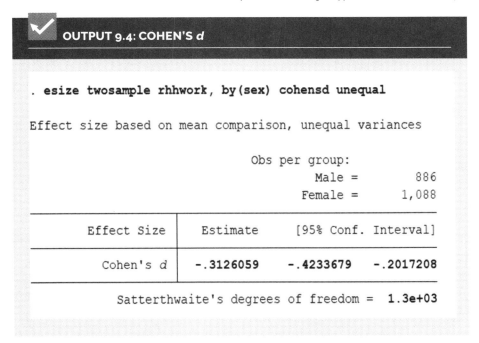

OUTPUT 9.4: COHEN'S d

```
. esize twosample rhhwork, by(sex) cohensd unequal

Effect size based on mean comparison, unequal variances

                                    Obs per group:
                                        Male =         886
                                      Female =       1,088

     Effect Size  │   Estimate     [95% Conf. Interval]

       Cohen's d  │  -.3126059    -.4233679    -.2017208

           Satterthwaite's degrees of freedom =   1.3e+03
```

9.6 PRESENTING THE RESULTS

Presenting the results for a nontechnical audience

To present these results to a lay audience who may not be familiar with statistical tests, we could write the following:

> On average, adults spend 10.24 hours per week on household chores. Our results show, however, that there is a statistically significant difference between the average hours spent on household chores per week by men and by women. Men spend 8.3 hours on average per week compared with women, who spend 11.9 hours, which is slightly more than a small difference in means.

Presenting the results in a scholarly journal

To present these results in a peer-reviewed scholarly journal, we would need to include more information. This could be written as follows:

> To test the hypothesis that men and women spend the same amount of time on housework each week, we used a two independent-samples *t* test. The

results indicated that on average, men spend 8.32 hours per week (SD = 9.43), compared with women, who spend 11.86 hours (SD = 12.7). This was a statistically significant difference at the 0.05 level ($t(1,255)$ = −5.7, $p < 0.001$). Examining the effect size or magnitude of the difference, Cohen's d revealed that the difference between the means is between a small and medium effect (d = −0.31).

9.7 SUMMARY OF COMMANDS USED IN THIS CHAPTER

As described in Chapter 4, this last section of each chapter summarizes all of the Stata code used in the chapter. In addition, all Stata code used throughout the book is summarized in Appendix 1.

Table

```
table sex, c(mean rhhwork) format(%3.2fc)
```

Test for equal variances

```
robvar rhhwork, by(sex)
```

Two independent-means test

```
ttest rhhwork, by(sex) unequal
```

Cohen's d effect size test

```
esize twosample rhhwork, by(sex) cohensd unequal
```

EXERCISES

1. You want to determine if men and women watch the same number of hours of television per week. Assume that the robust variance test determined that there was no statistically significant difference in the variances to answer this question.

	Mean Hours of TV Watched per Week	Sample Size	Variance
Men	14	20	100
Women	6	8	88

a. Based on the information in the table, determine if this is a statistically significant difference. (Hint: The degrees of freedom would be equal to $n_1 + n_2 - 2$).

b. Use the information to calculate a 95% confidence interval of the mean difference.

2. Use the National Survey on Drug Use and Health 2015 to determine if there is a difference in age when men and women first try alcohol by following the instructions below.

   a. Determine if there is a significant difference in the average age when men and women (irsex) first try alcohol (alctry). For each command that you use, you will need to eliminate all observations above the age of 71 since there are observations with large numeric codes that represent bad data, individuals who never used alcohol, and individuals who didn't know or refused to answer. To do this, include the code, **if alctry < 72** at the end of each command line.

   b. Use Cohen's *d* to examine the effect size, again using **if alctry < 72** at the end of the command line.

   c. Write the results of your findings for a nontechnical audience.

   d. Write the results of your findings for a journal article.

3. One of the arguments for school uniforms is that they will deter crime and increase student safety. We can explore this by using the School Survey on Crime and Safety data set from the 2015–2016 school year, which offers data on school characteristics, crimes, practices, and policies. The data represent 2,092 public schools in the United States. In particular, we can look at the total number of disciplinary actions required at schools that do and do not require uniforms. One question, however, is whether uniforms lead to fewer incidents (a negative relationship) or more incidents lead schools to require uniforms (a positive relationship). The possibility that two variables may influence each other makes it difficult to identify and measure the causal relationship, a problem called "endogeneity" that is discussed in Chapters 12 and 13.

   Using the pu_ssocs16 data set, generate a table that shows the average, the standard deviation, and the sample size of the total number of disciplinary actions required (DISTOT16) among schools that require and those that do not require uniforms (C0134). Format the table so that there are two digits to the right of the decimal point.

a. Determine if there is a significant difference in the average number of disciplinary actions required between schools that require and those that do not require uniforms.

b. What is the null hypothesis?

c. Can you reject the null hypothesis? Use statistics to support your conclusion.

REFERENCES

Cohen, J. (1988). *Statistical power analysis for the behavioral sciences* (2nd ed.). Hillsdale, NJ: Lawrence Erlbaum.

Kolhatkar, S. (2015, June 26). *Women in the U.S. still do way more housework than men*. Retrieved from www.bloomberg.com/news/articles/2015–06-26/women-in-the-u-s-still-do-way-more-housework-than-men

10

ONE-WAY ANALYSIS OF VARIANCE

Chapter Preview

Research question	Are children from wealthier families more likely to earn higher scores on the SAT than those from lower income families?
Null hypothesis	There is no difference in SAT scores among college students from families with different levels of income.
Test	One-way analysis of variance
Types of variables	One dependent continuous variable: SAT scores (SAT)
	One independent categorical variable with three or more categories: 1 = "Less than $60,000," 2 = "$60,000 to $99,999," 3 = "$100,000 to $149,000" ... (FAMILYINC)
When to use	Comparing three or more means
Assumptions	1. Each sample is an independent random sample.
	2. Normal distribution of the continuous variable
	3. Homogeneity of variances
Additional tests needed	Bartlett's test of equality of variances
Stata code: generic	**Oneway continuousvar categoricalvar**
Stata code: example	**oneway SAT FAMILYINC**

10.1 INTRODUCTION

ARTICLE 10.1

The Washington Post

Wonkblog

These four charts show how the SAT favors rich, educated families

By Zachary A. Goldfarb March 5, 2014

The College Board announced Wednesday that it is overhauling the SAT, dropping the timed essay and focusing less on fancy vocabulary in order to level the playing field a bit for high school students from a wider range of families. The organization's own data show that wealthier Americans, from more educated families, tend to do far better on the test. As do white and Asian Americans, and those students who had the opportunity to take the PSAT in high school before taking the SAT. Almost certainly, these four findings have common origins in that the SAT benefits families who can provide their kids with a better education and more test prep. But here are four charts that show how the SAT advantages specific demographics.

Many studies have shown that children from higher income families earn higher scores on the Scholastic Aptitude Test (SAT). There are several reasons for this including the fact that wealthier families can afford expensive preparation courses or private tutors for their children. This gap in test results has led to several changes. The College Board, which administers the test, has revised the exam to level the playing field by eliminating obscure vocabulary and using texts that are more typical of what students use in school. They have also offered free online tutoring (see Article 10.1).

In this chapter, we will learn how to test for a statistically significant difference between three or more means. The test is called a one-way analysis of variance (ANOVA). It is used with one continuous variable (SAT scores in the example above) and one categorical variable with three or more categories (different family income levels). Examples from different fields are given below along with a review of assumptions, procedures, and interpretation of the output.

10.2 WHEN TO USE ONE-WAY ANOVA

Table 10.1 shows examples from different fields where you may have three or more means. Each categorical variable must have at least three categories, and only one continuous variable is used. In all of these examples, we are testing the impact of the categorical variable on the continuous variable. This means that the continuous variable, SAT scores for example, is the dependent variable since its value will depend on family income levels. Family income is then the independent variable.

TABLE 10.1 ● EXAMPLES OF ONE-WAY ANALYSIS OF VARIANCE				
Field	**Research Question**	**Null Hypothesis**	**Continuous Variable**	**Categorical Variable**
Criminal Justice	Does birth order have an effect on the number of self-reported delinquent acts?	There is no difference in the average number of self-reported delinquent acts by birth order.	Number of self-reported delinquent acts	1. First born (or only child) 2. Middle born (if three or more children) 3. Last born
Economics	Does annual income vary across regions in the United States?	There is no difference in annual income across regions in the United States.	Annual income	1. Northeast 2. Mid-Atlantic 3. South 4. Midwest 5. West
Political Science	Is voter participation affected by the type of government?	There is no difference in voter participation in countries with different types of government.	Voter turnout rate	1. Liberal democracy 2. Communist/post-communist 3. Socialist
Psychology	Does the type of car ownership affect behavior toward bicyclists on the road?	There is no difference in behavior.	Number of feet of clearance given to bicyclists on the road	1. High-end cars 2. Medium-priced cars 3. Low-priced cars

(Continued)

Field	Research Question	Null Hypothesis	Continuous Variable	Categorical Variable
Public Health	Is there a difference in average bone density among respondents who take three levels of calcium supplement?	There is no difference in bone density.	Bone density level	1. Low calcium intake 2. Medium calcium intake 3. High calcium intake
Sociology	What is the average number of children among families from different religions?	There is no difference in the average number of children by religion.	Number of children	1. Christians 2. Muslims 3. Hindus 4. Buddhists

TABLE 10.1 ● *(Continued)*

10.3 CALCULATING THE *F* RATIO

The *F* ratio, which is used to determine if there is a statistically significant difference among several means, is calculated in two parts. The first part, or numerator, estimates the between-group variability and is expressed in Equation 10.1.

$$\text{Numerator} = \frac{\sum_{i=1}^{n} n_i (\overline{X}_i - \overline{X})^2}{K - 1} \tag{10.1}$$

where

n_i = sample size for group i

$\overline{X}_i$ = average for group i

$\overline{X}$ = the overall average of all observations

K = number of groups

Notice that the numerator examines how much the mean of each individual group differs from the overall mean of all groups combined. This is then weighted by the sample size, n, so that larger samples are given a greater weight. The denominator is the degrees of freedom, or the number of groups (K) minus 1.[1] Overall, this is a measure of how much variation there is "between" the groups, or the between-groups mean square.

---

[1] Refer to Chapter 8 for a discussion of degrees of freedom.

The second part of the F ratio is the within-group variability. As its name suggests, we are now looking at how much variation there is within each sample or group. This is expressed in Equation 10.2.

$$\text{Denominator} = \frac{\sum_{i=1}^{n} s_i^2 (n_i - 1)}{\sum_{i=1}^{n} (n_i - 1)} \tag{10.2}$$

where

S_i^2 = the variance of group i

n_i = sample size for group i

In this case, the numerator adds up the variance of each group and gives weight to each variance by multiplying by the sample size minus 1. When we then divide by the sum of the sample sizes minus 1, we are essentially getting the average variation within the groups. It is expressed as the within-groups mean square.

To calculate the F ratio, we then divide Equation 10.1 by Equation 10.2, which can be written as follows:

$$F = \frac{\text{Between-group variability}}{\text{Within-group variability}}$$

FIGURE 10.1 ⬡ BETWEEN-GROUP VARIANCE IS LARGER THAN WITHIN-GROUP VARIANCE ILLUSTRATION

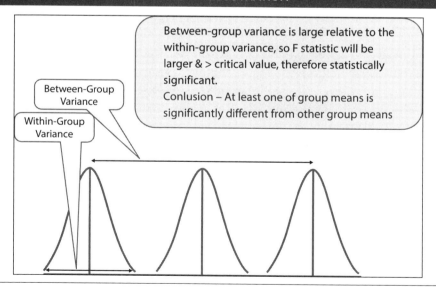

Source: Khatri (2014). "Analysis of Variance (ANOVA)." *LinkedIn SlideShare*, 9 Aug. 2014, www.slideshare.net/snehkhatri/analysis-of-variance-anova.

FIGURE 10.2 ● WITHIN-GROUP VARIANCE IS LARGER THAN BETWEEN-GROUP VARIANCE ILLUSTRATION

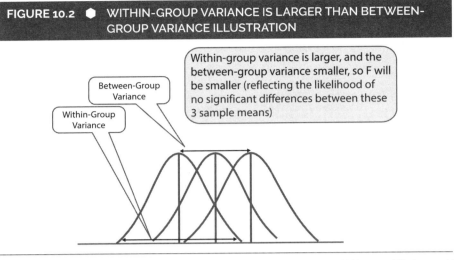

Source: Khatri (2014). "Analysis of Variance (ANOVA)." *LinkedIn SlideShare*, 9 Aug. 2014, www.slideshare.net/snehkhatri/analysis-of-variance-anova.

In other words, if the variability between the groups is greater than the variability within each group, you would expect a large *F* ratio. The larger the *F* ratio, the more likely you are to find a significant difference in the means. Figures 10.1 and 10.2 illustrate the concept of between- and within-group variance.

10.4 CONDUCTING A ONE-WAY ANOVA TEST

As described earlier, many people criticize the use of SAT scores because of their high correlation with income. Using the Admitted Student Questionnaire data set, we will examine the relationship between SAT scores and family income to see if there is a statistically significant difference among SAT scores in different income categories.

Output 10.1 shows five income groups and the average SAT scores within each group along with the standard deviation and the number of students in each group. Although we can easily see that the average SAT score does increase as family incomes rise, we cannot make the conclusion that there is a statistically significant difference until we run the one-way ANOVA test, which is described below.

OUTPUT 10.1: AVERAGE SAT SCORE BY FAMILY INCOME

```
. table FamilyInc, c(mean SAT sd SAT n SAT) format (%4.0fc)
```

FamilyInc	mean(SAT)	sd(SAT)	N(SAT)
<59K	1277	225	779
60-99K	1312	189	641
100-149K	1359	179	666
150-199K	1369	176	296
>200K	1434	143	796

Research question

Are children from wealthier families more likely to earn higher scores on the SAT than those from lower income families?

Null hypothesis

There is no difference in SAT scores among college students from families with different levels of income.

The alternative hypothesis would be that at least one of the group means is not the same as the others.

Variables

Continuous variable—SAT scores of combined reading and math (SAT)

Categorical variable—family income before taxes broken into five income categories (FamilyInc)

Assumptions

As described earlier, a one-way ANOVA test is used with one categorical variable with three or more categories and one continuous variable. We also make the following assumptions to generate valid results.

1. *Independence of observations:* Each individual or observation can only appear in one of the three or more groups. In addition, they can only appear once in each group.

2. *Normal distribution:* The continuous variable, SAT score, should be approximately normally distributed within each category. It only needs to be approximately normally distributed since minor violations of normality do not affect the results.

3. *Homogeneity of variances:* The variances of the three or more groups must be equal. This is tested with Bartlett's test. For large samples, however, the equality of variances assumption is not required.

Procedures using code

Using a do-file, we would run the commands below:

```
oneway SAT FamilyInc, tabulate
```

Procedures using menus

Using menus in Stata, we would click on the sequence listed below that would bring us to Dialog Box 10.1. In the dialog box, we would select the variables SAT and FamilyInc in the two drop-down menus as displayed.

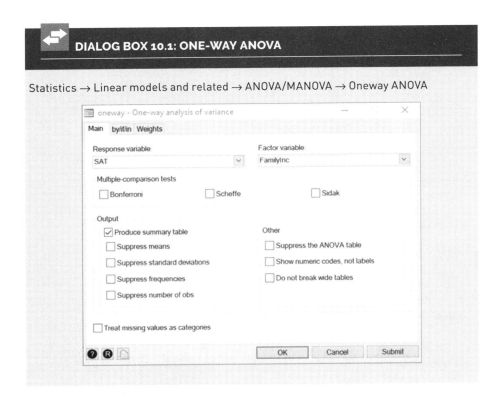

DIALOG BOX 10.1: ONE-WAY ANOVA

Statistics → Linear models and related → ANOVA/MANOVA → Oneway ANOVA

10.5 INTERPRETING THE OUTPUT

The first step to determine if there is a significant difference in SAT scores among different income groups is to check for equality of variances. In Stata, Bartlett's test for homogeneity of variances is automatically included in the output. The null hypothesis is that the variance for each of the five groups is equal. As illustrated in Output 10.2, the chi-square statistic is 159.5 and the significance level is 0.000. Because the significance level is less than 0.05, we reject the null hypothesis that the variances are equal. Although this means that one of the three assumptions for the one-way ANOVA is violated, the ANOVA is considered robust to heterogeneity of variance, and these results are typically ignored. This is particularly true for large samples. In a final report, the reader can be cautioned about the unequal variances.

Examining the F ratio, we see that the value is 78.69 with a significant level that is less than 0.05. We then reject the null hypothesis that there is no difference in SAT scores among college students from families with different levels of income.

As we learned in Chapter 9, we may also want to examine the effect size or the magnitude of the difference between the two groups. When running an ANOVA test, we would use eta-square (η^2). This is calculated as the between-groups sum of squares

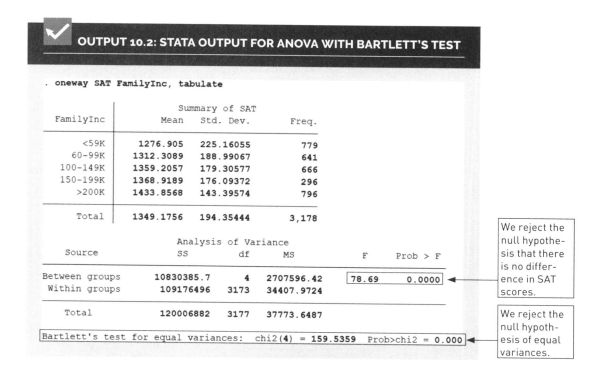

OUTPUT 10.2: STATA OUTPUT FOR ANOVA WITH BARTLETT'S TEST

```
. oneway SAT FamilyInc, tabulate
```

	Summary of SAT		
FamilyInc	Mean	Std. Dev.	Freq.
<59K	1276.905	225.16055	779
60-99K	1312.3089	188.99067	641
100-149K	1359.2057	179.30577	666
150-199K	1368.9189	176.09372	296
>200K	1433.8568	143.39574	796
Total	1349.1756	194.35444	3,178

Analysis of Variance

Source	SS	df	MS	F	Prob > F
Between groups	10830385.7	4	2707596.42	78.69	0.0000
Within groups	109176496	3173	34407.9724		
Total	120006882	3177	37773.6487		

Bartlett's test for equal variances: chi2(4) = 159.5359   Prob>chi2 = 0.000

We reject the null hypothesis that there is no difference in SAT scores.

We reject the null hypothesis of equal variances.

divided by the total sum of squares. Using the numbers from Output 10.2 above, this would be expressed as follows:

$$\eta^2 = \frac{\text{Between-group sum of squares}}{\text{Total sum of squares}} = \frac{10{,}830{,}385.7}{120{,}006{,}882} = 0.09$$

Turning this into a percentage, we can say that 9% of the variation in SAT scores can be explained by differences in family income. Although 9% seems low, our results did show that there was a significant difference in the mean SAT scores among income groups. Furthermore, it shows that the income accounts for a small amount of that variation and that we would need to examine other factors. It is important to keep in mind that insignificant or less dramatic results can be equally important when doing research. Not being able to show a significant difference is also a result.

10.6 IS ONE MEAN DIFFERENT OR ARE ALL OF THEM DIFFERENT?

As mentioned earlier, the null hypothesis is that there is no difference in SAT scores among college students from families with different levels of income. The alternative hypothesis is that at least one of the means is not the same. Once we have rejected the null hypothesis, we may want to know which mean or means are different. To find out which means are different, we would run a multiple comparison procedure. Although you could use multiple two independent t tests to compare each pair of means, the likelihood of finding a statistically significant difference in at least one pair of means increases as the number of comparisons increases, even when the means are equal. To account for the chance of this error, a multiple comparison test adjusts the observed significance level, making it more difficult to find a statistically significant difference. The Bonferroni test, for example, multiplies the observed significance by the number of comparisons being made.

Output 10.3 shows the commands to run a Bonferroni test and the output. The first row in the Bonferroni table compares the SAT score of students from families earning $60,000 to $99,000 with the scores of students from families earning less than $60,000. Within the first cell, 35.4039 is the average SAT score of children from families earning $60,000 to $99,000 minus the average SAT score of children from families earning less than $60,000. The significance level is reported underneath at 0.003. When comparing the two means independently, the significance level would have been 0.0003. The Bonferroni test multiplies this by 10 (because there are 10 comparisons) with the final significance level of 0.003. Because this is below our alpha level of 0.05, we would say that this is a statistically significant difference. Examining all of the cells in this table, 9 of the 10 comparisons show a statistically

---

✓ OUTPUT 10.3: ONE-WAY ANALYSIS OF VARIANCE TEST WITH THE BONFERRONI TEST

```
. oneway SAT FamilyInc, bonferroni
```

                              Analysis of Variance

Source	SS	df	MS	F	Prob > F
Between groups	10830385.7	4	2707596.42	78.69	0.0000
Within groups	109176496	3173	34407.9724		
Total	120006882	3177	37773.6487		

Bartlett's test for equal variances: chi2(4) = **159.5359** Prob>chi2 = **0.000**

                    Comparison of SAT by FamilyInc
                              (Bonferroni)

Row Mean- Col Mean	<59K	60-99K	100-149K	150-199K
60-99K	35.4039 0.003			
100-149K	82.3007 0.000	46.8968 0.000		
150-199K	92.0139 0.000	56.61 0.000	9.71321 1.000	
>200K	156.952 0.000	121.548 0.000	74.6511 0.000	64.9379 0.000

significant difference with the exception of a comparison of scores in the income groups of $100,000 to $149,999 and $150,000 to 199,000.

10.7 PRESENTING THE RESULTS

Presenting the results for a nontechnical audience

To present these results to a lay audience who may not be familiar with statistical tests, we could write the following:

Our results indicate that there is a statistically significant difference in SAT scores among children from families in five different income categories.

In the lowest category of income (less than $59,999), students earn on average 1,277 points on their combined reading and math SAT scores. In the wealthiest category of income (more than $200,000), students from these families earn 1,434 points on average. The results also show, however, that only 9% of the variation in SAT scores can be explained by income differences. It is therefore important to consider other factors that may affect SAT scores.

Presenting the results in a scholarly journal

In a peer-reviewed journal, we would include more information. These results could be explained as follows:

A one-way ANOVA was used to compare the combined math and reading SAT scores of students who come from families in five different income categories. The results indicate that there is a statistically significant difference at the 0.05 significance level among the SAT scores; $F(4, 3173) = 79.79$, $p < 0.001$. In particular, the scores rise as family income increases with students from the lowest income category earning 1,276.91 on average ($SD = 225.2$) compared with 1,433.86 points earned on average ($SD = 143.3$) among students from families in the wealthiest income category. Although Bartlett's test revealed unequal variances among the five income groups, the large sample sizes make the results robust. Using eta-square to examine the effect size, only 9% of the variation in SAT scores could be explained by income.

10.8 SUMMARY OF COMMANDS USED IN THIS CHAPTER

As described in Chapter 4, this last section of each chapter summarizes all of the Stata code used in the chapter. In addition, all Stata code used throughout the book is summarized in Appendix 1.

Table

```
table FamilyInc, c(mean SAT sd SAT count SAT) format(%4.0f)
```

One-way analysis of variance

```
oneway SAT FamilyInc, tabulate
```

One-way analysis of variance with Bonferroni test

```
oneway SAT FamilyInc, bonferroni
```

EXERCISES

1. Use the GSS2016 data set to answer this question. You want to examine whether the number of hours that individuals work per week (hrs1) varies by education level (degree). To do this, you must first eliminate all part-time workers from the data set. This can be done by running the commands **keep if partfull==1**. Next, eliminate anyone who worked less than 24 hours in the past week by running the commands **keep if hrs1 > 23**. Finally, remove observations that were coded as NA by running the command **keep if degree != .n**. *When you have completed the assignment, do not save the data set since this will permanently remove part-time workers!*

   a. Generate two tables. In the first table, show the overall average of hours worked per week (hrs1) for all respondents in the sample. In a second table, show the average hours worked (hrs1), the standard deviation for hours worked, and the count for hours worked by education level (degree). Format the table so that there is one digit to the right of the decimal point.

   b. Use a one-way analysis of variance test to examine the number of hours worked per week by degree level.

   c. What is the null hypothesis?

   d. What is the alternative hypothesis?

   e. Write a paragraph that would explain your findings to a nontechnical audience.

   f. Write a paragraph that would explain your findings in a scholarly journal.

2. You want to compare the average number of hours that teenagers play video games on weeknights based on three age categories: (1) 10 to 12 years, (2) 13 to 15 years, and (3) 16 to 18 years. You are given the following information on the mean, variance, and sample size of each group. The overall average for all individuals combined is 2. Based on this information, calculate the *F* statistic. Show all of your work.

Age-Groups	Average Hours of Gaming on a Weeknight	Variance	Sample Size
10–12 years old	1	4	22
13–15 years old	3	25	31
16–18 years old	2	9	52

3. Use the College Results 2013 data set to determine if there are regional differences in the endowment per full-time student among regional universities. To examine this, begin by removing national universities, national liberal arts colleges, and all regional colleges. This can be done by running the commands **drop if Ranktype < 3 | RankType > 6**. *When you have completed the assignment, do not save the data set since this will permanently remove other types of colleges!*

   a. Generate a table that shows the average endowment per full-time student (EndowmentTotalFTE) by the type of university (RankType). Format the table so that it uses commas and only whole numbers.

   b. Run a one-way analysis of variance to determine if there is a statistically significant difference in the average endowment per full-time student across regions.

   c. What is the null hypothesis?

   d. What is the alternative hypothesis?

   e. What can you conclude from your results?

4. Socioeconomic mobility theories suggest that students from certain regions are more likely to go to college, earn higher incomes, or move from a low-income category to a higher income category. Use the School Survey on Crime and Safety from 2015 to 2016 (pu_ssocs16.dta) to explore this issue by answering the following questions:

   a. Generate a table that shows the average, standard deviation, and sample size for the percentage of students who are likely to go to college (C0534) by location (FR_URBAN). Format the table so that there are only whole numbers.

   b. Run a one-way analysis of variance to determine if there is a statistically significant difference in the percentage of students who are likely to go to college.

   c. Use the Bonferroni test and explain the results.

   d. What can you conclude from your results?

REFERENCES

Goldfarb, Z. A. (2014, March 5). *These four charts show how the SAT favors rich, educated families* [Web log post]. Retrieved from www.washingtonpost.com/news/wonk/wp/2014/03/05/these-four-charts-show-how-the-sat-favors-the-rich-educated-families/

Khatri, S. (2014, August 9). *Analysis of variance* (LinkedIn SlideShare). Retrieved from www.slideshare.net/snehkhatri/analysis-of-variance-anova

CROSS TABULATION AND THE CHI-SQUARED TEST

Chapter Preview

Research question	Do views about the death penalty differ among men and women?
Null hypothesis	There is no difference in the percentage of men and women who oppose the death penalty.
Test	Chi-squared test
Types of variables	Two categorical variables with two or more categories in each: Sex—male or female Oppose—favor or oppose the death penalty
When to use	Comparing percentages
Assumptions	1. Independent observations 2. Minimum expected cell frequency should be five or greater in 80% of the cells.
Stata code: generic	**tab categoricalvar1 categoricalvar2, chi2 row** (or column if the independent variable is in the column)
Stata code: example	**tab Sex Oppose, chi2 row**

11.1 INTRODUCTION

The Washington Post
Democracy Dies in Darkness

Politics · Analysis

On death penalty, pope diverges from his U.S. flock

By Bonnie Berkowitz, Joe Fox and Madison Walls Aug. 3, 2018

The pope's official opposition to the death penalty in all cases, which was announced August 2, pits the Catholic Church's stance against the laws and practices of several dozen countries, including the United States.

It also differs from the views of more than half of U.S. Catholics — and Americans in general — according to a recent survey.

Catholics account for about 21 percent of the U.S. population, according to Pew Research Center. Some areas with the largest Catholic populations are in the 31 states that have the death penalty, most notably Texas, which has carried out more than a third of U.S. executions since 1976.

A split in public opinion

Despite a long-term downward trend in support for the death penalty, the United States may be on a different philosophical wavelength from the pope at the moment.

Support for capital punishment rose a bit this year after decades of decline, according to a Pew Research Center survey conducted this spring. And it went up among U.S. Catholics more than among the nation in general, from 43 percent in 2016 to 53 percent this year.

The death penalty has always been a controversial issue. Currently, the United States is the only Western country that uses it. Within the United States, 31 states have the death penalty and the remaining 19 have abolished it. Within the Catholic church, opinions are divided with slightly more than half of all Catholics supporting the death penalty despite the Pope's recent denouncement of the death penalty as described in Article 11.1.

In this chapter, we will learn how to test for a statistically significant difference in percentages using Pearson's chi-squared test. We use this test when there are two categorical variables with at least two categories in each variable. For example, we will examine if the same percentage of men and women believe in capital punishment. In other words, if 65% of the overall population believes in capital punishment, do 65% of men and 65% of women believe in capital punishment? Before turning to the General Social Survey (GSS) to examine views about the death penalty, however, examples of how the chi-squared test can be used in different fields is given below.

11.2 WHEN TO USE THE CHI-SQUARED TEST

Table 11.1 shows examples from different fields where the chi-squared test can be used. As mentioned above, there must be two categorical variables with at least two categories in each.

TABLE 11.1 ⬥ EXAMPLES OF THE CHI-SQUARED TEST			
Field	**Research Question**	**Null Hypothesis**	**Categorical Variables**
Criminal Justice	Are men and women equally likely to support decriminalization of marijuana?	Men and women are equally likely to support decriminalization of marijuana.	1. Gender 2. View on decriminalizing marijuana (yes or no)
Economics	Is income more equally distributed in developed countries?	There is no difference in income distribution between developed and developing countries.	1. Level of development (developed or developing) 2. Three levels of classification of equality based on ranges of the Gini coefficient (high equality, medium equality, and low equality)
Political Science	Are men and women equally likely to vote for a Republican candidate for president?	Men and women are equally likely to vote for a Republican candidate for president.	1. Gender 2. Party they will vote for (Republican, Democrat, Green, Independent)
Psychology	Does the ability to delay gratification among children lead to lower obesity?	There is no difference in obesity levels among those who were able to delay gratification and those who were not.	1. Ability to delay gratification (yes or no) 2. Obese at a later age (yes or no)

TABLE 11.1 ● (Continued)			
Field	**Research Question**	**Null Hypothesis**	**Categorical Variables**
Public Health	Is opioid abuse higher among men?	There is no difference in opioid abuse among men and women.	1. Opioid abuse (yes or no) 2. Gender
Sociology	Do men and women have the same reaction when a stranger invades their personal space?	There is no difference in the way men and women react when a stranger invades their personal space.	1. Gender 2. Reaction (negative, positive, or no reaction)

11.3 CALCULATING THE CHI-SQUARE STATISTIC

In previous chapters, we examined differences in means and used the normal or the t distribution. When examining counts or percentages, we need to calculate a chi-square statistic and compare it with the chi-square distribution. Unlike the normal or t distributions that are bell shaped, the chi-square distribution is skewed to the right and is illustrated in Figure 11.1. Because the chi-square distribution is based on one or more squared variables, it can never be negative.

FIGURE 11.1 ● CHI-SQUARE DISTRIBUTION

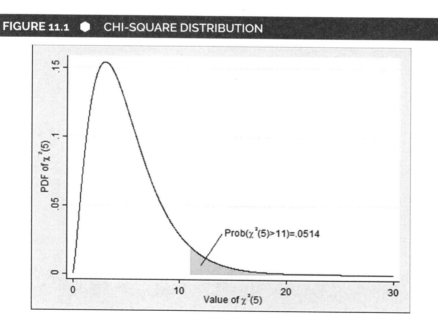

We use the chi-square statistic to determine the probability of observing our results when the null hypothesis is true. The formula for the chi-square statistic is illustrated in Equation 11.1.

$$\chi^2 = \sum_{i=1}^{n} \frac{(O_i - E_i)^2}{E_i}$$

(11.1)

where

O_i = the number of observations of type i

E_i = the expected number of type i

n = the number of cells in the table

This equation can be more easily understood with an example. Output 11.1 uses data from the GSS2012 data set to show the observed number, the expected number, and the percentage of men and women who support or oppose the death penalty. In this case, sex is our independent variable and the view on the death penalty is the dependent variable. In other words, someone's views on the death penalty may be influenced or depend on their sex.

OUTPUT 11.1: CROSS TABULATION OF DEATH PENALTY VIEWS BY GENDER WITH OBSERVED AND EXPECTED COUNTS

574 is the observed number of observations of men who favor the death penalty.

538.3 is the expected number of observations. It is equal to the percentage of the total population that favors the death penalty (64.86%) multiplied by the total number of men in the sample (830).

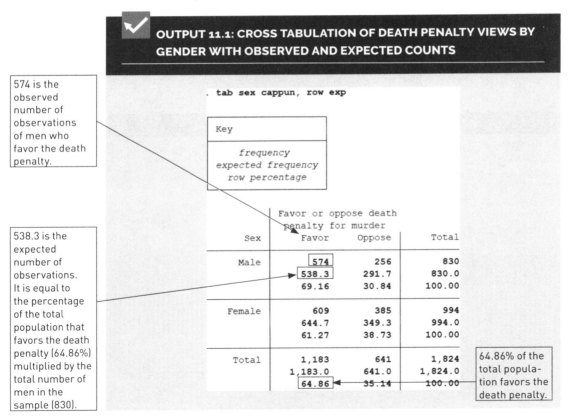

```
. tab sex cappun, row exp


  Key

      frequency
   expected frequency
     row percentage


                    Favor or oppose death
                    penalty for murder
       Sex          Favor      Oppose          Total

       Male          574          256             830
                    538.3        291.7           830.0
                    69.16        30.84           100.00

     Female          609          385             994
                    644.7        349.3           994.0
                    61.27        38.73           100.00

      Total        1,183          641           1,824
                  1,183.0        641.0         1,824.0
                    64.86        35.14          100.00
```

64.86% of the total population favors the death penalty.

The first cell shows that 574 men favor the death penalty out of a total of 830 men. This is the observed count. In the general population or the "total" row, we see that 1,183 people favor the death penalty, or 64.86%. Our null hypothesis would suggest that 64.86% of men and 64.86% of women would favor the death penalty. The expected count in the first cell is therefore 64.86% * 830 or 538.3. For females who favor the death penalty, the expected count is 64.86% * 994 or 644.7. After calculating the expected count for each cell, we can use Equation 11.1 to generate the chi-square statistic:

$$\chi^2 = \frac{(574-538.3)^2}{538.3} + \frac{(256-291.7)^2}{291.7} + \frac{(609-644.7)^2}{644.7} + \frac{(385-349.3)^2}{349.3} = 12.36$$

To determine if this is usual, we would compare this with the chi-square distribution. As with the t distribution, you would need to use degrees of freedom. For the chi-square statistic, the degrees of freedom is based on the number of rows and columns rather than the number of cases. In this case, the degrees of freedom is calculated as follows:

Degrees of freedom = (Number of rows in the table – 1) * (Number of columns – 1)

There are a number of online calculators that can determine the probability of observing a chi-square statistic at least as large as the one you observed when the null hypothesis is true. One example is the chi-square calculator by DI Management[1] (www.di-mgt.com.au/chisquare-calculator.html) that will calculate the p-value and show you the graph.

When plugging in 12.36 for the chi-square value and 1 degree of freedom, the p-value is 0.00044. Fortunately, however, we will not need to calculate the chi-square statistic using the observed and expected counts since Stata will do this for us. This is illustrated in the next section.

11.4 CONDUCTING A CHI-SQUARED TEST

As described in the introduction, capital punishment is a controversial issue in the United States. Using the GSS data from 2012, we could examine several factors that may be related to views about capital punishment—gender, education, income, and so on. In this section, we will use the same example from the previous section to determine if men and women hold the same views about capital punishment. We can then compare the results calculated above with the same test generated by Stata.

---

[1] Stata can calculate the p-value as well using the commands **display chi2tail(1,12.36)**, but it will not show the graph.

Research question

Is there a difference in the percentage of men and women who favor the death penalty for murder?

Null hypothesis

There is no difference in the percentage of men and women who favor the death penalty for murder.

Variables

Categorical variable—favor or oppose the death penalty for murder (cappun)

Categorical variable—gender (sex)

Assumptions

1. *Independence of observations:* There should be only one observation for each participant.

2. *Minimum expected cell frequency:* There should be at least five observations per cell in the table in at least 80% of the cells.

Procedures using code

Using a do-file, we would run the commands below:

```
tab sex cappun, nofreq row chi2 V
```

Procedures using menus

Using menus in Stata, we would click on the sequence listed below that would bring us to Dialog Box 11.1. In the dialog box, we would select the variables "sex" and "cappun" in the drop-down menu as displayed.

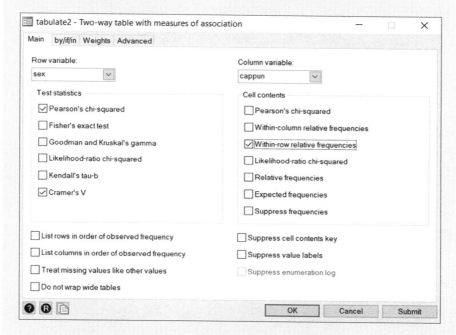

DIALOG BOX 11.1: CROSS TABULATION WITH THE CHI-SQUARED TEST

Statistics → Summaries, tables, and tests → Frequency tables → Two-way table with measures of association

11.5 INTERPRETING THE OUTPUT

Output 11.2 shows the output for the chi-squared test. As illustrated, the chi-square statistic is almost identical to the number that we calculated in Section 11.3. There is only a slight difference due to rounding. Our results indicate that when the null hypothesis is true (that the same percentage of men and women favor the death penalty), the probability of observing a chi-square statistic at least as large as 12.3507 is less than 0.05. We therefore reject the null hypothesis and can state that there is a statistically significant difference in the views of men and women about the death penalty.

As we saw in previous chapters, we may want to examine effect size or the magnitude of the difference in views between men and women. This is particularly important because larger samples will often indicate a significant difference even when the difference is quite small.

There are several measures to examine the effect size, but Cramér's V is the most common test used.[2] It is calculated as follows:

$$\text{Cramér's } V = \sqrt{\frac{\chi^2}{n[\min(k-1, r-1)]}} \tag{11.2}$$

where

   n = number of observations
   k = number of columns
   r = number of rows

Cramér's V generates a correlation coefficient that can range from 0 to 1 with 0 representing no association and +1 representing perfect correlation. In other words, a score of +1 would mean that gender can fully explain the difference in views on the death penalty. This would happen when 100% of men believe in the death penalty and 100% of women do not. In other words, the dependent variable, views on the death penalty, is dependent on gender.

For a 2 × 2 table, as in this example, a Cramér's V <0.1 is considered small, <0.3 is medium, and <0.5 is a large difference between the two proportions. Based on our example, the V of 0.0823 indicates that there is a very weak correlation between the two variables. In other words, gender is a significant factor in determining views on the death penalty, but it has only a small effect.[3]

---

[2] In the case of a 2 × 2 table, the Cramér's V is equivalent to the Phi coefficient, which is used to test the effect size for 2 × 2 tables.

[3] For a more complete explanation of Cramér's V and other measures of association, please refer to the website www.statisticssolutions.com/nominal-variable-association

OUTPUT 11.2: STATA OUTPUT FOR THE PEARSON CHI-SQUARED TEST

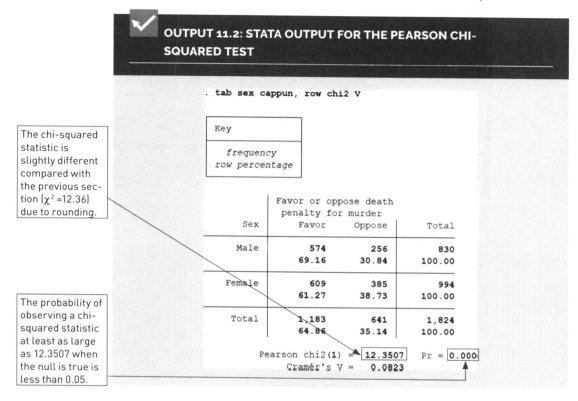

. tab sex cappun, row chi2 V

Key
frequency
row percentage

The chi-squared statistic is slightly different compared with the previous section (χ^2 =12.36) due to rounding.

	Favor or oppose death penalty for murder		
Sex	Favor	Oppose	Total
Male	574	256	830
	69.16	30.84	100.00
Female	609	385	994
	61.27	38.73	100.00
Total	1,183	641	1,824
	64.86	35.14	100.00

Pearson chi2(1) = 12.3507   Pr = 0.000
Cramér's V =   0.0823

The probability of observing a chi-squared statistic at least as large as 12.3507 when the null is true is less than 0.05.

11.6 PRESENTING THE RESULTS

Presenting the results for a nontechnical audience

To present these results to a lay audience who may not be familiar with statistical tests, we could write the following:

> Our results indicate that there is a statistically significant difference in the percentage of men and women who favor the death penalty for murder. A larger percentage of men (69%) favor the death penalty compared with women (61%).

Presenting the results in a scholarly journal

In a peer-reviewed journal, we would include more information. These results could be explained as follows:

> A chi-squared test for independence indicated that there is a statistically significant difference in the percentage of men and women who favor the

death penalty: $\chi^2(1, n = 1,824) = 12.35, p = 0.00$, Cramér's $V = 0.08$. Sixty-nine percent of men favor the death penalty compared with 61% of women.

11.7 SUMMARY OF COMMANDS USED IN THIS CHAPTER

As described in Chapter 4, this last section of each chapter summarizes all of the Stata code used in the chapter. In addition, all Stata code used throughout the book is summarized in Appendix 1.

Chi-square statistic with Cramér's V

```
tab sex cappun, nofreq row chi2 V
```

EXERCISES

1. Misuse of prescription pain relievers has become a national crisis in the United States. Use the National Survey on Drug Use and Health data set to examine differences in prescription pain reliever abuse between men and women in the United States.

   a. Generate a table that compares the percentage of men and women (irsex) who have ever misused pain relievers (pnrnmflag). Be sure to use row or column percentages, depending on which one is appropriate. Also include Cramér's *V*.

   b. What is the null hypothesis?

   c. Based on your results, would you reject the null hypothesis?

   d. Using the appropriate statistics from your results, explain your answer to Part "c."

   e. Interpret Cramér's *V*. What does it mean in the context of this example?

   f. Explain your results in a few sentences to a nontechnical audience.

   g. Explain your results in a few sentences for a scholarly journal.

2. Use the same data set and research question from Question 1 to generate a new table that shows the observed and expected frequencies for each cell.

Based on your table, write out the full equation for the chi-square statistic and calculate it using a calculator. Round each expected frequency to the nearest whole number in your equation.

3. Use Stata and the GSS2016.dta file to examine whether people with different levels of education (degree) believe in life after death (postlife).

   a. What is the null hypothesis?

   b. Explain why you would or would not reject the null hypothesis using output from your analysis.

   c. Calculate the effect size and interpret the number.

   d. In a few sentences, explain your results for a nontechnical audience.

   e. In a few sentences, explain your results for a scholarly journal.

REFERENCES

Berkowitz, B., Fox, J., & Walls, M. (2018, August 3). On death penalty, pope diverges from his U.S. flock. *The Washington Post.*

EXPLORING RELATIONSHIPS

PART FOUR

LINEAR REGRESSION ANALYSIS

Chapter Preview

Research question	How much does the value of used cars decline with additional mileage?
Null hypothesis	The mileage of a used car has no effect on its value.
Test	*t* test of the mileage coefficient in multiple regression analysis
Types of variables	One continuous dependent variable (price) and multiple independent variables (including mileage)
When to use	To examine the relationship between one continuous dependent variable and one or more independent variables
Assumptions	Independent variables are measured without error. All relevant variables are included. The functional form is correct. The variance of the residuals is constant. The error term is not correlated with any independent variables.
Additional tests needed	Tests for normality, omitted variables, multicollinearity, and heteroscedasticity (see Chapter 13)
Stata code: generic	**regress depvar indepvars** Where depvar is the dependent variable and indepvars is a list of one or more independent variables
Stata code: example	**regress Price Year Mileage**

12.1 INTRODUCTION

ARTICLE 12.1

Just What Factors Into The Value Of Your Used Car?

By Joseph A. Dallegro

About nine million used vehicles are sold in the U.S. each quarter. The companies tracking those sales provide an invaluable resource — detailed information on what sells and for how much. These are the figures anyone looking to buy or sell a used car needs to know to be sure they are getting a good — or at least fair — deal.

… In brief, the main factors affecting a used vehicle's price are mileage and condition, with options, location and color also playing a role.

"As mileage increases, so does wear and tear," said Alec Gutierrez, senior analyst for Kelley. "It goes without saying that a potential purchaser would be less inclined to pay top dollar for a 200,000-mile car verses one with 30,000 miles." Were my PT Cruiser to have 100,000 miles, its value would drop to $6,730, according to Kelley.

Condition is more subjective than mileage — someone selling a reliable, accident-free car with paint scratches and surface rust might describe it as "excellent," whereas most buyers might call it good to average — but it's as important as mileage in assessing value. "Although condition is closely associated with mileage, the two are not directly correlated," Gutierrez said. "Even a vehicle with low mileage can sustain more than its fair share of wear and tear, which negatively impacts the value. Vehicles with torn leather seats, electronic equipment that doesn't work, scratches or dents, or other similar issues will not be highly sought after and thus will see a negative impact to their value."

The location of a vehicle can also play a part, depending on the vehicle in question. Mid-priced family sedans are popular everywhere, but more specialized vehicles do better in certain areas. Convertibles and sports cars command higher prices along the coasts and in warmer climates, Gutierrez noted, while four-wheel-drive trucks and SUVs do best in the Northeast, Midwest and other areas that get a lot of snow.

Source: Dallegro (2018).

We are often interested in exploring the effect of different factors on a variable of interest. For example, Article 12.1 explores the factors that influence the market price of used cars. The author argues that used car prices are mainly affected by mileage and condition, but options, location, and color can also influence the value. This conclusion is based on an interview with an expert in the market for cars, with examples from the Kelley Blue Book, a guide to used car prices.

In this chapter, we will learn a statistical method called regression analysis, which is used to study the effect of one or more independent variables on one dependent variable. A *dependent variable* is an outcome variable that we wish to explain using a number of other variables. The *independent variables* are the variables used to "explain" the variation in the dependent variable (they are also called explanatory variables). Regression analysis uses data on the variables of interest to generate an equation that best describes the relationship between the dependent variable and the independent variables. Using the example from above, we can use regression analysis to generate an equation that predicts the price of used cars as a function of mileage, year, and model.

This chapter emphasizes the use of regression analysis and the interpretation of the results. It does not look "under the hood" to explain the calculation of coefficients, standard errors, and test statistics. For additional information on regression analysis, the reader may consult Bailey (2017), Greene (2018), or Woolridge (2016), which provide much more in-depth treatments of regression analysis.

12.2 WHEN TO USE REGRESSION ANALYSIS

Regression analysis is widely used in economics, sociology, psychology, business studies, and other fields. Table 12.1 shows examples from different fields where multiple regression can be used. In each case, there is a research question, a null hypothesis, a continuous dependent variable, and one or more independent variables. Each of these can be tested using multiple regression analysis.

The chapter begins with a description of correlation, a simple descriptive tool for measuring the strength of the relationship between two variables. Next, we consider simple linear regression, with a continuous dependent variable and one independent variable. Last, multiple linear regression is described, which has a continuous dependent variable and multiple independent variables. Chapter 13 describes diagnostic tools for regression analysis, including how to incorporate nonlinear relationships. And Chapter 14 considers types of regression analysis for use when the dependent variable is categorical rather than continuous.

TABLE 12.1 ● EXAMPLES OF MULTIPLE REGRESSION ANALYSIS				
Field	Research Question	Null Hypothesis	Continuous Dependent Variable	Independent Variables
Criminal Justice	Do youth sports programs predict a lower arrest rate among teenagers?	Youth sports programs are not associated with teenage arrest rate.	Number of arrests of teenagers per 100,000 teenagers in each county	Size of youth sports program and other county characteristics
Economics	How does meat demand vary with income?	Income has no effect on meat demand.	Household meat consumption from a survey	Income and other household characteristics
Political Science	How does county average education level predict county-level support for a candidate?	Education level does not predict support for the candidate.	Share of a county supporting the candidate	Average education and other voter characteristics in each county
Psychology	How are family history characteristics associated with psychological well-being?	Family history characteristics are not associated with psychological well-being.	Indicator of psychological well-being from a survey	Family history characteristics
Public Health	Is the incidence of measles related to the percentage of children vaccinated?	The share of children vaccinated in a county is not related to the prevalence of measles.	Share of children who contract measles in a given year in each county	Share of children receiving the measles vaccine and other health factors
Sociology	Is the number of children a couple has affected by the parents' education?	The parents' education has no effect on the number of children a couple has.	Number of children a couple has	Education of the father and education of the mother

12.3 CORRELATION

Suppose we are interested in examining the relationship between two continuous variables, such as the price and mileage of a sample of used cars. We can start by exploring the data visually with a scatter plot of the two variables. A scatter plot can tell us at a glance whether the two variables are positively related or negatively related. If the scatter plot shows an upward sloping trend, the two variables are positively correlated, meaning that high values of one variable are associated with high values of the other variable. For example, daily temperature and ice cream sales are positively correlated. If the scatter plot shows a downward sloping trend, the variables are negatively correlated: High values of one variable are associated with low values of the other. For example, number of sunny days in a month and umbrella sales are probably negatively correlated.

Scatter plots also tell us in a general sense how closely related the two variables are. The closer the points are to the central trend, the stronger the relationship between the two variables. Finally, the graph can let us know whether the relationship between the two variables is linear (following a straight line) or nonlinear (curved).

We have assembled a database of information on 382 used Chevrolet Malibus that were for sale in the Washington, D.C., area in mid-2017, drawing the data from the website autotrader.com. For each car, we recorded information on the price, mileage, model year, and trim level. The data are available in the file malibu.dta. After opening the file, we can create a scatter plot of price and mileage using the menu system (see Dialog Box 12.1) or with the following command:

twoway (scatter Price Mileage)

The command **twoway** means that we want to generate a graph with two variables, **scatter** indicates the type of graph, the first variable is plotted on the vertical axis, and the second on the horizontal axis. Because the variables are capitalized in the database, we must capitalize them whenever we refer to them in Stata commands.[1]

The output in Figure 12.1 shows that most of the cars have a price between $10,000 and $20,000 and have less than 100,000 miles on the odometer. As expected, price and mileage are negatively correlated, meaning that cars with high mileage tend to have low prices, and vice versa. The graph also indicates that the relationship is roughly linear, meaning that there is no obvious curvature in the pattern.

---

[1] The normal convention in Stata is to keep variables in lowercase. We capitalized the variables in the Malibu database to make it easier to distinguish Stata commands (always in lowercase) from the variables.

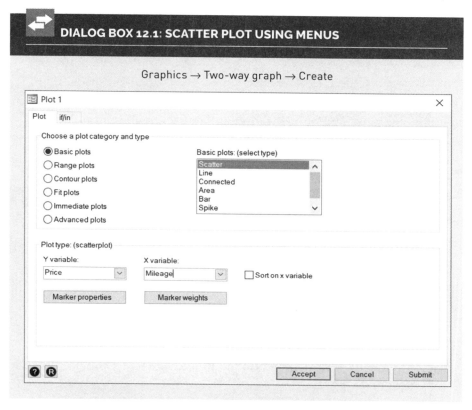

DIALOG BOX 12.1: SCATTER PLOT USING MENUS

Graphics → Two-way graph → Create

How can we measure the strength of the relationship between two continuous variables? One of the most common measures is the *Pearson correlation coefficient* or *r*. The correlation coefficient can be calculated using the following equation:[2]

$$\text{Correlation coefficient} = r = \frac{\sum_{i=1}^{n}[(x_i - \bar{x})(y_i - \bar{y})]}{\sqrt{\sum_{i=1}^{n}(x_i - \bar{x})^2 \sum_{i=1}^{n}(y_i - \bar{y})^2}} \tag{12.1}$$

where

n is the number of observations of x and y

$x_i = x_1, x_2, \ldots x_n$ are the values of x

$y_i = y_1, y_2, \ldots y_n$ are the values of y

$\bar{x}$ is the mean of x

$\bar{y}$ is the mean of y

---

[2] This equation has an intuitive interpretation for those with some statistics background. The correlation coefficient is the ratio of (a) the covariance of x and y and (b) the product of the standard deviation of x and the standard deviation of y.

FIGURE 12.1 ◆ SCATTER PLOT OF PRICE AND MILEAGE

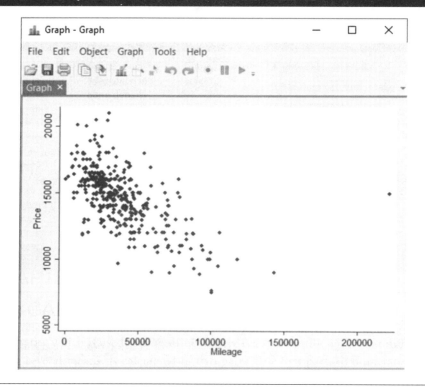

The value of *r* varies between –1 and 1, where –1 means a perfect negative correlation, 0 means no correlation, and 1 means a perfect positive correlation. When two variables are perfectly correlated, every observation lies on a straight line if graphed on a scatter plot. When two variables have a very low correlation coefficient, the scatter plot looks like a random collection of dots with no pattern.

To calculate the Pearson correlation coefficient for price and mileage in Stata, we can use the menu system (see Dialog Box 12.2) or the **pwcorr** command (see Output 12.1). Adding the **sig** option will give the statistical significance of the correlation.

The results, shown in Output 12.1, reveal that the correlation coefficient is –0.6229. The negative number indicates a negative correlation between price and mileage: As mileage increases, price declines. The magnitude suggests a relatively strong

Statistics → Summaries, tables, and tests → Summary and descriptive statistics →
Pairwise correlations of variables

correlation. The number below the correlation coefficient, 0.0000, indicates the *p*-value of the correlation, that is, the probability of finding a correlation coefficient this large (or larger) if there were in fact no correlation between the two variables. The low value indicates that the probability of this occurring "by chance" is very small. The two numbers along the diagonal are 1.0 because they represent the correlation coefficient of each variable with itself.

The **pwcorr** command can be used to calculate all the correlation coefficients for each pair of variables in a list. For example, if we list five variables, Stata will display a 5 × 5 table of correlation coefficients.

OUTPUT 12.1: PEARSON CORRELATION COEFFICIENT

```
. pwcorr Price Mileage, sig

                    Price   Mileage

        Price      1.0000

      Mileage     -0.6229   1.0000
                   0.0000
```

A closely related measure of correlation is the *coefficient of determination*, more commonly known as R^2. When measuring the association between two variables, R^2 can be calculated easily as the square of the Pearson correlation coefficient:

$$\text{Coefficient of determination} = R^2 = r^2 \qquad (12.2)$$

R^2 varies between 0 and 1. If $R^2 = 0$, the two variables are completely uncorrelated, and if $R^2 = 1$, they are perfectly correlated, either positively or negatively. One convenient feature of R^2 is that, under some circumstances, it represents the share of the variance in y that can be explained by the x variable.

Figures 12.2 to 12.7 provide some examples of scatter plots to give an intuitive sense of what different values of R^2 look like.

FIGURES 12.2 TO 12.4   ●   SCATTER PLOTS WITH DIFFERENT LEVELS OF POSITIVE CORRELATION

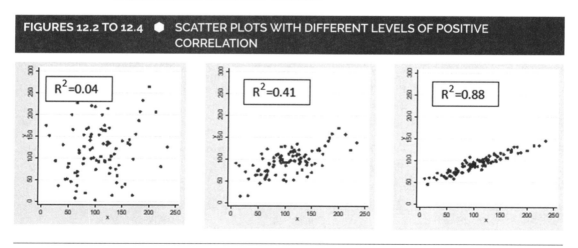

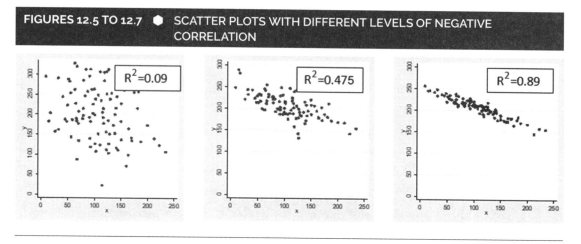

FIGURES 12.5 TO 12.7 ● SCATTER PLOTS WITH DIFFERENT LEVELS OF NEGATIVE CORRELATION

Correlation analysis has a number of limitations:

- It does not tell us anything about the mathematical relationship between the two variables, such as the slope of the line or where it crosses the vertical axis.

- It only considers the relationship between the two variables.

- It assumes a linear relationship between the two variables.

- It does not imply or confirm any causal relationship between the two variables.

As we will see in the next section, regression analysis gives an equation that describes the relationship among various variables, allows both linear and nonlinear relationships, and, subject to some assumptions, can identify causal relationships.

12.4 SIMPLE REGRESSION ANALYSIS

As mentioned above, regression analysis describes the relationship between a dependent variable and one or more independent variables. The distinction between dependent and independent variables is based on a key assumption in regression analysis: It assumes that the independent variables are *exogenous*, meaning that they are not affected by the dependent variable, nor are there any variables outside that model that affect both the dependent variable and the independent variables. If this assumption holds, then any relationship between y and x can be considered causal, meaning that the model describes how the independent variables *affect* the dependent variable. If these assumptions do not hold, then one or more of the independent variables are said to be *endogenous*. In this case, we cannot infer causality, but the regression analysis might still be useful as a descriptive tool. In this case, it would only describe the changes in *y* that are *associated* with changes in *x*. Chapter 13 describes in more detail the consequences of regression models that violate this or other assumptions behind regression analysis.

We start with the simple case of a linear relationship between one dependent variable and a single independent variable. Later in this chapter, we describe regression analysis with multiple independent variables. And in later chapters, we show how regression analysis can be used to describe nonlinear relationships.

The relationship between a dependent variable and one independent variable in a linear relationship can be described with the following equation:[3]

$$y = \beta_0 + \beta_1 x + \varepsilon \qquad (12.3)$$

where

y is the dependent variable
x is the independent variable
β_0 is the constant or y intercept
β_1 is the slope or coefficient on x
ε is the error term

The error term, ε, reflects the fact that the relationship between y and x is not exact, but rather is subject to some error. Note that β_0 and β_1 are parameters that cannot be directly observed; we can only estimate them using the values of y and x. Likewise, the error term, ε, cannot be directly observed.

The predicted value of y, written as $\hat{y}$, is defined as follows:

$$\text{Predicted value of } y = \hat{y} = \hat{\beta}_0 + \hat{\beta}_1 x \qquad (12.4)$$

where $\hat{\beta}_0$ is the estimated value of the true parameter β_0, and $\hat{\beta}_1$ is the estimated value of the parameter β_1 (we discuss how to estimate them shortly). As you can see, the "hat" indicates an estimate of a population parameter based on sample data.

---

[3] This equation is similar to one that may be familiar from algebra classes, $y = Mx + B$, with different notation and the addition of the error term, ε. The slope is M in this equation and β_1 in the regression equation, while the y-intercept is B here and β_0 in the regression equation.

FIGURE 12.8 ● REGRESSION CONCEPTS ILLUSTRATED ON HYPOTHETICAL DATA

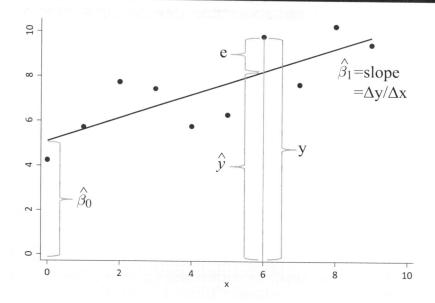

The *residual* is the difference between the actual value and the predicted value:

$$\text{Residual} = y - \hat{y} = e \tag{12.5}$$

It is important not to confuse ε and e: ε is the unobserved error term in the "true" relationship between y and x, while e is the observed difference between y and its predicted value, $\hat{y}$, the latter based on the estimated relationship between y and x.[4] We use the distribution of the (observed) residuals to infer the distribution of the (unobserved) error term.

The relationships among these concepts is shown in a simplified example in Figure 12.8. The 10 dots represent the observations of x and y, while the line reflects the predicted values of y ($\hat{y}$) as a function of x. For each of the 10 observations, the residual (e) is the vertical distance between the observation (y) and the line representing the predicted values ($\hat{y}$), where the distance is considered negative when y is less than $\hat{y}$.

Now we can ask this question: What do we mean when we say that regression analysis identifies the equation that "best describes" the relationship? In this case, regression

---

[4] To be consistent, we could label the residual $\hat{\varepsilon}$, since it is an estimate of the error term, but we follow the convention in statistics of labeling it e.

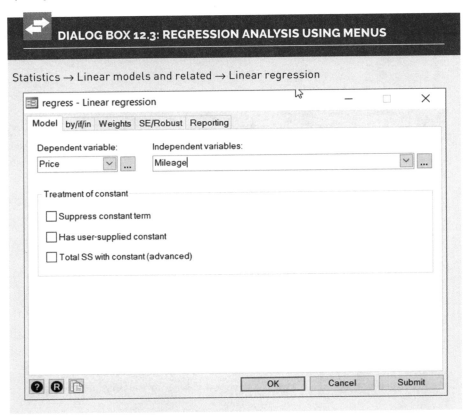

analysis finds the values of $\hat{\beta}_0$ and $\hat{\beta}_1$ that minimize the sum of squared residuals or $\sum e^2$ across all observations. For this reason, this type of regression analysis is also called ordinary least squares regression. The calculation of the estimated coefficients and related statistics uses matrix algebra and is beyond the scope of this book, but interested readers will find more information in Woolridge (2016), Greene (2018), and other books dedicated to regression analysis.

In addition to estimating β_0 and β_1, regression analysis generates other information to help us interpret the results. It is easier to explain the output of regression analysis using an example. Let's return to our database of the prices of used Chevrolet Malibus. We can run a regression analysis with the menu systems (see Dialog Box 12.3) or with the **regress** command, followed by the dependent variable and then any independent variables we wish to include (see Output 12.2).

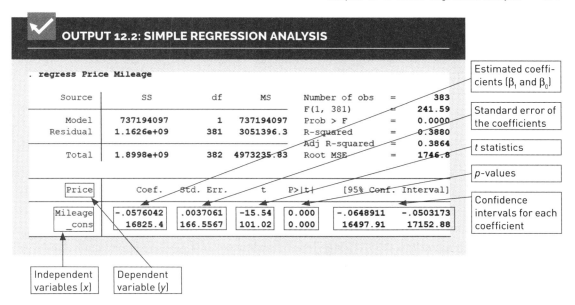

OUTPUT 12.2: SIMPLE REGRESSION ANALYSIS

. regress Price Mileage

Source	SS	df	MS
Model	737194097	1	737194097
Residual	1.1626e+09	381	3051396.3
Total	1.8998e+09	382	4973235.83

Number of obs =	383
F(1, 381) =	241.59
Prob > F =	0.0000
R-squared =	0.3880
Adj R-squared =	0.3864
Root MSE =	1746.8

Price	Coef.	Std. Err.	t	P>|t|	[95% Conf. Interval]
Mileage	-.0576042	.0037061	-15.54	0.000	-.0648911 -.0503173
_cons	16825.4	166.5567	101.02	0.000	16497.91 17152.88

Estimated coefficients (β_1 and β_0)

Standard error of the coefficients

t statistics

p-values

Confidence intervals for each coefficient

Independent variables (*x*)

Dependent variable (*y*)

How do we interpret the information in Output 12.2? In the upper right corner, we see that the number of observations (cars) is 383. The *F* statistic is a test of the null hypothesis that all coefficients (excluding the constant) are equal to 0. The "Prob > *F*" line gives the probability that an *F* statistic this large could be generated by chance if the null hypothesis were true. Since it is 0.0000, this indicates that the probability of getting this result would be very small if there were actually no linear relationship between price and mileage.

"*R*-squared" refers to R^2, the coefficient of determination of the observed values of *y* and the predicted values of *y* ($\hat{y}$). In a linear regression model with a constant, R^2 can also be interpreted as the proportion of the variance in *y* that can be explained by the model. In this case, mileage explains about 39% of the variance in price across our sample of Malibus.

"Adj *R*-squared" refers to adjusted R^2. One limitation of R^2 is that, when you add an independent variable to the model, R^2 will always increase, even if the new variable does not help predict the dependent variable. Adjusted R^2 is adjusted for the number of independent variables, so it will increase only if the new variable increases the explanatory power of the model more than would be expected by chance. Adjusted R^2 is calculated as $1 - (1 - R^2)(n - 1)/(n - k)$, where *n* is the number of observations and *k* is the number of independent variables including the constant.

Looking at the table at the bottom of Output 12.2, we see a table showing a list of the variables including the constant in the first column and a list of coefficients in the second column. The variables and coefficients can be rearranged to form the equation that best fits the data as follows:

$$\hat{y} = \hat{\beta}_0 + \hat{\beta}_1 * x \tag{12.6}$$

$$\text{Predicted price} = 16825.4 + (-0.0576042 * \text{Mileage})$$

The coefficient for mileage $(\hat{\beta}_1)$ is approximately −0.0576. It tells us how much y changes given a one-unit change in x. In this case, the coefficient tells us that the price declines by \$0.0576 or 5.76 cents for each additional mile on the car. In other words, these cars tend to depreciate \$576 for each additional 10,000 miles on the odometer. Graphically, −0.0576 is the slope of the line plotting predicted price against mileage.

The constant $(\hat{\beta}_0)$ is 16,825. This represents the value of $\hat{y}$ (predicted price) when x (mileage) is 0, given this simple linear model. It is also called the y intercept because, graphically, it indicates the value of $\hat{y}$ where the best-fit line passes through the vertical (or y) axis.[5]

The second column shows the standard error of the coefficient estimates. The standard error is a measure of the precision of the estimate of the coefficient. If the model fits the data well, then the residuals and the standard error will be small.

The third column gives the t statistic for each coefficient, calculated as the ratio of the coefficient and its standard error. As a rule of thumb, a t statistic greater than 2 or less than −2 indicates that the coefficient is significantly different from 0. However, the rule of thumb is redundant because Stata and other statistical software packages also report p-values, which are a more direct measure of statistical significance.

As described in Chapter 7, the p-value tells us the probability that we could get a value of $\hat{\beta}$ this large or larger (in absolute value) if the null hypothesis (that the coefficient is 0) were true. In this case, the p-value on the mileage variable indicates that there is less than 0.0005 probability (less than 0.05% probability) that we would get a result this strong (or stronger) if there were no relationship between price and

---

[5] Note that the prices of new Chevrolet Malibus in 2017 started at \$22,000, substantially more than our estimate of β_0. This suggests that the relationship between price and mileage is not linear: the price probably drops sharply in the first few 1,000 miles, when the car goes from "new" to "used," and then drops more gradually after that. This also highlights the risks of using regression analysis to make predictions outside the observed range of x.

mileage ($\beta_1 = 0$). Similarly, the p-value on the constant suggests that it is unlikely that the true intercept is 0 ($\beta_0 = 0$). These probabilities are based on the assumption that there is a linear relationship between price and mileage, as well as other assumptions discussed in Chapter 13. By convention, if a p-value is less than 0.05, the coefficient is considered "significantly different from zero" or "statistically significant." If the p-value is less than 0.01, it is considered "statistically significant at the 1% level."

The last two columns show the lower and upper limits of the 95% confidence interval. This means that we are 95% sure that the true value of the parameter lies between these two numbers. The more precise the coefficient estimate, the smaller the standard error, the larger the t statistic, the smaller the p-value, and the narrower the confidence interval.

As discussed in Chapter 7, there is some controversy over the use of p-values. Sometimes, the p-value is misinterpreted. Some researchers argue for a stricter standard, requiring a smaller p-value to consider a relationship statistically significant. For example, social scientists have traditionally considered p-values greater than 0.05 but less than 0.10 to be "weakly significant," but recently, some have argued that it is not worth reporting coefficients with p-values greater than 0.05. There is a growing consensus that researchers should focus more on the confidence interval and less on the p-value.

To see the best-fit line generated by the regression analysis, we can return to the graphing command. We can show both the scatter plot and the regression line with the following Stata command:

```
twoway (scatter Price Mileage) (lfit Price Mileage)
```

The first set of parentheses in the command tell Stata that we want Stata to display a scatter plot of price and mileage. The second set of parentheses indicates that we would like to add the "linear fit" line of price and mileage to the same graph. The line in Figure 12.9 corresponds to the equation described in Output 12.2 and Equation 12.6. The constant coefficient in Output 12.2 (16,825.4) is the value of $\hat{\beta}_0$ in Equation 12.2 and corresponds to the price at which the line crosses the vertical axis in Figure 12.9. Similarly, the mileage coefficient in Output 12.2 (−0.0576042) is the value of $\hat{\beta}_1$ in Equation 12.2 and corresponds to the slope of the line in Figure 12.9.

FIGURE 12.9 ⬣ SCATTER PLOT OF PRICE AND MILEAGE

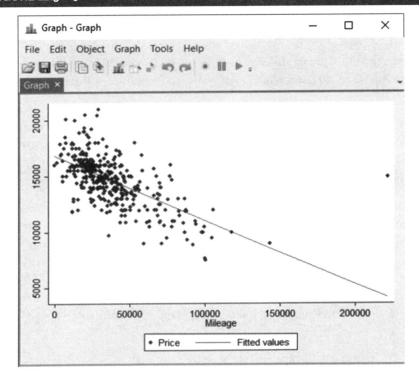

12.5 MULTIPLE REGRESSION ANALYSIS

Simple regression analysis refers to the case where there is just one independent variable in addition to the constant. However, regression analysis can also be used with multiple independent variables in addition to the constant. A linear multiple regression model assumes that the data follow a pattern like this:

$$y = \beta_0 + \sum_{i=1}^{k-1} \beta_i x_i + \varepsilon \qquad (12.7)$$

where

k is the number of independent variables (including the constant)

β_i is one of the k coefficients

x_i is one of the $k-1$ independent variables

ε is the error term

As with simple regression analysis, the true values of the βs in Equation 12.7 are unknown, but we can estimate them from the observed values of y and the independent variables, x_i. The estimated coefficients (denoted by $\hat{\beta}_0, \hat{\beta}_1, \hat{\beta}_2, \ldots, \hat{\beta}_{k-1}$) are those that minimize the sum of squared residuals $\left(\sum e^2\right)$. Each estimated coefficient $\hat{\beta}_i$ is interpreted as the effect of a one-unit increase in the corresponding independent variable, x_i, while holding constant all other independent variables.

Let's return to the model of Malibu prices. We know that mileage is not the only characteristic that affects the price of used cars. For example, the price is also influenced by the trim level. In the case of the Chevrolet Malibu, there are three trim levels: (1) the Malibu LS is the base model, (2) the LT is midrange, and (3) the LTZ is the luxury version. The variable Trim takes the value 1 for the LS, 2 for the LT, and 3 for the LTZ. The trim level is an ordinal categorical variable, meaning that there is a natural order but we cannot assume that the intervals between them are the same. In other words, we cannot assume that the difference in value between the LS and the LT is the same as the difference in value between the LT and the LTZ. If we used the variable Trim in the regression model, its coefficient would reflect both the increase in price associated with moving from LS to LT and the increase associated with moving from LT to LTZ. In other words, it would assume that the LS–LT and the LT–LTZ price differences were equal, which may not be true.

To avoid this problem, independent variables that are categorical (nominal or ordinal) are represented by one or more dummy variables, each taking a value of 0 or 1. Dummy variables are also called dichotomous, binary, or indicator variables. For example, the LT dummy variable will be equal to 1 for LT models and 0 for the other two models (LS and LTZ).

However, the number of dummy variables included in the regression analysis must be equal to the number of categories minus one.[6] In other words, one category is omitted from the regression. The coefficients of the included dummy variables represent the effect on the dependent variable of being in that category rather than the omitted category, as illustrated in Table 12.2.

In the case of the Malibu, there are three trim levels, so we need two dummy variables. We could define the LS dummy variable like this:

```
gen LS = 0
replace LS = 1 if Trim==1
```

---

[6] The intuitive explanation is that the independent variables in a regression model cannot include any redundant information. If there are three categories, they can be represented by two dummy variables. Adding a third dummy variable would not add any new information.

Categorical Variable	Categories	Number of Categories	Number of Dummy Variables Needed	Example of Dummy Variables to Include	Interpretation of Coefficients
Gender	Male, female	2	1	Female	Effect of being female relative to male
Marital status	Single, married, divorced, widowed	4	3	Single, divorced, widowed	Effect of having each status relative to being married
Region	North, South, Central, East, West	5	4	North, South, East, West	Effect of living in each region relative to living in the Central region

TABLE 12.2 ● EXAMPLES OF USING DUMMY VARIABLES TO REPRESENT A CATEGORICAL VARIABLE

However, this is risky: If Trim has any missing values, the first line will set LS to 0 for those observations, which would be an error. A better approach is to specify values for LS depending on the value of Trim, as shown below. If any observations of Trim are missing, the corresponding values of LS, LT, and LTZ will also be missing, as they should be.

```
gen LS = 0 if Trim==2 | Trim==3
replace LS = 1 if Trim==1
gen LT = 0 if Trim==1 | Trim==3
replace LT = 1 if Trim==2
gen LTZ= 0 if Trim==1 | Trim==2
replace LTZ= 1 if Trim==3
```

The first line creates a new variable LS and sets it equal to 0 if Trim is 2 or 3. The second line revises the variable LS to be equal to 1 if Trim is 1. Keep in mind that Stata is case sensitive, so the variable LTZ is different from a variable named ltz. We use uppercase variable names to avoid the lowercase "l," which can be confused with the number 1 or an uppercase I.

Using **gen** and **replace** to create dummy variables is effective, but somewhat cumbersome. We can streamline the code by using the **recode ... gen** command. The

recode command was described in Chapter 5, but adding the **gen** option creates a new variable rather than changing the values of the original variable. With this command, we can create three dummy variables with three commands. The first line below says to create a new variable LS, which will be equal to 1 if Trim is 1 and equal to 0 if Trim is 2 or 3:

```
recode Trim (1=1) (2 3=0), gen(LS)
recode Trim (2=1) (1 3=0), gen(LT)
recode Trim (3=1) (1 2=0), gen(LTZ)
```

Finally, the most streamlined approach to converting a categorical variable such as Trim into a set of dummy variables is to use what Stata calls "factor variables" by attaching an "i." prefix to the categorical variable in the **regress** command itself:

```
regress Price Mileage i.Trim
```

Instead of the six **gen** and **replace** commands or the three **recode … gen** commands, the factor variable approach requires just two characters! For now, we will use the **recode … gen** method to calculate dummy variables because it is more transparent, but the factor variable notation will be used in Chapter 14.

If we only need to include dummy variables for two of the three categories, how do we choose which one to omit? One convention is to omit the dummy associated with the category with the largest number of observations. Another convention is to omit the category associated with the lowest values of the dependent variable so that the dummy coefficients will be positive. But it does not really matter. The R^2 and the coefficients and p-values of all other variables will be the same. The decision of which category to omit will only affect the constant and the coefficients on the dummy variables representing the categorical variable, but even these differences do not affect the predicted values of the dependent variable. In this example, the choice of which trim level is omitted has no effect on the predicted price of a Malibu, as we will show later.

Let's calculate the dummy variables using the **recode … gen** command and run a version of the Malibu price model omitting the LS variable, since the Malibu LS is the least expensive version. The commands and results are shown in Output 12.3.

As shown in Output 12.3, the value of R^2 is 0.4908, indicating that the three independent variables explain 49% of the variation in price. Not surprisingly, three independent variables plus the constant explain a larger share of the variation in price than mileage and the constant alone. The adjusted R^2 is also higher than in the earlier model, indicating that the new variables are contributing significantly to the

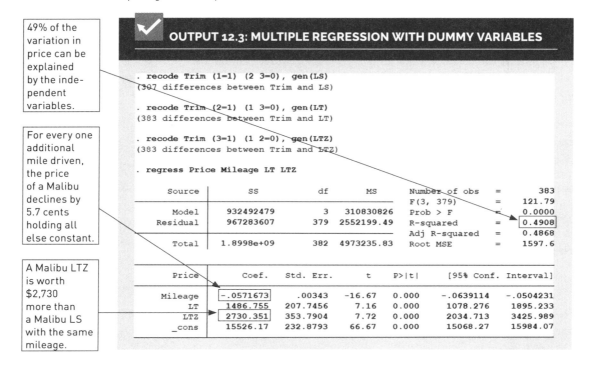

49% of the variation in price can be explained by the independent variables.

For every one additional mile driven, the price of a Malibu declines by 5.7 cents holding all else constant.

A Malibu LTZ is worth $2,730 more than a Malibu LS with the same mileage.

OUTPUT 12.3: MULTIPLE REGRESSION WITH DUMMY VARIABLES

```
. recode Trim (1=1) (2 3=0), gen(LS)
(307 differences between Trim and LS)

. recode Trim (2=1) (1 3=0), gen(LT)
(383 differences between Trim and LT)

. recode Trim (3=1) (1 2=0), gen(LTZ)
(383 differences between Trim and LTZ)

. regress Price Mileage LT LTZ
```

Source	SS	df	MS
Model	932492479	3	310830826
Residual	967283607	379	2552199.49
Total	1.8998e+09	382	4973235.83

Number of obs = 383
F(3, 379) = 121.79
Prob > F = 0.0000
R-squared = 0.4908
Adj R-squared = 0.4868
Root MSE = 1597.6

Price	Coef.	Std. Err.	t	P>|t|	[95% Conf. Interval]
Mileage	-.0571673	.00343	-16.67	0.000	-.0639114 -.0504231
LT	1486.755	207.7456	7.16	0.000	1078.276 1895.233
LTZ	2730.351	353.7904	7.72	0.000	2034.713 3425.989
_cons	15526.17	232.8793	66.67	0.000	15068.27 15984.07

explanatory power of the model. This is confirmed by the fact that the *p*-values of the LT and LTZ coefficients are less than 0.01, indicating that both are statistically significant at the 1% level.

The coefficients for each variable give us information on the linear equation that best fits our data:

$$Price = 15526.17 + (-0.0571673 * Mileage) + (1486.755 * LT) + (2730.351 * LTZ)$$

The coefficient on mileage is about −0.057, meaning that each additional mile on the car is associated with a price reduction of $0.057 or 5.7 cents. This is similar but not identical to the coefficient in the previous regression model that did not include the dummy variables to represent trim levels (see Output 12.2). The coefficient on LT is 1,486.755, indicating that a Malibu LT is worth about $1,487 more than a Malibu LS (the omitted category) given the same mileage. Similarly, a Malibu LTZ is worth $2,730 more than a Malibu LS with the same mileage.

From the regression equation, what is the predicted price of a Malibu LS with zero miles? We can use the equation above, keeping in mind that Mileage = 0, LT = 0, and LTZ = 0:

$$Price = 15526.17 + (-0.0571673 * 0) + (1486.755 * 0) + (2730.351 * 0) = 15526.17$$

For a Malibu LT with zero mileage, the calculation is similar except that the variable LT = 1:

$$Price = 15526.17 + (-0.0571673 * 0) + (1486.755 * 1) + (2730.351 * 0) = 17012.925$$

And for a Malibu LTZ with zero mileage, LTZ = 1, so the calculation is as follows:

$$Price = 15526.17 + (-0.0571673 * 0) + (1486.755 * 0) + (2730.351 * 1) = 18256.521$$

These three numbers represent the intercept for each type of Malibu on a graph of price and mileage. Our regression equation assumes that cars in all three trim levels lose about 5.7 cents/mile, so the mileage coefficient (or slope) is the same.

We can graph the best-fit line for the LS, LT, and LTZ models separately using the fact that Stata stores the coefficients from the most recent model as **_b[*varname*],** where *varname* is the name of the independent variable for that coefficient. Thus, we can calculate predicted values for each model and graph them as in Figure 12.10:

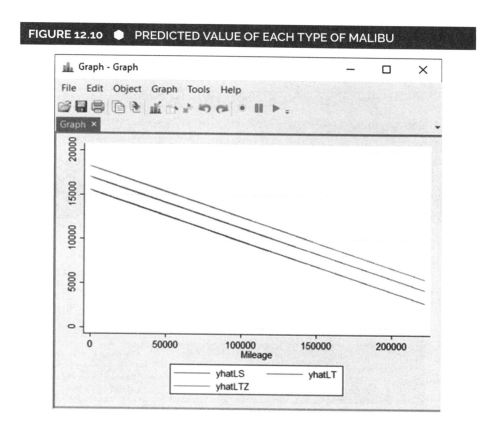

FIGURE 12.10 ⬥ PREDICTED VALUE OF EACH TYPE OF MALIBU

```
gen yhatLS = _ b[ _ cons]+ _ b[Mileage]*Mileage
gen yhatLT = _ b[ _ cons]+ _ b[Mileage]*Mileage + _ b[LT]
gen yhatLTZ = _ b[ _ cons]+ _ b[Mileage]*Mileage + _ b[LTZ]
twoway (line yhatLS Mileage) (line yhatLT Mileage) ///
   (line yhatLTZ Mileage)
```

Now we can show that it does not matter which category we choose to omit. Suppose we ran a different version of this model using LTZ as the omitted category rather than LS (see Output 12.4).

The results in Output 12.4 (with LTZ omitted) are almost identical to those in Output 12.3 (with LS omitted). The only differences are in the rows for the constant and the variables LS and LT. The constant in Output 12.4 is higher than it was in Output 12.3 because it now represents the price of a zero-mileage LTZ rather than a zero-mileage LS. The two dummy variable coefficients are negative rather than positive because they now reflect the fact that the Malibu LS and LT have lower prices than the omitted LTZ. However, these differences do not change the predicted prices of any cars. Below are the predicted intercepts for a Malibu LS, LT, and LTZ, respectively:

$$Price = 18256.52 - 0.0571673*(0) - 2730.351*(1) - 1243.596*(0) = 15526.169$$

$$Price = 18256.52 - 0.0571673*(0) - 2730.351*(0) - 1243.596*(1) = 17012.924$$

$$Price = 18256.52 - 0.0571673*(0) - 2730.351*(0) - 1243.596*(0) = 18256.521$$

✔ OUTPUT 12.4: MULTIPLE REGRESSION WITH A DIFFERENT OMITTED CATEGORY

```
. regress Price Mileage LS LT
```

Source	SS	df	MS			
				Number of obs	=	383
				F(3, 379)	=	121.79
Model	932492479	3	310830826	Prob > F	=	0.0000
Residual	967283607	379	2552199.49	R-squared	=	0.4908
				Adj R-squared	=	0.4868
Total	1.8998e+09	382	4973235.83	Root MSE	=	1597.6

Price	Coef.	Std. Err.	t	P>|t|	[95% Conf. Interval]	
Mileage	-.0571673	.00343	-16.67	0.000	-.0639114	-.0504231
LS	-2730.351	353.7904	-7.72	0.000	-3425.989	-2034.713
LT	-1243.596	319.4179	-3.89	0.000	-1871.65	-615.5431
_cons	18256.52	343.8593	53.09	0.000	17580.41	18932.63

Comparing these numbers with those calculated using the previous regression model (which omitted the LS), we see that the intercepts are the same, other than differences in rounding. Likewise, the coefficient on the variable Mileage is the same. This means that the predicted price of each Malibu is the same whether we omit the LS or LTZ category. Likewise, a model in which the LT dummy variable is omitted would generate the same predicted prices for each car.

One final issue related to the choice of omitted categories is that it will affect the standard errors, t statistics, and confidence intervals of the dummy variables. For example, LTZ may be statistically significant when LS is omitted but not when LT is omitted. However, the decision whether to include the set of dummies should be based on a joint test, where the null hypothesis is that all the coefficients on the dummy variables representing the categorical variable are equal to zero. The joint test will give the same result regardless of which category is omitted.

We can do a joint test of the hypothesis that all the coefficients on the dummy variables are equal to zero using the **test** command. This command can be used to test a variety of null hypotheses, but if the command is followed by a list of variables, it will test the hypothesis that all the corresponding coefficients are equal to zero. The **test** command uses the most recently estimated coefficients, so if we rerun the model from Output 12.3, then we could test the joint significance of LT and LTZ using the menu system (see Dialog Box 12.4) or the **test** command (see Output 12.5).

The first two lines of Output 12.5 show the null hypothesis that the LT and LTZ coefficients are both equal to zero. The last line of the output gives the p-value, which suggests that we can reject the null hypothesis that the two coefficients are both equal to zero at the 1% confidence level. We would get the same result if we ran the model from Output 12.4 and tested the joint significance of LS and LT.

In summary, when using a set of dummy variables to represent a categorical independent variable, one of the set must be omitted from the regression model. The choice of which dummy to omit has no effect on the predicted values of the dependent variable. Likewise, the choice of which dummy to omit will have no effect on the joint test of the statistical significance of the set of dummy variables.

DIALOG BOX 12.4: HYPOTHESIS TESTING USING MENUS

Statistics → Postestimation → Tests, contrasts, and comparisons of parameter estimates → Linear tests of parameter estimates → Create

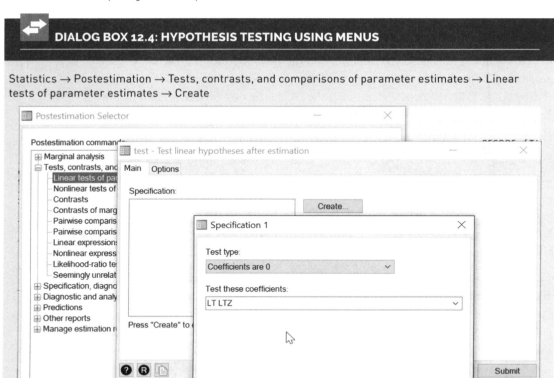

OUTPUT 12.5: TESTING JOINT HYPOTHESES

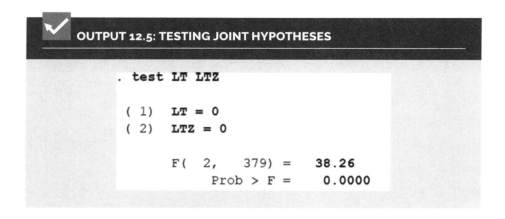

12.6 PRESENTING THE RESULTS

To describe the results, the researcher should focus on the independent variables that have a statistically significant and meaningful effect on the dependent variable. By statistically significant, we mean that the p-value is less than 0.05, indicating that the finding is unlikely to have occurred by chance if there is, in fact, no relationship. By meaningful, we mean that the size of the effect is important enough to affect policy or other decisions related to the topic of the study. With a large sample size, it is quite possible that a relationship is statistically significant (measured with little error) but too small to be of practical importance.

In addition, it may be worth identifying independent variables that did not have a statistically significant relationship with the dependent variable if this contradicts or challenges widely held beliefs. However, the size of the coefficient should not be discussed unless it is statistically significant.

For a newspaper or magazine targeting a nontechnical audience, we might summarize the Malibu regression results as follows:

> Statistical analysis reveals that the price of used Chevrolet Malibu cars is influenced by mileage and the model type: LS, LT, or LTZ. For example, each additional mile on the odometer is associated with a reduction in value of 5.7 cents. Similarly, holding mileage constant, the upscale Malibu LTZ is worth $2,730 more than the base-model LS, while the midrange Malibu LT is worth $1,487 more than the Malibu LS.

For an academic audience, we can assume some familiarity with regression analysis and provide some additional details. We can use the **outreg** command[7] to generate a table of regression results in Word format. In its simplest form, the **outreg** command uses the most recent regression analysis and sends the output to a Word file.

```
outreg using "c:/Malibu model"
```

The "**c:/Malibu model**" is used to indicate the name and location of the new Word file to be created. There are numerous options that allow you to specify the statistics to be included and the layout of the table. If no options are specified, the default is a simple table showing the coefficients, t statistics, level of significance, number of observations, and R^2, as shown in Output 12.6.

---

[7] The **outreg** command is a user-defined command, meaning that it is not officially part of Stata software. However, it can be easily downloaded and installed by typing **ssc install outreg** in the command line. Stata will install both the command itself and help files associated with it. There are hundreds of other user-defined commands available for download in this way.

> ✔ **OUTPUT 12.6: REGRESSION OUTPUT IN WORD FORMAT USING OUTREG**

	Price
Mileage	-0.057
	(16.67)**
LT	1,486.755
	(7.16)**
LTZ	2,730.351
	(7.72)**
_cons	15,526.170
	(66.67)**
R^2	0.49
N	383

$* p<0.05; ** p<0.01$

The options can be used to include standard errors, confidence intervals, or other statistics, or to modify the format such as changing parentheses to brackets or changing the number of digits to the right of the decimal point.

In writing up the results, it is important to consult the journal for which you are writing. For example, some journals are encouraging greater use of confidence intervals (CIs) rather than reporting only the statistical significance of the coefficients. Below is a possible write-up for a technical audience:

We used regression analysis to explore the determinants of the price of used Chevrolet Malibus advertised in the Washington, D.C., region in 2017. The results indicate that mileage is statistically significant at the 1% confidence level. The coefficient on mileage is 0.057 (CI 0.050–0.064), indicating that each additional mile reduces the value of the car by 5.7 cents. In addition, the coefficient on the dummy variable representing the intermediate LT model was 1,487 (CI 1,078–1,875), indicating that the LT model is worth $1,487 more than the base LS model (the omitted category). The coefficient on the luxury

LTZ model was 2,730 (CI 2,035–3,426), suggesting that the price of a used LTZ is $2,730 above the base LS model, other things being equal. A Wald test of the joint significance of the two trim dummy variables rejects the null hypothesis that both coefficients are equal to zero at the 1% confidence level.

These results would normally be followed by a discussion that places the findings in the context of previous research, identifying areas of agreement and areas where these results differ from previous studies. Finally, it is often useful to identify questions that remain unanswered and suggest future areas for research. Chapter 15 provides more information on organizing the research paper.

12.7 SUMMARY OF COMMANDS USED IN THIS CHAPTER

This section summarizes all of the Stata code used in the chapter. In addition, all Stata code used throughout the book is summarized in Appendix 1.

Scatter plots and line of best fit

```
twoway (scatter Price Mileage)
twoway (scatter Price Mileage) (lfit Price Mileage)
```

Correlation

```
pwcorr Price Mileage
```

Regression

```
regress Price Mileage
regress Price Mileage LT LTZ
```

Three methods to generate dummy variables

Method 1:

```
gen LS = 0 if Trim==2 | Trim==3
replace LS = 1 if Trim==1
gen LT = 0 if Trim==1 | Trim==3
replace LT = 1 if Trim==2
gen LTZ = 0 if Trim==1 | Trim==2
replace LTZ = 1 if Trim==3
```

Method 2:

```
recode Trim (1=1) (2 3=0), gen(LS)
recode Trim (2=1) (1 3=0), gen(LT)
recode Trim (3=1) (1 2=0), gen(LTZ)
```

Method 3:

```
regress Price Mileage i.Trim
```

Calculate and graph predicted values

```
gen yhatLS = _b[_cons]+_b[Mileage]*Mileage
gen yhatLT = _b[_cons]+_b[Mileage]*Mileage + _b[LT]
gen yhatLTZ = _b[_cons]+_b[Mileage]*Mileage + _b[LTZ]
twoway (line yhatLS Mileage) (line yhatLT Mileage) ///
(line yhatLTZ Mileage)
```

Test the joint hypothesis that a set of coefficients are all equal to zero

```
test LT LTZ
```

Generate a table of regression results in Word format

```
outreg using "c:/Malibu model"
```

EXERCISES

1. You want to examine the relationship between a college's rank according to U.S. News and World Report and factors that may influence it such as their acceptance rate and the amount of the college's endowment or financial assets per full-time student.

   a. Using the "College Results 2013" data set, run a regression with the college rank (Rank) as the dependent variable and the acceptance rate (PctAdmit00) and endowment per full-time student in hundred thousand dollars per full-time equivalent (endow100000FTE) as the independent variables for national universities (if RankType==1). Then run the same regression for national liberal arts colleges (if RankType==2).

   b. Write out the equation for each of the two models using the coefficients from your results, rounding each coefficient to the nearest whole number.

c. If a national university has an endowment of 0.12 hundred thousand dollars per full-time student (or 12,000 dollars per full-time student) and its acceptance rate is 55%, what does the model predict for the rank of this university rounded to the nearest whole number?

d. What percentage of the variation in rank is explained by the model for national liberal arts colleges?

e. What is the null hypothesis for the F value in the two models? In each model, would you reject this hypothesis and why?

f. How would you interpret the coefficient for PctAdmit00 in each models? In other words, write out a full sentence that explains the meaning of the coefficient. Are they statistically significant?

g. Write a paragraph that explains the results of the two models for a scholarly journal. Be sure to comment on how the results of the two models compare with each other.

2. Suppose you have sample of 200 college students who are economics majors, business majors, and math majors. You run a regression to determine how absences affect their grades and generate the equation below. All of the coefficients are statistically significant at the 0.05 alpha level.

Grade point average = 3.5 – 0.2 Absences – 0.3 Economics major – 0.1 Business major

where

Grade point average = the cumulative grade point average of a student

Absences = the number of times that a student skips a class per term on average

Economics major = 1 if the student is an economics major and 0 if not

Business major = 1 if the student is a business major and 0 if not

Math major is the omitted category for major

a. Draw a graph of the equation and label the vertical intercept(s).

b. What is the slope of your line or lines in your graph?

c. Explain in words the meaning of the coefficient on absences.

d. Explain in words the meaning of the coefficient on economics major.

3. Violence in public schools has led to an increase in the total number of full-time security guards and other sworn law enforcement officers on school campuses. Use the School Survey on Crime and Safety (pu_ssocs16.dta) to examine the relation between the total number of disciplinary actions taken by a school (DISTOT16—the dependent variable) and the number of full-time security guards or officers on campus (SEC_FT16). Include the school size by creating dummy variables for size based on the variable FR_SIZE.

   a. Based on your results, interpret the coefficients on your dummy variables related to size.

   b. Interpret your results for the number of full-time security guards or officers on campus.

   c. Comment on the endogeneity problem of this regression equation related to disciplinary actions and security guards or law officers.

REFERENCES

Bailey, M. A. (2017). *Real econometrics: The right tools to answer important questions*. New York, NY: Oxford University Press.

Dallegro, J. A. (2018). Just what factors into the value of your used car. *Investopedia*. Retrieved from www.investopedia.com/articles/investing/090314/just-what-factors-value-your-used-car.asp?ad=dirN&qo= investopediaSiteSearch&qsrc=0&o=40186

Greene, W. H. (2018). *Econometric analysis*. New York, NY: Pearson.

Woolridge, J. M. (2016). *Introductory econometrics: A modern approach*. Mason, OH: South-Western Cengage Learning.

13

REGRESSION DIAGNOSTICS

Chapter Preview

Background	Linear regression analysis generates the best equation to describe the relationship between one dependent variable and one or more independent variables, but it depends on several assumptions about the data. This chapter discusses ways to test these assumptions and remedy the problem if it is found.
Measurement error	*Assumption:* Regression analysis assumes the independent variables are measured without error.
	Diagnosis: **sum ... detail, predict ... resid, predict ... cooksd**
	Remedies: Minimize errors in data collection. Try alternative indicators. Take into account in interpretation.
Specification error	*Assumption:* Functional form is correct and all relevant independent variables are included.
	Diagnosis: **rvpplot, rvfplot, ovtest**, test significance of new variables, quadratic terms, and interaction terms
	Remedy: Include new variables, quadratic terms, or interaction terms if statistically significant.
Multicollinearity	*Assumption:* Independent variables are not highly correlated with one another.
	Diagnosis: **correl, vif** test
	Remedy: Test joint significance of correlated variables and explain in text.

Heteroscedasticity	*Assumption:* Variance of residuals is constant.
	Diagnosis: **rvpplot, rvfplot, hettest**
	Remedy: **vce(robust)** option, generalized least squares
Nonnormality	*Assumption:* Residuals are normally distributed.
	Diagnosis: **sktest**
	Remedy: Transform variables, take into account in interpretation.
Endogeneity	*Assumption:* Independent variables are exogenous.
	Diagnosis: Largely based on theory and experience rather than statistical tests
	Remedy: Instrumental variables regression, panel data regression, and experimental methods

13.1 INTRODUCTION

In Chapter 12, we said that ordinary least squares (OLS) regression analysis gives us the equation that best fits the data, in the sense that it is the equation that minimizes the sum of squared residuals ($\sum e^2$). Under certain conditions, OLS gives us the best linear unbiased estimates (BLUE) of the coefficients.

- "Best" means the lowest variance of the error terms.

- "Linear" means that the dependent variable is a linear function of the independent variables.

- "Unbiased" means that the estimated coefficients will not be systematically higher or lower than the true coefficients across different samples.

What are the conditions needed for OLS results to be BLUE?

- The independent variables are measured without error.

- The regression equation is correctly specified, meaning there are no omitted variables and it uses the right functional form (e.g., linear, quadratic, logarithmic, etc.).

- None of the independent variables is perfectly correlated with any other independent variable.

- The variance of the errors is constant, and the error terms are not correlated with each other.

- The independent variables are exogenous.

One additional condition is convenient for the interpretation of the OLS results but not necessary for BLUE: that the error terms are normally distributed.

In this chapter, we look at what happens to OLS regressions if these conditions do not hold. We focus on the following issues:

- *Measurement error:* The independent variables are measured with error.

- *Specification error:* The equation in the model is missing important variables or has the wrong functional form.

- *Multicollinearity:* Two or more independent variables are perfectly or closely correlated with each other.

- *Heteroscedasticity:* The variance of the error term is not constant.[1]

- *Endogeneity:* The "independent" variables are influenced by the dependent variable or both dependent and independent variables are influenced by factors omitted from the model.

- *Nonnormality:* The error terms in the regression model are not normally distributed.

Below, we discuss each of these problems in turn. We consider the consequences of violating each assumption, how to test to see if the assumption is valid, and how to improve the analysis if the assumption is not valid.

13.2 MEASUREMENT ERROR

Regression analysis assumes that the dependent variable is measured with some error, but that the independent variables are measured without error. In actual research, particularly social science research, the independent variables are almost always subject to some measurement error, meaning that values of the variable in the database differ from the true values of the variable, due to errors or deception by the respondent, mistakes by the enumerator, data entry errors, or possibly corruption of the data in processing. In general, measurement error in an independent variable will cause its regression coefficient to be biased toward zero.[2] This will underestimate the size of the effect of the independent variable and will reduce the likelihood of detecting a real effect (this is Type II error of not rejecting a null hypothesis when it is false).

---

[1] We do not cover the problems associated with autocorrelation, meaning correlation between the error terms in different observations. This is a problem that mainly affects time-series regression analysis, which is a large topic that cannot be adequately summarized here.

[2] This is always true when there is just one independent variable and usually true when there are multiple independent variables.

We can demonstrate this by adding a random number to one of the independent variables in our Malibu data to simulate measurement error. Then we compare the results with and without the simulated "error." The Stata function **rnormal(*m,s*)** generates a normally distributed random variable with mean *m* and standard deviation *s*. In the example in Output 13.1, we add some artificial "measurement error" to the variable Mileage by adding a random number with mean 0 and standard deviation 3,800, roughly 10% of the mean value of Mileage. The **set seed** command ensures that anyone running these commands will get the same random numbers and the same results.[3]

The results in Output 13.1 show that the coefficient on the Mileage variable is now −0.054 rather than −0.057 in Output 12.3. By adding some "measurement error" to the Mileage variable, the estimated coefficient is now smaller in absolute value, reflecting the bias toward zero.

How do we find measurement errors? One approach is to look at the extreme values of individual variables. The **summarize** command with the **detail** option will show us some useful information about the distribution of a variable (Output 13.2).

✔ OUTPUT 13.1: MULTIPLE REGRESSION WITH ADDITIONAL MEASUREMENT ERROR

```
. set seed 2314

. gen MileageErr = Mileage + rnormal(0,3800)

. regress Price MileageErr LT LTZ
```

Source	SS	df	MS		
Model	891585092	3	297195031	Number of obs =	383
Residual	1.0082e+09	379	2660134.55	F(3, 379) =	111.72
				Prob > F =	0.0000
				R-squared =	0.4693
				Adj R-squared =	0.4651
Total	1.8998e+09	382	4973235.83	Root MSE =	1631

Price	Coef.	Std. Err.	t	P>|t|	[95% Conf. Interval]	
MileageErr	-.0544219	.0034341	-15.85	0.000	-.0611742	-.0476696
LT	1467.022	212.289	6.91	0.000	1049.61	1884.434
LTZ	2682.371	361.0611	7.43	0.000	1972.437	3392.305
_cons	15434.41	236.9127	65.15	0.000	14968.58	15900.24

[3] Like all statistical software, Stata generates pseudo-random numbers starting with a "seed." By fixing the seed, we can ensure that Stata generates the same set of random numbers in multiple runs or runs by different users. The "2314" is arbitrary, but the seed must be a positive integer.

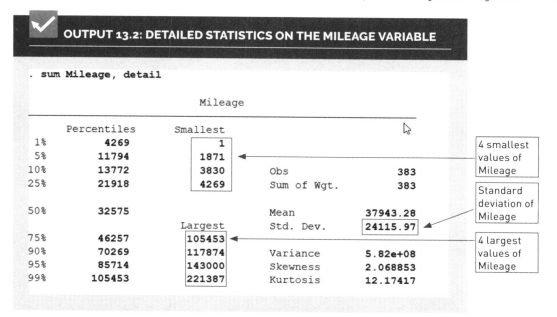

OUTPUT 13.2: DETAILED STATISTICS ON THE MILEAGE VARIABLE

```
. sum Mileage, detail

                              Mileage

          Percentiles      Smallest
   1%          4269              1
   5%         11794           1871
  10%         13772           3830        Obs               383
  25%         21918           4269        Sum of Wgt.       383

  50%         32575                       Mean         37943.28
                            Largest       Std. Dev.    24115.97
  75%         46257         105453
  90%         70269         117874        Variance      5.82e+08
  95%         85714         143000        Skewness      2.068853
  99%        105453         221387        Kurtosis      12.17417
```

A rule of thumb is to check observations where a value is more than 3 standard deviations below or above the mean. In this case, it would be 37,943 ± 3 * 24,116 or between –34,405 and 110,291. Of course, any negative numbers for Mileage would raise a red flag. The five largest values show that three of them (117,874, 143,000, and 221,387) are above the upper limit. Outliers are not necessarily errors but should be checked, if possible.

A second approach to finding suspicious data is to examine observations that are outliers in the relationship between dependent and independent variables. In other words, we check cases with large residuals (e), defined as the observed value of the dependent variable (y) minus the predicted value ($\hat{y}$). To calculate the residuals from the most recent regression analysis, we use the command **predict *newvar*, resid**, where *newvar* is the name we wish to assign to the residual. The first command below will calculate the residual and give it the name "e". The second command will give us various statistics about the residual, including the five largest and the five smallest (negative) values:

```
predict e, resid
sum e, detail
```

If we run these commands after the regression model in Output 12.3 (without the added measurement error), the results (not shown) reveal that the largest outlier is 10,598, meaning the actual price is $10,598 greater than the predicted price. We can look at the data for all observations with residuals greater than 10,000 with the following command (though we already know there is just one observation this large):

```
browse if e>10000
```

The observation (car) with the large residual turns out to be the one that has more than 200,000 miles, suggesting that it deserves further investigation.

The third approach is to look for observations that have the greatest influence, or "leverage," on the coefficients. An observation will have a lot of leverage if the value of an independent variable is far from its mean. Cook's distance indicator, or Cook's *D*, measures the effect of removing an observation on the estimated coefficients. Some researchers define an outlier as an observation with a Cook's *D* value greater than 1. Others look for observations where the Cook's *D* is at least three times greater than the mean value of Cook's *D*.

In Stata, we can calculate Cook's *D* for the most recent regression analysis with the **predict *newvar*, cooksd** command, where *newvar* is the name we want to give to

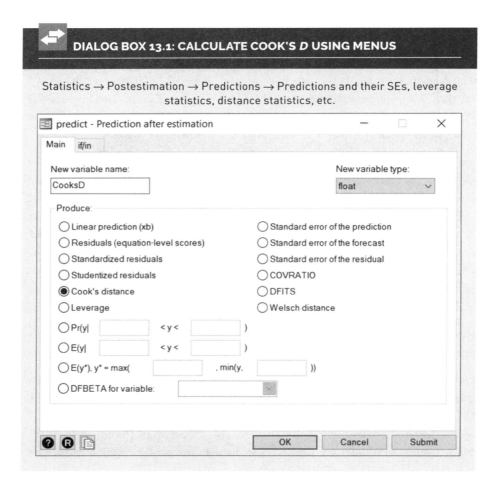

DIALOG BOX 13.1: CALCULATE COOK'S *D* USING MENUS

Statistics → Postestimation → Predictions → Predictions and their SEs, leverage statistics, distance statistics, etc.

the new variable, or by using the menu system (see Dialog Box 13.1). Then we can examine the outliers with the browse commands, as shown below.

```
predict CooksD, cooksd
browse if CooksD>1
```

In the Malibu data set, there is only one observation for which the Cook's D is greater than 1. It is the same car that had an extreme value of Mileage and a large residual. It is also visible in the scatter plot in Figure 12.9 as the car with more than 200,000 miles being sold for $14,955. This is a surprisingly high price for a car with more than 200,000 miles. After checking with the original online advertisement, we discovered that this was a data entry error: An extra digit had been added to the Mileage by mistake. We can correct the error with the **replace** command and rerun the regression as illustrated in Output 13.3.

After correcting the error, the coefficient on Mileage is −0.068 compared with −0.057 in the original model. In addition, the value of R^2 has increased from 0.49 in the original to 0.56 in this model. This illustrates the impact that an error in a single extreme observation can have on the estimated coefficients and the goodness of fit.

Finding this error was relatively easy: The same observation was an extreme value of one of the independent variables (Mileage), had the largest residual, and had a Cook's D larger than 1. Furthermore, we were able to check the original data (online

OUTPUT 13.3: REGRESSION MODEL AFTER CORRECTING ERROR

```
. replace Mileage=22138 if Mileage==221387
(1 real change made)

. regress Price Mileage LT LTZ

      Source |       SS           df       MS            Number of obs   =       383
-------------+----------------------------------         F(3, 379)       =    161.44
       Model | 1.0658e+09          3   355256326         Prob > F        =    0.0000
    Residual |  834007107        379  2200546.46         R-squared       =    0.5610
-------------+----------------------------------         Adj R-squared   =    0.5575
       Total | 1.8998e+09        382  4973235.83         Root MSE        =    1483.4

       Price |      Coef.   Std. Err.      t    P>|t|     [95% Conf. Interval]
-------------+----------------------------------------------------------------
     Mileage |  -.0679225   .0034718   -19.56   0.000    -.074749   -.0610961
          LT |     1373.3   193.3688     7.10   0.000    993.0901    1753.51
         LTZ |   2795.833   328.6218     8.51   0.000    2149.683   3441.984
       _cons |   15976.78   223.8593    71.37   0.000    15536.62   16416.95
```

advertisements) and correct the mistake. Unfortunately, not all data cleaning is this easy. To begin with, not all outliers are caused by measurement error; some cars really do have more than 200,000 miles. In addition, not all errors are outliers: It is quite possible for a measurement error not to be an extreme value and to have a low value of Cook's *D*. Nonetheless, the remedies for measurement error often depend on errors being outliers. Below are a few guidelines to reduce measurement error:

- The best way to minimize measurement errors is to avoid them in the first place with careful data collection and data entry. Software for online surveys or for electronic data collection often allow the researcher to set upper and lower limits. If one tries to enter a number outside this range, the program can be designed so that the user is either warned that it is an extreme value or blocked from entering an extreme value.

- In cleaning the data, the researcher should replace a number that is impossible (e.g., age = 140) with a missing value. However, it is not good practice to replace numbers that are merely unlikely (e.g., age = 100). As mentioned above, not all outliers are data errors.

- Some researchers use rules for "trimming" data, such as eliminating values that are more than 3 standard deviations from the mean. This practice should be used conservatively and must be disclosed in writing up the results.

- Some researchers choose to use alternative regression methods that are less sensitive to outliers. These methods are briefly described at the end of Section 13.6.

- Finally, it is always useful to take into account possible effects of measurement error in interpreting the results of regression analysis. As mentioned above, measurement errors tend to bias regression coefficients toward zero.

Researchers must take care that data cleaning follows transparent and consistent rules and that the procedures are documented when describing the results. Furthermore, the cleaning should never be driven by an effort to achieve a certain outcome. Aggressive data cleaning to achieve a desired finding has resulted in several high-profile cases of research fraud, with severe professional consequences.

13.3 SPECIFICATION ERROR

OLS regression assumes that the specification of the regression equation is correct, meaning it has the right independent variables and uses the right function to describe the relationship between dependent and independent variables. Below, we describe three types of specification errors, how to diagnose each type, and some methods to address the problem.

13.3.1 Types of Specification Errors

Three common ways that the functional form may be incorrect are (1) a relevant variable is missing from the equation, (2) it fails to take into account nonlinearity in the relationship between the dependent variable and one or more independent variables, and (3) it does not incorporate interaction between independent variables.

13.3.1.1 Omitted Variables

The first type of specification error is omitted variables. Suppose a relevant independent variable is omitted from a linear regression model, where "relevant" means that it influences the dependent variable. If the omitted variable is uncorrelated with the other independent variables, then the estimated coefficients in the model are unbiased. In this case, the only problem associated with omitting the variable is that the explanatory power of the model (measured by the adjusted R^2) is not as high as it could be. On the other hand, if the omitted variable *is* correlated with one or more independent variables in the model, it creates another problem: The estimated coefficients of those variables will be biased.

For example, if the price of used cars is affected by both the mileage and the age, but only mileage is included in the model, the coefficient on mileage will "pick up" some of the effect of age (given that older cars tend to have higher mileage). Thus, the coefficient on mileage will be too large, in absolute value, reflecting the effect of both age and mileage. Later in this section, we will test this using our Malibu data set.

13.3.1.2 Incorrect Functional Form

The second type of specification error is incorrect functional form, meaning the use of an incorrect function describing the relationship between dependent and independent variables. The most common problem with functional form is that the model is linear but the data follow a nonlinear pattern. For example, in Figure 13.1, the data clearly follow a nonlinear U-shaped relationship. If we estimate the relationship as if it were linear, we will get the best straight line that fits the data (the upward sloping red line), but it will not be a good description of the data. The predicted values of the dependent variable would overestimate the observed values over some range of the independent variable and underestimate them over another range. Modeling a nonlinear relationship as linear could also result in heteroscedasticity, which could invalidate the estimated standard errors (as discussed later). Finally, using a linear model on a nonlinear relationship reduces the explanatory power of the model. If

FIGURE 13.1 ● MODELING A NONLINEAR RELATIONSHIP WITH A LINEAR MODEL

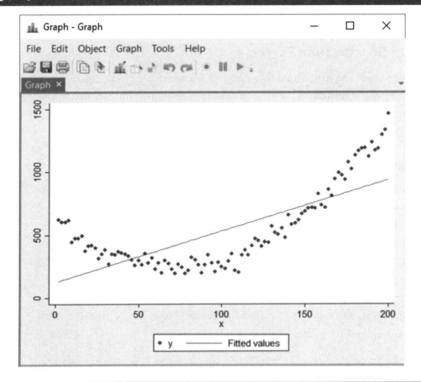

the nonlinearity is strong (as in Figure 13.1), the predictions from a linear model are almost worthless.

In the Malibu regression model, we use a linear equation to represent the relationship between Price and Mileage, meaning that each additional mile has the same effect on the value of the car (−6.8 cents in the most recent version) regardless of the mileage on the car. But what if the actual relationship is nonlinear? For example, one would think that the per-mile depreciation would be greater for relatively new cars with low mileage than for high-mileage cars. Later, we will test this hypothesis.

13.3.1.3 Missing Interaction Terms

The third type of specification error is that interaction between the independent variables is ignored in the model. In the regression models we have considered so far, the effect of each independent variable on the dependent variable is not affected by the other independent variables. However, the effect of one independent variable on the dependent variable may depend on one or more other independent variables.

In the model of Malibu prices, we assume that the effect of mileage on price is not affected by the trim level. In other words, the model assumes that an additional 1,000 miles has the same effect on the price of a Malibu LS as it does on the price of a Malibu LT and a Malibu LTZ. This is reflected in Figure 12.10, where the three lines are parallel. The reason these lines are parallel is *not* because the data tell us that all three trim models depreciate at the same rate. Instead, they are parallel because the functional form forces them to be parallel. Specifically, there is only one coefficient to represent the effect of mileage on price.

Interaction between two independent variables can be represented by a term with the product of the two independent variables, as shown at the end of the following equation:

$$y = \beta_0 + \beta_1 x_1 + \beta_2 x_2 + \beta_3 x_1 x_2 \tag{13.1}$$

In Section 13.3.3, we show how this approach can be used to test whether the effect of mileage on price differs across models.

13.3.2 Diagnosing Specification Error

How do we diagnose specification error? It is useful to start by examining patterns in the residuals. A scatter plot of the residuals as a function of each of the continuous independent variables may show a U pattern or inverted-U pattern indicating a non-linear relationship. For example, we can plot the residuals against any independent variable using the **rvpplot** command ("rvp" refers to residual vs. predictor).

As mentioned above, we suspect that the relationship between Price and Mileage might be nonlinear, with per-mile depreciation being stronger (more negative) when the mileage is low and weaker (less negative) as the mileage increases. We can run **rvpplot** after the Malibu regression model to check this using the menu system (see Dialog Box 13.2) or with the following command:

```
rvpplot Mileage
```

As shown in Figure 13.2, the scatter plot does not indicate any obvious nonlinearity, but later we show how to test for nonlinearity. It is also useful to inspect the pattern of residuals against the predicted (or fitted) values of the dependent variable. This can be done with the command **rvfplot**, where "rvf" means residuals versus fitted. This command is illustrated in Section 13.5 in the discussion of heteroscedasticity.

Another method to test for specification error is to apply the Ramsey Regression Equation Specification Error Test (RESET). In Stata, the Ramsey test is implemented using the command **estat ovtest**, which is short for postestimation statistic omitted variable test.[4]

---

[4] This and other post-estimation statistics will work without including **estat**, but Stata's online help files warn that the shorter form is out-of-date.

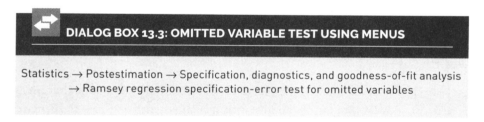

The default version (**estat ovtest**) adds powers of the predicted dependent variable ($\hat{y}$) to the original list of independent variables. An alternative version (**estat ovtest, rhs**) adds powers of the independent variables as explanatory variables ("rhs" refers to right-hand side variables). If the coefficients on the new variables are jointly significant, we reject the null hypothesis of no specification error.

FIGURE 13.2 ● SCATTER PLOT OF RESIDUALS AGAINST MILEAGE

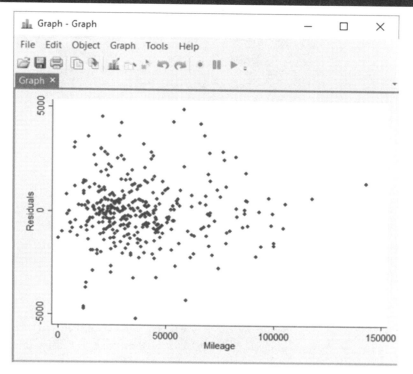

To demonstrate the omitted variable test, we run the default version after the Malibu regression using the menu system (see Dialog Box 13.3) or the command in Output 13.4.

The null hypothesis is that the model has no omitted variables, and the result in Output 13.4 indicates that we cannot reject the null hypothesis that there are no omitted variables. We also ran the **rhs** version of the test (not shown), which also fails to reject the null hypothesis. In other words, these tests do not reveal evidence of omitted variables. This does not mean that other variables would not be statistically significant in this model. But at least, we can be assured that there are no powers of the existing variables that would be statistically significant if added.

13.3.3 Correcting Specification Error

The remedy for specification error is relatively straightforward if we have additional relevant variables in our data set: We add to the model any omitted variables that are statistically significant and experiment with alternative functional forms to find a better fit. Below, we consider ways to check for specification error due to (a)

```
  ✓    OUTPUT 13.4: OMITTED VARIABLE TEST

. estat ovtest

Ramsey RESET test using powers of the fitted values of Price
      Ho:  model has no omitted variables
                  F(3, 376) =        0.69
                  Prob > F =        0.5608

.
end of do-file
```

omitted variables, (b) nonlinear relationships, and (c) interaction between independent variables.

First, we consider the case of specification error due to omitted variables. As discussed earlier, any correlation between an omitted variable and an included variable will bias the estimate of the coefficient on the included variable.

For example, the age of the car is not taken into account in our Malibu regression model, and age is likely to be correlated with mileage. For this reason, it is important to add an age variable to get an unbiased estimate of the coefficient for mileage. We first calculate the age from the model year of the car, then run the regression as illustrated in Output 13.5.

Output 13.5 shows that the coefficient on the Age variable is negative and statistically significant. With each additional year, the price of a Malibu declines by about $684 after controlling for mileage and trim level. Also, the coefficient on Mileage changed from −0.068 in Output 13.3 to −0.058 in this version. Mileage and Age are positively correlated, so in the earlier regression, the variable Mileage was picking up the effect of both mileage and age. When Age is included as a variable, the coefficient on Mileage is closer to zero and probably more accurate.

Second, theory or inspection of the data may lead us to believe that the relationship between the dependent variable and one or more independent variables is nonlinear. One way to represent a nonlinear relationship between the dependent variable (y) and an independent variable (x) is to add variables representing powers of the independent variable, usually x^2 and occasionally higher power such as x^3. Although the relationship between y and x is now nonlinear, it is still considered a linear regression

OUTPUT 13.5: REGRESSION CORRECTING FOR SPECIFICATION ERROR

```
. gen Age = 2017-Year

. regress Price Mileage Age LT LTZ
```

Source	SS	df	MS		
Model	1.1377e+09	4	284413289	Number of obs =	383
Residual	762122931	378	2016198.23	F(4, 378) =	141.06
				Prob > F =	0.0000
				R-squared =	0.5988
Total	1.8998e+09	382	4973235.83	Adj R-squared =	0.5946
				Root MSE =	1419.9

Price	Coef.	Std. Err.	t	P>|t|	[95% Conf. Interval]	
Mileage	-.0580374	.0037127	-15.63	0.000	-.0653376	-.0507372
Age	-683.8149	114.5219	-5.97	0.000	-908.9947	-458.6351
LT	1221.144	186.8379	6.54	0.000	853.7722	1588.516
LTZ	2478.576	319.0117	7.77	0.000	1851.316	3105.836
_cons	17578.08	343.2694	51.21	0.000	16903.13	18253.04

model because it is *linear in the parameters*, meaning that (a) the left side of the equation is the dependent variable (*y*) or some transformation of *y* and (b) the right side of the equation is a linear combination of independent variables (*x*) and/or transformed versions of those *x* variables.

In the analysis of the prices of used Malibus, we considered whether the per-mile depreciation might be greater for low-mileage cars than for high-mileage cars. In other words, is the relationship between Price and Mileage nonlinear? We can test this directly by calculating a quadratic term (Mileage2) and adding it to the regression model, as shown in Output 13.6.

The low *t* statistic and the high *p*-value on Mileage2 indicate that the quadratic term is not statistically significant at the 5% level (or even at the 10% level). This confirms our intuition from the graph in Figure 13.2 that the relationship between price and mileage does not have any obvious curvature. It should be noted that there may be nonlinearities that are too small for our sample to detect. If we had a much larger sample, say 2,000 cars, including more relatively new cars, the standard errors would be smaller and we would be able to detect smaller effects, possibly including nonlinear effects.

OUTPUT 13.6: MULTIPLE REGRESSION WITH QUADRATIC TERM

```
. gen Mileage2 = Mileage^2

. regress Price Mileage Mileage2 Age LT LTZ
```

Source	SS	df	MS			
				Number of obs	=	383
				F(5, 377)	=	113.50
Model	1.1415e+09	5	228297847	Prob > F	=	0.0000
Residual	758286851	377	2011370.96	R-squared	=	0.6009
				Adj R-squared	=	0.5956
Total	1.8998e+09	382	4973235.83	Root MSE	=	1418.2

Price	Coef.	Std. Err.	t	P>|t|	[95% Conf. Interval]	
Mileage	-.071764	.0106087	-6.76	0.000	-.0926237	-.0509043
Mileage2	1.36e-07	9.87e-08	1.38	0.168	-5.78e-08	3.31e-07
Age	-704.6508	115.3754	-6.11	0.000	-931.5109	-477.7908
LT	1202.033	187.1265	6.42	0.000	834.0904	1569.975
LTZ	2483.554	318.65	7.79	0.000	1857	3110.108
_cons	17903.16	415.8842	43.05	0.000	17085.41	18720.9

New Mileage squared variable

Adding a quadratic term is only one way to represent nonlinear relationships in regression analysis. Other widely used transformations include logarithms of y and/or the x variables:

$$y = \beta_0 + \beta_1 \ln(x_1) + \beta_2 \ln(x_2)$$

$$\ln(y) = \beta_0 + \beta_1 x_1 + \beta_2 x_2$$

$$\ln(y) = \beta_0 + \beta_1 \ln(x_1) + \beta_2 \ln(x_2)$$

Because these examples are linear in the parameters, they can be estimated using OLS and implemented by the **regress** command in Stata. Appendix 8 illustrates graphically examples of these nonlinear functional forms and explains how to calculate the marginal effect of x on y for each one.

The third type of specification error is missing interaction terms. Now we can return to the question of whether the three trim levels (the Malibu LS, LT, and LTZ) lose value at the same rate. In other words, is the mileage coefficient the same for all three models? Or is there interaction between the Mileage variable and the dummy variables representing the model? To answer this question, we calculate new variables that are the product of the Mileage variable and trim dummy variables. The new model can be written as follows:

$$Price = \beta_0 + \beta_1 * Mileage + \beta_2 * Age + \beta_3 * LT + \beta_4 * LTZ$$
$$+ \beta_5 * Mileage * LT + \beta_6 * Mileage * LTZ + \varepsilon$$

The first two terms on the second line are the interaction terms. The effect of Mileage on Price can be derived as follows:

$$\frac{\partial Price}{\partial Mileage} = \beta_1 + \beta_5 * LT + \beta_6 * LTZ$$

Based on this, we know that for the Malibu LS, for which LT = LTZ = 0:

$$\frac{\partial Price}{\partial Mileage} = \beta_1$$

For the Malibu LT, for which LT = 1 and LTZ = 0:

$$\frac{\partial Price}{\partial Mileage} = \beta_1 + \beta_5$$

And for the Malibu LTZ, for which LT = 0 and LTZ = 1:

$$\frac{\partial Price}{\partial Mileage} = \beta_1 + \beta_6$$

These equations show that the two interaction terms allow the three trim levels (LS, LT, and LTZ) to have different per-mile depreciation rates. On the other hand, if β_5 and β_6 are not significantly different from zero, it implies that all three types of Malibu depreciate at the same rate, that is, β_1. Output 13.7 shows the calculation of the two interaction terms, the **regress** command, and the output.

The results in Output 13.7 indicate that neither of the two interaction terms, MilexLT and MilexLTZ, is statistically significant. We can use the **test** command to carry out a joint test of the null hypothesis that both coefficients are zero. The results (not shown) indicate that we cannot reject the hypothesis that both coefficients are zero. In other words, there is no evidence that the per-mile depreciation rate differs across the Malibu LS, LT, and LTZ models.

In Output 13.7, we calculated the two interaction terms using the **gen** command because it clearly shows how they are defined. However, Stata offers an alternative approach that is more efficient, though somewhat less transparent. In Chapter 12, we described "factor variable" notation, which allows us to insert i.Trim in the **regress** command to indicate that we want the two dummy variables representing Trim (LT and LTZ), saving us the trouble of defining the two dummy variables with the **gen** command. We can also use this notation to add interaction terms to a regression model. In the command below, **i.Trim#c.Mileage** inserts the two interaction terms in the list of independent variables.

```
regress Price Mileage Age i.Trim i.Trim#c.Mileage
```

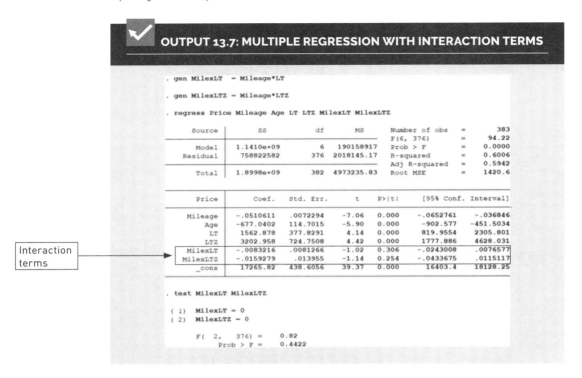

Interaction terms

```
OUTPUT 13.7: MULTIPLE REGRESSION WITH INTERACTION TERMS

. gen MilexLT = Mileage*LT

. gen MilexLTZ = Mileage*LTZ

. regress Price Mileage Age LT LTZ MilexLT MilexLTZ

      Source |       SS           df       MS            Number of obs   =       383
-------------+------------------------------            F(6, 376)       =     94.22
       Model | 1.1410e+09          6   190158917        Prob > F        =    0.0000
    Residual | 758822582         376   2018145.17       R-squared       =    0.6006
-------------+------------------------------            Adj R-squared   =    0.5942
       Total | 1.8998e+09        382   4973235.83       Root MSE        =    1420.6

-------------+----------------------------------------------------------------------
       Price |      Coef.   Std. Err.      t    P>|t|     [95% Conf. Interval]
-------------+----------------------------------------------------------------------
     Mileage |  -.0510611   .0072294    -7.06   0.000    -.0652761    -.036846
         Age |  -677.0402   114.7015    -5.90   0.000    -902.577    -451.5034
          LT |   1562.878   377.8291     4.14   0.000     819.9554    2305.801
         LTZ |   3202.958   724.7508     4.42   0.000     1777.886    4628.031
     MilexLT |  -.0083216   .0081266    -1.02   0.306    -.0243008    .0076577
    MilexLTZ |  -.0159279    .013955    -1.14   0.254    -.0433675    .0115117
       _cons |   17265.82   438.6056    39.37   0.000     16403.4     18128.25
-------------+----------------------------------------------------------------------

. test MilexLT MilexLTZ

 ( 1)  MilexLT = 0
 ( 2)  MilexLTZ = 0

       F( 2,  376) =    0.82
            Prob > F =    0.4422
```

As in Chapter 12, i.Trim represents LT and LTZ, # refers to interaction, and c.Mileage indicates that Mileage is a continuous variable.[5] This **regress** command will generate the same model and same results as those in Output 13.7 without the need to define MilexLT and MilexLTZ. The advantage of this notation becomes even greater with a large number of interaction terms.

In summary, we addressed the problem of specification error in three ways. First, we ran the Ramsey RESET, which did not find evidence of specification error. Second, we tried including a mileage-squared term, but it was not statistically significant, implying that the relationship between price and mileage is not quadratic. Last, we tested the use of interaction terms between trim level and mileage, but the results do not suggest that the rate of depreciation differs across the three types of Malibu. Since the quadratic term and the interaction terms were not statistically significant, the rest of this chapter will use the model from Output 13.5 for additional diagnostic tests.

---

[5] To be more precise, the # symbol refers to multiplication. For example, we could represent the Mileage squared variable as c.Mileage#c.Mileage in the **regress** command, making it unnecessary to define Mileage2 with the **gen** command.

13.4 MULTICOLLINEARITY

Multicollinearity refers to a condition in which two or more independent variables are closely correlated with one another. The technical definition is that a linear combination of some set of independent variables is exactly zero or close to zero.

Perfect multicollinearity refers to the case where there is a linear combination of independent variables that is exactly equal to zero. For example, if one mistakenly includes variables for the male population, the female population, and the total population, then there exists a linear combination (males + females − total) that is equal to zero for all observations. If there is perfect multicollinearity, the model cannot be estimated. In this case, Stata will simply omit one of the collinear variables and report results for the rest of the model. As an aside, this explains why we must omit one of the dummy variables representing a categorical variable if there is a constant. For example, if we include dummy variables for all three trim levels in our Malibu regression model, then the sum of the three dummies minus the variable associated with the constant (1) would be zero for all observations.

Imperfect multicollinearity refers to the case where there is a linear combination of independent variables that is close to zero. Because perfect multicollinearity is rare (and often the result of a mistake in coding), imperfect multicollinearity is often referred to simply as multicollinearity. Multicollinearity can occur if the model includes multiple variables that are measuring similar concepts, such as household income and expenditure or two tests of intelligence. It results in large standard errors of the coefficients and thus large confidence intervals. This is because the data do not allow us to estimate the effect of each variable independently with much accuracy. However, (imperfect) multicollinearity is not a violation of the assumptions behind OLS regression, so OLS results are still the best linear unbiased estimates (BLUE).

A simple way to identify multicollinearity is by creating a correlation matrix with the independent variables. If any of the correlation coefficients are greater than 0.8 or 0.9,

OUTPUT 13.8: CORRELATION AMONG INDEPENDENT VARIABLES

```
. correl Mileage Age LT LTZ
(obs=383)

             |  Mileage      Age       LT      LTZ

     Mileage |   1.0000
         Age |   0.4465   1.0000
          LT |  -0.1682  -0.1353   1.0000
         LTZ |   0.1337  -0.0450  -0.4600   1.0000
```

there is likely to be a problem of multicollinearity. The results (shown in Output 13.8) indicate that none of the pairs of independent variables is highly correlated.

A more advanced test is the variance inflation factor, or VIF, which is calculated for each independent variable. The VIF for independent variable i is calculated as follows:

$$\text{VIF}_i = \frac{1}{1 - R_i^2}$$

where R_i^2 is obtained from regressing X_i on all the other independent variables. If an independent variable is closely correlated with other independent variables, the R^2 of this regression will be close to 1.0 and the VIF factor will be large. If an independent variable is not correlated with any other independent variable, R^2 will be close to 0 and the VIF will be close to 1. There is no consensus on the VIF threshold for considering multicollinearity a problem, but a rule of thumb is that a VIF greater than 10 deserves attention, but some researchers prefer a threshold of 4 (O'Brien, 2007).

In Stata, this test can be implemented with the **estat vif** command or with the menu system (see Dialog Box 13.4). Like other postestimation commands, it uses the results from the most recent regression model. The test in Output 13.9 is based on the model from Output 13.5, which included the variables Mileage, Age, LT, and LTZ, but did not include the quadratic term or the interaction terms.

Since the VIF values are less than 2, they indicate that multicollinearity is not an issue in our analysis of the price of used Malibu cars.

What is the remedy for multicollinearity that renders two closely correlated independent variables statistically insignificant? Ideally, the researcher would collect a larger sample of data so that each coefficient can be measured with greater precision despite the multicollinearity. In cases where this is not possible, some researchers propose dropping one of the correlated variables so that the remaining one becomes statistically significant. However, this "solution" just introduces omitted variable bias, because the included variable picks up some of the effect of the omitted variable. In other words, the results are misleading because they exaggerate the effect

---

DIALOG BOX 13.4: TEST OF MULTICOLLINEARITY USING MENUS

Statistics → Postestimation → Specification, diagnostics, and goodness-of-fit analysis → Variance inflation factors

---

OUTPUT 13.9: TEST FOR MULTICOLLINEARITY

```
. estat vif
```

Variable	VIF	1/VIF
LT	1.31	0.762368
LTZ	1.31	0.763365
Age	1.29	0.774836
Mileage	1.29	0.775296
Mean VIF	1.30	

of the included variable and ignore the effect of the excluded variable. For this reason, O'Brien (2007) cautions that some of the remedies for multicollinearity may be worse than the original problem.

A better approach is to test the combined effect of the two variables by running an F test of the joint hypothesis that both coefficients are equal to zero. In Stata, this is implemented with the command **test x1 x2**. If the null hypothesis is rejected, the researcher can report that two variables are jointly significant, but the effects of each variable cannot be independently measured because of the close correlation between the two.

13.5 HETEROSCEDASTICITY

An important assumption behind OLS regression is that the variance of the error term is constant. In other words, OLS assumes that the dispersion of the errors is the same throughout the sample of observations. This is called homoscedasticity. However, in practice, the variance of the errors may vary, a condition called heteroscedasticity. Figure 13.3 shows what heteroscedasticity looks like on a graph. The residuals (e) terms are small (in absolute value) for some values of x but are much larger for other values of x, suggesting that the variance of the (unobserved) errors is not constant.

In a regression model of food spending as a function of income, the errors might be larger among high-income households than among low-income households. This is an example of heteroscedasticity being a function of an independent variable. Or in our model of Malibu prices, the errors might be greater for more expensive cars. In this case, heteroscedasticity would be a function of the dependent variable.

FIGURE 13.3 ● **EXAMPLE OF HETEROSCEDASTICITY**

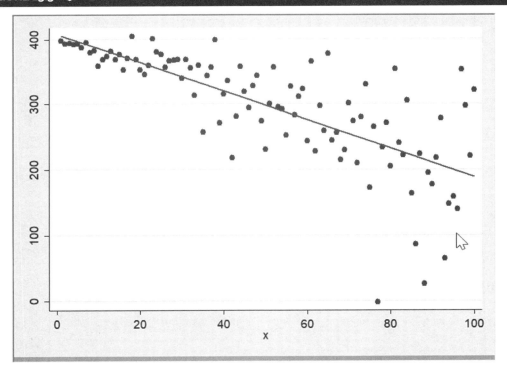

DIALOG BOX 13.5: PLOT OF RESIDUALS AND FITTED DEPENDENT VARIABLE USING MENUS

Graphics → Regression diagnostic plots → Residual-versus-fitted

What are the consequences of using OLS regression when heteroscedasticity is present? The estimated coefficients are still unbiased but (a) the estimated coefficients are not *efficient*, meaning that they do not make use of all available data, and (b) the OLS standard errors of the coefficients are incorrectly measured.

We can visually check for heteroscedasticity using the **rvfplot** command, which plots the residuals $(e = y - \hat{y})$ against the fitted (or predicted) values of the dependent variable $(\hat{y})$ for the most recent regression analysis run in Stata. If we run the **rvfplot** command or use the menu system (see Dialog Box 13.5) after the regression analysis of the Malibu data in Output 13.5, we get the graph in Figure 13.4.

FIGURE 13.4 ● SCATTER PLOT OF RESIDUALS AGAINST PREDICTED PRICES

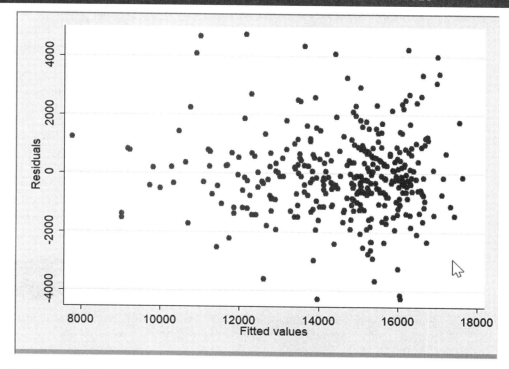

In this graph, the variance of the residuals is represented by the degree of vertical dispersion of the dots around the horizontal center line. The degree of dispersion does not seem to vary much from left to right, suggesting that heteroscedasticity is weak or nonexistent.

We can also check for heteroscedasticity by plotting the residuals against each of the continuous independent variables using the command **rvpplot**. In the Malibu regression, we would run **rvpplot Mileage** and **rvpplot Age** to see if the variance of the residuals differs across values of these variables. This command was demonstrated in Section 13.3 as a tool to check for nonlinearity.

The main statistical test for heteroscedasticity is the Breusch–Pagan/Cook–Weisberg, which assumes that the variance of the error term is a function of either the predicted value of the dependent variable ($\hat{y}$) or some set of independent variables (x). Multiple versions of the Breusch–Pagan/Cook–Weisberg test can be implemented with the Stata command **estat hettest**. Here are some of the more common options:

- **estat hettest** tests whether the variance of the residuals is a function of the predicted values of the dependent variable and that the errors are normally distributed.

- **estat hettest** *varlist* (where *varlist* is a list of independent variables) tests whether the variance of the residuals is a function of the independent variables listed. It also assumes that the errors are normally distributed.

- **estat hettest rhs** tests whether the variance of the residuals is a function of all the independent variables ("rhs" refers to variables on the right-hand side of the equation).

- **estat hettest, iid** tests for heteroscedasticity without assuming that the errors are normally distributed. It can be combined with *varlist* or **rhs**.

To run the Breusch–Pagan/Cook–Weisberg test for heteroscedasticity in the Malibu price model, we can use the **estat hettest** command with the **iid** option or the menu system (see Dialog Box 13.6; we use the **iid** option because, in the next section, we

DIALOG BOX 13.6: HETEROSCEDASTICITY TEST USING MENUS

Statistics → Postestimation → Specification, diagnostics, and goodness-of-fit analysis → Tests for heteroscedasticity → Select N*R2 version of the score test

✓ OUTPUT 13.10: TEST FOR HETEROSCEDASTICITY

```
. estat hettest, iid

Breusch-Pagan / Cook-Weisberg test for heteroskedasticity
        Ho: Constant variance
        Variables: fitted values of Price

        chi2(1)     =       0.04
        Prob > chi2 =     0.8441
```

test and reject the null hypothesis of normally distributed residuals). Like all the post-estimation commands in this chapter, **estat hettest** will analyze the most recently run regression model.

Following the model of Malibu prices from Output 13.5 again, Output 13.10 shows the test for heteroscedasticity and the results. The high p-value indicates that we cannot reject the null hypothesis of homoscedasticity in our model. In other words, we did not find evidence that our residuals violate the OLS assumption of constant variance of the error term.

If we find evidence of heteroscedasticity, there are two types of remedy. The first is to run a regression with robust standard errors, also called Huber–White or sandwich standard errors. This is the easiest and most common approach. It uses a different method to calculate the standard error of each coefficient, resulting in a different confidence interval and p-value for each coefficient. However, the estimated coefficients are the same as the OLS estimates. In Stata, robust standard errors can be implemented by adding the **vce(robust)** option to the **regress** command, as shown below.

regress y x1 x2, vce(robust)

A second approach to dealing with heteroscedasticity is to use a generalized least squares (GLS) analysis, in which the variance of the residuals is estimated as a function of variables in the model. The variance estimates are then used to give greater weight to observations with lower variance. The advantage of GLS is that it adjusts the coefficients, making use of information about the differences in the variance of the error terms. The disadvantage is that it requires good knowledge of how the variance varies across observations, which can be difficult to obtain. A more detailed description of GLS regression is, however, beyond the scope of this book. Interested readers may consult Greene (2018) and Woolridge (2016).

13.6 ENDOGENEITY

It is true that "correlation does not imply causation," but with careful use of data and methods, regression analysis *can* imply causality. The challenge is to ensure that the independent variables are *exogenous*. In statistical terms, independent variables are exogenous if they are uncorrelated with the error term (ε). If any of the independent variables are correlated with the error term, the model has an endogeneity problem. With endogeneity, the OLS coefficients are biased and may also be inconsistent, in that, as the sample size increases, the estimated coefficient will not converge toward the true value of the coefficient.

Under what conditions would an independent variable be correlated with the error terms? There are at least two situations where this may occur.[6]

- The independent variable is influenced by the dependent variable. This is called reverse causation.

- The independent variable and the dependent variable are both affected by a variable that has been omitted from the model. The omitted variable is sometimes called a confounding factor.

Endogeneity is a serious problem in the use of regression analysis, particularly in the social sciences and other fields where it is difficult to run a controlled experiment. Most of the techniques for addressing endogeneity involve advanced methods that are beyond the scope of this book. Nonetheless, we provide a brief description because it is important to recognize the nature of the problem, even before we have learned the techniques for controlling it.

In our Malibu regression model, we can be fairly confident that trim level, mileage, and age of the car are not influenced by the price because these characteristics predate the setting of the price. But there may be omitted variables that are correlated with both the dependent variable and one or more independent variables. For example, suppose LTZ owners keep their cars cleaner than LS and LT owners. If cleanliness improves the resale value of a car, then the LTZ dummy coefficient will be biased upward because it captures the effect of being the upscale model *and* the effect of being cleaner than average.

And consider the case of a study estimating the effect of the size of the police force on the crime rate (see Levitt, 1997). The research question is, "Does hiring more

---

[6] Technically, correlation between the independent variables and the error term is the underlying cause of problems associated with using OLS when there is measurement error in the independent variables (described in Section 13.2) and specification error (described in Section 13.3). However, for teaching purposes, we find it useful to consider these separate topics.

police officers reduce the crime rate?" The problem is that areas with high crime rates are likely to hire more officers to address the problem. In other words, both variables influence each other. If we ignore the endogeneity and use OLS regression to estimate the crime rate per 1,000 inhabitants (y) as a function of the size of the police force per 1,000 inhabitants (x) and other factors, we may even get a positive coefficient. But clearly, we cannot conclude that expanding the police force increases the crime rate. The explanation is that when the crime rate increases, local governments respond by increasing the size of their police force. In other words, the crime rates (y) can influence the size of the police force (x), an example of reverse causation. This demonstrates the point that endogeneity can generate biased coefficients, even changing the sign of the coefficient.

One strategy for dealing with endogeneity is to use *panel data*, that is, data covering multiple units (e.g., households or counties) over multiple time periods (e.g., months or years). If we could assemble data for crime rates and size of police force for 1,000 counties over 20 years, we could estimate the changes in crime rates as a function of changes in the size of the police force in previous year(s). The time difference can reduce or eliminate the endogeneity caused by reverse causation. Stata has a set of commands for implementing panel data analysis, including **xtreg** (x refers to cross-sectional and t refers to time series), but panel data analysis is a large topic and is outside the scope of this book.

A second strategy is to use instrumental variables, defined as one or more variables that are correlated with the endogenous "independent" variable (size of police force) but not associated with the dependent variable (crime rate). Levitt (1997) used the number of firemen as an instrument for the size of the police force. The two are likely to be correlated because they are both affected by changes in the local government budget and decisions about how much to spend on public services, but the crime rate probably has little effect on the number of firemen employed by the city. First, we estimate the size of the police force (x) as a function of the number of firemen (z), and then we estimate the crime rate (y) as a function of the *predicted* size of the police force ($\hat{x}$) based on the first-stage analysis. The coefficient in the second regression is based on only those changes in the police force that were exogenous (changes in county budget and priorities), rather than changes driven by the variation in the crime rate. Stata will implement instrumental variables regression with the **ivregress** command. However, identifying a good instrument is often difficult. We can test statistically whether the instrument is a good predictor of the endogenous independent variable, but it is not possible to test whether it has an independent effect on the dependent variable. Weak instruments will cause biased estimates of the parameters, which may be worse than the bias caused by the endogeneity.

A third strategy for addressing endogeneity is to carry out an experiment. Suppose we could provide funding to increase the police force by 10% in 100 randomly selected counties, while selecting another 100 counties that would not get any additional funding. We could then use regression analysis to compare the change in crime in the two groups of counties. This is a randomized controlled trial (RCT), considered the most reliable method of estimating causation with endogenous variables. Some versions of randomized trials have been used in medical research since studies of treatments of scurvy among 18th-century sailors. The use of RCTs in the social science research is more recent, but it has grown rapidly in the past few decades. Although RCTs are considered the gold standard for measuring causal effects, they can be costly and cannot be applied to some research topics for reasons of scale (e.g., the effect of trade policy) or ethical considerations (e.g., the effect of length of prison sentence).

As mentioned above, Stata has a series of commands for addressing the problem of endogeneity, but these methods are beyond the scope of this book. Nonetheless, it is important to be aware of the issue of endogeneity. With OLS regression in a nonexperimental setting, we must be very cautious in inferring that relationship as causal. To do so, we must have strong reasons to believe that there is no reverse causality and that there are no confounding variables that influence both the dependent and the independent variables. Bailey (2016) describes numerous topics in regression analysis with particular emphasis on the problem of, and solutions to, endogeneity.

13.7 NONNORMALITY

Normally distributed error terms are sometimes considered an "optional" assumption for OLS regression. This is because normality is not necessary for OLS, but it is convenient. It is not necessary in that, even without normally distributed errors, OLS will still generate the best linear unbiased estimates (BLUE) of the coefficients. On the other hand, normality is convenient in that it ensures that the estimated coefficients are normally distributed so that the p-values and confidence interval will be correct even in small samples.

However, even if the error terms are not normally distributed, the estimated coefficients may still be normally distributed. Because OLS coefficients can be interpreted as a type of weighted average, the central limit theorem tells us that the distribution of the estimated coefficients ($\hat{\beta}_i$) becomes more normal as the sample size increases, even if the error term (ε) is not normally distributed. As few as 100 observations may be sufficient to ensure that the OLS coefficients are normally distributed, implying that the standard p-values and confidence intervals are reliable. Thus, the problem of normality is not one of the more serious problems for regression analysis unless the sample is quite small (Bailey, 2016).

How do we visually inspect the normality of residuals? As described in Section 13.2, we can use the **predict** command to calculate the residual for each observation (car) in the Malibu database and give it the variable name "e." We can then compare the distribution of the residual and the normal distribution using a histogram (Figure 13.5), as described in Chapter 6.

```
lab var e Residuals
histogram e, normal start(-6000) width(500) ///
  xlabel(-6000(1000)5000)
```

The **normal** option adds a line showing the normal distribution with the same mean and standard deviation for comparison. The **start** and **width** options tell Stata where to begin the bars and how wide to make them, while the **xlabels** option indicates which labels to use.

FIGURE 13.5   ●   HISTOGRAM OF RESIDUALS AND THE NORMAL DISTRIBUTION

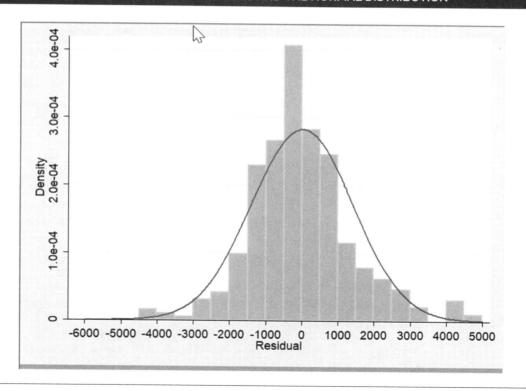

TABLE 13.1 ● INTERPRETING SKEWNESS AND KURTOSIS		
	Skewness	**Kurtosis**
Range	−∞ to +∞	1 to +∞
Value in the normal distribution	0	3
Interpretation of low values	Negative skewness means the distribution is skewed to the left. In other words, the left tail is longer or thicker.	Kurtosis less than 3 means fewer outliers and thinner tails than a normal distribution.
Interpretation of high values	Positive skewness means the distribution is skewed to the right. In other words, the right tail is longer or thicker.	Kurtosis greater than 3 means more outliers and thicker tails than a normal distribution.

The histogram in Figure 13.5 shows that the distribution of the residuals diverges from the normal distribution. There are too many residuals between −1,500 and 0 and too few between 1,000 and 2,500.

We can measure the divergence from normality by calculating skewness and kurtosis. Skewness is generally considered a measure of symmetry, but this is not always the case. All symmetric distributions have a skewness of zero, but a skewness of zero does not guarantee that the distribution is symmetric. For example, a distribution may have zero skewness and still be asymmetric if the left tail of the distribution is thick and the right tail is long.

Kurtosis generally measures the presence of thick tails, defined as the portion of the distribution more than 1 standard deviation from the mean. The normal distribution has a kurtosis value of 3, so "excess kurtosis" is defined as kurtosis minus 3. In other words, positive excess kurtosis implies that the tails are thicker than in the normal distribution, while negative excess kurtosis means the tails are thinner than in the normal distribution. Table 13.1 provides some guidance in interpreting skewness and kurtosis.

In Stata, the command **sum e, detail** will calculate skewness, kurtosis, and many other statistics for the variable e. Alternatively, we can use the **tabstat** command to calculate these two statistics alone.

As shown in Output 13.11, the skewness of the residual from the Malibu regression is 0.44, indicating that it has a slight positive skew, though this is not easily visible in the graph. The kurtosis of the residual is 4.35, indicating that the tails are thicker than in a normal distribution.

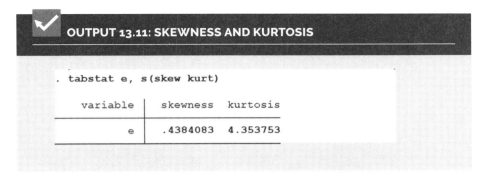

OUTPUT 13.11: SKEWNESS AND KURTOSIS

```
. tabstat e, s(skew kurt)

    variable │  skewness   kurtosis
    ─────────┼────────────────────────
           e │  .4384083   4.353753
```

Is the distribution of the residual significantly different from normal? In Stata, the skewness–kurtosis test (sometimes called the D'Agostino K^2 test) checks skewness and kurtosis separately, then runs a joint test of the null hypothesis that skewness = 0 and kurtosis = 3, which would be consistent with normality. Using the Malibu price data, we can run the test using the menu system (see Dialog Box 13.7) or using the command (see Output 13.12).

DIALOG BOX 13.7: NORMALITY TEST USING MENUS

Statistics → Summaries, tables, and tests → Distributional plots and tests → Skewness and kurtosis normality test

OUTPUT 13.12: TEST FOR NORMALITY

```
. sktest e

                     Skewness/Kurtosis tests for Normality
                                                      ——— joint ———
  Variable |    Obs   Pr(Skewness)   Pr(Kurtosis)  adj chi2(2)    Prob>chi2
-----------+---------------------------------------------------------------
         e |    383      0.0006         0.0002         20.94        0.0000
```

The number under "Pr(skewness)" gives the probability of getting the observed distribution of the residual if the skewness were actually zero, while the number under "Pr(Kurtosis)" indicates the probability of getting this result if the kurtosis were 3. Both null hypotheses can be rejected at the 1% level. Naturally, the joint hypothesis that skewness = 0 and kurtosis = 3 is also rejected at the 1% level. In summary, we reject the null hypothesis that the residuals from the Malibu regression are normally distributed.

How do we address the problem of nonnormality in the residuals? The most common approach is to try transforming the dependent variable. For example, some variables such as household income, individual health care spending, and county population data have many small, positive values and a few very large values. In statistical terms, these variables are positively skewed. However, if we transform the variable by taking the natural logarithm, the new variable is often much closer to a normal distribution. This makes it more likely that residuals from a regression model will be normally distributed, particularly if the independent variables are normally distributed.

We can take the example of the population of U.S. counties. The **kdensity** command gives us a "smoothed" histogram of a variable. The left side of Figure 13.6 shows the distribution of counties by population. Most counties have populations less than 25,000, but a few have more than 1 million inhabitants. The right side of Figure 13.6 shows that the distribution of the natural log of population is clearly much more similar to a normal distribution.

```
kdensity population
gen logpop = log(population)
kdensity logpop
```

Running the command **tabstat pop logpop, s(skew kurt)** reveals that the skewness is 14.1 for the original population but just 0.28 for the log population (recall that skewness is 0 for the normal distribution). Likewise, kurtosis is 337 in the original

FIGURE 13.6 ● DISTRIBUTION OF COUNTY POPULATION AND THE LOGARITHM OF COUNTY POPULATION

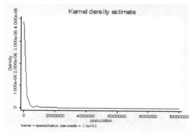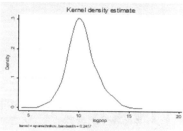

population variable, but 3.4 in the log population (kurtosis is 3.0 for the normal distribution). Transforming the dependent variable so that it is normally distributed (or closer to a normal distribution) improves the chances that the residual will be normally distributed. This is particularly important when the sample size is small.

If transforming the dependent variable is not successful in producing normally distributed residuals, some researchers suggest setting a stricter criterion for statistical significance of the coefficients. For example, one might insist on a p-value of less than 1% to conclude that the coefficient is significantly different from zero. There are also regression models that give less weight to the outliers, including robust regression (implemented with **rreg** in Stata) and quantile regression (implemented with **qreg**). However, these methods are beyond the scope of this book.

As mentioned above, in the absence of other problems, even if the errors are not normally distributed, OLS gives the best linear unbiased estimates (BLUE) of the coefficients. Furthermore, unless the number of observations is small, the coefficients are likely to be normally distributed if even the errors are not normally distributed. In this case, OLS will generate reliable p-values and confidence intervals regardless of the distribution of the error terms.

13.8 PRESENTING THE RESULTS

In this section, we normally give examples of how to write results for a nontechnical publication (e.g., a newspaper) and for a technical publication (e.g., an academic journal). However, newspapers and other nontechnical publications rarely describe regression diagnostics, so for this chapter, we will only provide the example of how to describe the results for a journal or other technical publication.

For a journal article, the write-up should include a description of the results of each test, expressed in terms of rejecting or failing to reject the null hypothesis. The value of the test statistic and the p-value can be included in parentheses. Thus, the regression diagnostics for the Malibu regression could be described as follows:

This model was subjected to various diagnostic tests of the specification. First, we ran the Ramsey RESET using powers of the dependent variable. The test fails to reject the null hypothesis as there are no omitted variables, $F(3, 376)$ = 0.69, p = 0.561. Second, we tried including a mileage-squared term, but it was not significantly different from zero, t = 1.38, p = 0.168. We also tried an alternative specification including interaction terms between Mileage and the trim levels to see if the three trim levels depreciate at different rates. A joint test failed to reject the null hypothesis that both interaction terms were equal to zero, $F(2, 376)$ = 0.82, p = 0.442.

Heteroscedasticity was checked using the Breusch–Pagan/Cook–Weisberg test. We failed to reject the null hypothesis of homoscedasticity when modeling the variance of the errors as a function of the predicted values of Price, $\chi^2(1)$ = 0.04, p = 0.847.

There was also no evidence of multicollinearity, as indicated by the fact that the variance inflation factors (VIFs) for all the independent variables were less than 2.0. However, the D'Agostino K^2 test rejected the null hypothesis that the residuals were normally distributed, $\chi^2(2)$ = 20.94, p = 0.000. When the residuals are not normally distributed, caution must be taken in assigning statistical significance when p-values are marginal. Fortunately, all four coefficients in our model have quite low p-values (<0.0005), providing confidence that the coefficients are significantly different from zero.

13.9 SUMMARY OF COMMANDS USED IN THIS CHAPTER

As described in Chapter 4, this last section of each chapter summarizes all of the Stata code used in the chapter. In addition, all Stata code used throughout the book is summarized in Appendix 1.

Adding a random number to independent variables

```
gen MileageErr = Mileage + rnormal(0,3800)
```

```
regress Price MileageErr LT LTZ
```

Cook's D to look for outliers

```
predict CooksD, cooksd
browse if CooksD>1
```

Replace

```
replace Mileage=22138 if Mileage==221387
```

Adding a squared independent variable to a regression

```
gen Mileage2 = Mileage^2
regress Price Mileage Mileage2 Age LT LTZ
```

Checking for specification error

```
twoway (scatter ehat Mileage)
rvpplot Mileage
rvfplot
```

Omitted variable test

```
estat ovtest
estat ovtest, rhs
```

Interaction terms

```
gen MilexLT = Mileage*LT
gen MilexLTZ = Mileage*LTZ
regress Price Mileage Age LT LTZ MilexLT MilexLTZ
```

Correlation

```
correl Mileage Age LT LTZ
```

Multicollinearity test

```
estat vif
```

Checking for heteroscedasticity

```
rvpplot Mileage
ryfplot
```

Testing for heteroscedasticity

```
estat hettest
estat hettest, iid
```

Calculate the residual

```
predict e, resid
```

Histogram

```
histogram e, normal start(-6000) width(500) ///
xlabel (-6000(1000)5000)
```

Testing for nonnormality

```
tabstat e, s(skew kurt)
sktest e
```

REFERENCES

Bailey, M. A. (2016). *Real econometrics the right tools to answer important questions*. New York, NY: Oxford University Press.

Greene, W. H. (2018). *Econometric analysis*. New York, NY: Pearson.

Levitt, S. D. (1997). Using electoral cycles in police hiring to estimate the effect of police on crime. *American Economic Review, 87*(3), 270–290.

O'Brien, R. M. (2007). A caution regarding rules of thumb for variance inflation factors. *Quality & Quantity, 41*, 673–690.

Woolridge, J. M. (2016). *Introductory econometrics: A modern approach*. Mason, OH: South-Western Cengage Learning.

REGRESSION ANALYSIS WITH CATEGORICAL DEPENDENT VARIABLES

Chapter Preview

Research question	Do views on legalization of marijuana vary by age and education?
Null hypothesis	Age and education have no effect on views on legalization of marijuana.
Test	Logit analysis and z test of coefficients on age and education
Types of variables	Dependent variable is binary (support or oppose legalization). Independent variables can include continuous variables, categorical variables, or a mix of both.
When to use	When dependent variable is binary (0 or 1)
Assumptions	For the logit model: The log odds is a linear function of the independent variables. For the probit model: The probability that $y = 1$ is a cumulative normal density function of the independent variables.
Stata code: generic	**logit depvar indepvars** **probit depvar indepvar**
Stata code: example	**logit legmar age i.sex educ** **probit legmar age i.sex educ**

14.1 INTRODUCTION

Chapter 12 introduced regression analysis, which estimates the equation that best describes the relationship between a dependent variable and one or more independent variables. We focused on ordinary least squares (OLS) regression in which the dependent variable is continuous and the model is linear in the parameters. However, in many cases, we want to estimate a relationship in which the dependent variable is not continuous. Suppose we want to predict whether a household will purchase a car this year, whether an adult is working or not, whether a student will graduate from high school, or whether a patient will survive surgery. This chapter explains how to apply regression analysis to these types of problems. In particular, we focus on two types of nonlinear regression analysis used on categorical dependent variables: logit[1] and probit regression.

Let's take a concrete example. A recent poll by CBS News found that 61% of Americans now support legalization of marijuana, a 5 percentage point increase from the year before (see Article 14.1). The survey found that support for legalization varies by age and political affiliation. This survey did not find a difference in views of men and women, but the article notes that previous surveys found that men were more likely to support legalization of marijuana than women. The news story examines the relationships between support for legalization and each characteristic separately, but regression analysis allows us to predict whether an individual supports legalization based on a combination of different characteristics.

How would we analyze the determinants of support for legalization of marijuana? The dependent variable (y) takes just two possible values, "no" and "yes," which we represent mathematically as 0 and 1. Although the observed values of y are either 0 or 1, the predicted value of y is a number between 0 and 1, which is interpreted as the probability that $y = 1$ given the values of the independent variables. In our example, regression analysis would generate an equation that predicts the probability that a person with certain characteristics (e.g., a 32-year-old female Republican) will support legalization of marijuana. It would also allow us to test the statistical significance of each independent variable.

This chapter focuses on regression methods that can be used when the dependent variable is binary. First, the relevance of this type of analysis is demonstrated by describing studies from various fields where the dependent variable is binary. Then, we briefly discuss the use of a linear OLS model to analyze data with a binary dependent variable. This leads to a more extended discussion of the logit model, including the functional form, the method used to find the solution, and the interpretation of

---

[1] The terms *logit regression* and *logistic regression* can be used interchangeably.

ARTICLE 14.1

CBS NEWS / *April 20, 2017, 7:00 AM*

Marijuana legalization support at all-time high

825 Comments / f Share / ✈ Tweet / ◎ Stumble / @ Email

Last Updated Apr 20, 2017 11:57 AM EDT

By Jennifer De Pinto, Fred Backus, Kabir Khanna and Anthony Salvanto

The belief that pot should be legal has reached a new high in CBS News polls. Sixty-one percent of Americans now say that it should be, a five-point increase from a year ago. This sentiment has increased each year we've measured it since 2013, with the turning point to majority support coming in 2014. Back in 1979, this poll found just 27 percent saying it should be legal.

Those over 65 are the most opposed to legalization, but most under age 65 support it. And women are now as much in favor of legal marijuana as men are; in previous years they were less so.

... Support for legalization has risen among all age groups – particularly those under 55. Americans under 35 show the strongest support. Three in four adults between 18 and 34 support legal marijuana use, as do six in 10 Americans between 35 and 64. Seniors remain the one age group for whom a majority still think marijuana use should be against the law.

There are partisan differences. Most Democrats and independents increasingly think marijuana use should be legal, while Republicans are divided....

Source: De Pinto, Backus, Khanna, and Salvanto (2017).

the coefficients. We also briefly consider the closely related probit model and how it differs from the logit model. Finally, we consider regression models that are designed to handle categorical dependent variables with more than two values, such as political party affiliation or marital status. A more in-depth description of regression analysis for categorical dependent variables can be found in Long and Freese (2006) and Greene (2018).

14.2 WHEN TO USE LOGIT OR PROBIT ANALYSIS

Table 14.1 shows examples of research questions from different fields where the dependent variable is binary. Each row gives a research question, the corresponding null hypothesis, the binary dependent variable, and one or more independent variables. The table demonstrates that binary dependent variables are common in empirical research, highlighting the importance of statistical tools for analyzing data of this type.

TABLE 14.1 ● EXAMPLES OF RESEARCH QUESTIONS WITH BINARY DEPENDENT VARIABLES

Field	Research Question	Null Hypothesis	Binary Dependent Variable	Independent Variables
Criminal Justice	Does job counseling reduce the probability of ex-convicts being arrested within a year of release?	Job counseling has no effect on the rearrest rate.	Whether or not an ex-convict is rearrested within a year of release	Job counseling and personal characteristics
Economics	Is the likelihood of being employed affected by the level of education?	Level of education has no effect on the probability of being employed.	Whether or not an individual is employed	Level of education and other individual and community characteristics
Political Science	Are voters who live near a polling station more likely to vote?	Distance to polling station has no effect on probability of voting.	Whether or not an individual voted in a recent election	Distance to polling station and other voter characteristics
Psychology	What factors affect an individual's likelihood of completing a 4-week therapy session?	Personal characteristics do not affect likelihood of completing therapy session.	Whether or not patients complete the therapy session	Age, sex, education, and other personal characteristics
Public Health	How does the proportion of children vaccinated in a county affect the likelihood of a whooping cough outbreak over 1 year?	Proportion of children vaccinated has no effect on the probability of a whooping cough outbreak.	Whether or not there is a whooping cough outbreak in the county	Proportion of children vaccinated, demographic characteristics, and indicators of access to health care
Sociology	Is the decision to attend church affected by attendance by neighbors?	Church attendance is not affected by attendance by one's neighbors.	Whether or not a person attends church regularly	Church attendance by neighbors and other personal and social factors

One option is to simply apply the linear OLS model described in Chapters 12 and 13 to the case where the dependent variable is binary. This is called the linear probability model (LPM). Perhaps the main advantage of the LPM is that it is easy to interpret the coefficient(s). Each coefficient in the LPM represents the effect of a one-unit increase in the corresponding independent variable on the probability that $y = 1$. Thus, if $\beta = 0.02$, then each one-unit increase in the corresponding independent variable is associated with a 0.02 or 2 percentage point increase in the probability that $y = 1$.

The main disadvantage of the LPM is that it will generate predicted values of the dependent variable that are less than 0 or greater than 1 over some ranges of x, which are not valid as probabilities.[2] To demonstrate this, suppose we have 20 observations, where x takes the values between 1 and 20 and y is either 0 or 1. Figure 14.1 shows the data as points on the graph, all of which are along the $y = 1$ line or the $y = 0$ line. The LPM model generates the straight line that best fits the data, which is also shown in the figure. At the left of the graph, the line representing the predicted value of y dips below 0, while at right, it rises above 1. Since the predicted value of y represents the probability that $y = 1$, the model is predicting probabilities outside the 0 to 1 range.

FIGURE 14.1 ● LINEAR REGRESSION WITH A BINARY DEPENDENT VARIABLE

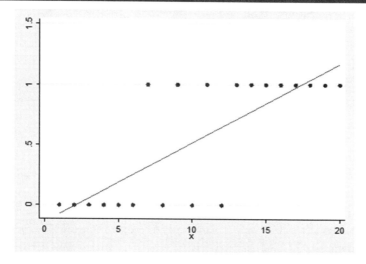

---

[2] This problem is relevant only in the case of continuous independent variables. If the independent variable, x_i, is a dummy variable, the only relevant values are where $x_i = 0$ and $x_i = 1$, and at those two points, the predicted probability will be between 0 and 1.

On the other hand, if we apply a logit model to the same data, the predicted value of y is a curved line that remains greater than 0 and less than 1 throughout the range of x (Figure 14.2). This is only possible because the relationship between the predicted probability (P) and independent variable (x) is nonlinear. As discussed in Chapter 13, a nonlinear relationship between the dependent variable and an independent variable means that the marginal effect (the slope on the graph) varies across observations. However, Stata can be used to calculate the marginal effects of each independent variable on the predicted probability in a logit model.

FIGURE 14.2 ● LOGIT REGRESSION WITH A BINARY DEPENDENT VARIABLE

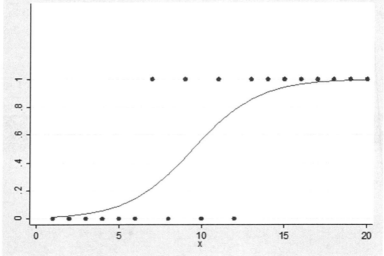

14.3 UNDERSTANDING THE LOGIT MODEL

The logit model is based on the concept of the odds, defined as the probability of an event occurring (P) divided by the probability of the event not occurring. Mathematically, we can express the odds as follows:

$$\text{Odds} = \frac{P}{1-P} \tag{14.1}$$

Odds are commonly used to describe payoffs in sports gambling, but they also reflect the perceived probability of winning. For example, if a racetrack offers 3-to-1 odds on a horse, this means they will pay out three times the value of the bet if the horse wins. This implies that the perceived probability that the horse will lose is three times greater than the perceived probability that it will win.[3] In other words, the horse has a 3/(3 + 1) = 0.75 = 75% probability of losing and a 25% probability of winning.

The logit regression model expresses the natural logarithm of the odds (sometimes called the "log odds") as a linear function of a constant and a set of k–1 independent variables:

$$\ln\left(\frac{P}{1-P}\right) = \beta_0 + \sum_{i=1}^{k-1}\beta_i x_i \qquad (14.2)$$

This equation can be rewritten in terms of P as follows:

$$P = \frac{\exp(\beta_0 + \sum\beta_i x_i)}{1 + \exp(\beta_0 + \sum\beta_i x_i)} \qquad (14.3)$$

To give a better sense of how these concepts are related to one another, Table 14.2 provides the odds (expressed two ways) and the log odds for selected probabilities. Although probabilities range from 0 to 1, the odds start at 0 (when P = 0) and approach infinity (as P approaches 1). The logarithm of the odds ranges from negative infinity (when P = 0) to positive infinity (when P = 1).

TABLE 14.2 ● SELECTED PROBABILITIES, ODDS RATIOS, AND LOG ODDS RATIOS			
Probability (P)	**Odds**	**Odds [P/(1 – P)]**	**Log Odds [ln(P/(1 – P))]**
0.00	0:1	0.00	$-\infty$
0.10	1:9	0.11	−2.20
0.25	1:3	0.33	−1.10
0.50	1:1	1.00	0
0.75	3:1	3.00	1.10
0.90	9:1	9.00	2.20
1.00	1:0	∞	∞

[3] Strictly speaking, in order to make a profit, betting companies offer payout odds slightly less than implied by the perceived probabilities. For example, if two evenly matched teams are playing, the perceived probabilities that each will win is 50%, implying payoff odds of 1-to-1. However, betting companies offer slightly lower payoffs for each team, say 9-to-10. For this reason, the sum of implied probabilities across outcomes is slightly greater than 100%, in this case 1 – [9/(9 + 10)]=0.526=52.6% for each team.

Because the logit regression model is nonlinear, it cannot be estimated using OLS. OLS involves a fixed set of calculations using matrix algebra that will always generate a set of estimated coefficients and related statistics. In contrast, running a logit model involves maximum likelihood estimation (MLE). MLE starts with a function that describes the likelihood of getting the observed data as a function of the coefficients. Then, there is an iterative search process to find the set of coefficients that maximizes this function. Fortunately, the calculations behind the search procedure are carried out by Stata.

One implication of MLE for the researcher is that, because the search procedure is computationally intensive, it takes somewhat more time to run a logit model than an OLS model. In addition, the procedure will occasionally fail to converge, meaning that it cannot "find" a set of coefficients that is better than other sets of coefficients. In graphic terms, this means that the likelihood function is "flat" over some range of coefficient estimates, making it impossible to identify a point of maximum likelihood.

The logit model relies on a set of assumptions similar to those behind OLS regression. Below are some of the more important ones:

- The dependent variable takes just two possible values (0, 1).

- The independent variables are measured without error.

- The log odds of the event ($y = 1$) are a linear function of the independent variables.

- The model includes all relevant variables.

- There is no correlation between the independent variables and the error term.

In addition, it is important to keep in mind several limitations of logit (and probit) models. First, logit and probit models are relatively sensitive to heteroscedasticity. In OLS regression, heteroscedasticity does not result in biased coefficients, but with probit and logit, it does cause the estimated coefficients to be biased.

Second, because logit models are estimated with MLE, they require larger samples. A common rule of thumb is that the sample size should be at least $10k/p$, where k is the number of independent variables and p is the probability of the less likely outcome of the dependent variable. For example, if we have six independent variables and the dependent variable is zero 90% of the time, the sample size should be at least $10 * 6/0.1 = 600$ (Peduzzi, Concato, Kemper, Holford, & Feinstein, 1996).

Finally, probit and logit models have a "zero cell" problem. Each 2×2 cross tabulation between the (binary) dependent variable and the independent dummy variables must have observations in all four cells of the table. Otherwise, the model cannot be estimated.

14.4 RUNNING LOGIT AND INTERPRETING THE RESULTS

14.4.1 Running Logit Regression in Stata

The 2016 General Social Survey (GSS) is an annual survey covering a wide range of economic, social, and political variables. It uses a multistage stratified random sample of 2,867 respondents in the United States. We can use the GSS to demonstrate how to use Stata to run logit models and interpret the results. More specifically, we explore the factors associated with people's views on legalization of marijuana. We can load the data with the following commands:

```
clear
use GSS2016
```

As described in Chapter 2, to get population estimates from the survey data, we need to apply sampling weights. In addition, it is necessary to adjust the standard errors in regression analysis for the sample design. For example, the clustering of observations in the sample increases the standard error of parameter estimates compared with a simple random sample, while stratification may reduce them. Stata can calculate standard errors taking into account the sample design if we give it information about the design using the **svyset** command. The following command informs Stata of the characteristics of the sample of the 2016 GSS:

```
svyset [weight=wtss], strata(vstrat) psu(vpsu) ///
   singleunit(scaled)
```

The portion in brackets, **[weight=]**, tells Stata the name of the variable that contains the sampling weights. In the GSS data, wtssl is a relative sampling weight. As described in Chapter 2, relative weights are useful for calculating weighted means and percentages but cannot be used to estimate population totals. This is not a problem for us because we are not interested in estimating, for example, the total number of people in the United States who support marijuana legalization.

The **strata()** option is used to indicate the name of the variable in the database that indicates the strata. The GSS is based on 65 strata, identified by the variable vstrata. The **psu()** option is used to tell Stata the name of the variable that identifies the primary sampling unit, that is, the sampling unit of the first stage of selection. In the GSS data, the vpsu variable indicates the primary sampling unit. Finally, the **singleunit()** option tells Stata how to deal with special cases that are not relevant to our purposes.[4]

The information about the sample design can be used in a regression model by putting the prefix **svy:** before the command. For linear regression, it looks like this:

```
svy: regress y x1 x2
```

Below, we apply this approach to the logit analysis of the GSS data on opinions regarding the legalization of marijuana. But first, we need to prepare the dependent and independent variables for the analysis.

Using the **describe** command, we see that the survey includes data for 960 variables on 2,867 respondents. The **describe** command also reveals that the value labels in the GSS are usually the variable name in uppercase. The variable "grass" records the opinion of respondents about legalization of marijuana, as shown by the variable label "should marijuana be made legal."

Before working with new categorical variables, it is important to understand how they are coded. If we know the name of the value labels, we can use **label list** to show the value labels for the variable grass (see Output 14.1).

Output 14.1 shows that when the variable grass = 1, this means the respondent supports legalization of marijuana, while 2 indicates that the respondent opposes legalization. The other three codes are for different types of missing values (observations with missing values are omitted from regression analysis). For the **logit** command, the dependent variable should take the values of 0 and 1, so we need to create a binary variable from the variable grass. We can use the **recode ... gen** command to change values and create the new variable:

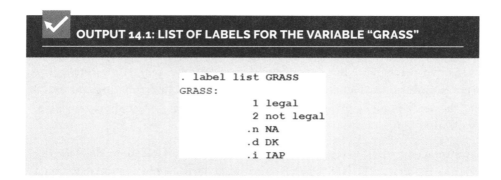

OUTPUT 14.1: LIST OF LABELS FOR THE VARIABLE "GRASS"

```
. label list GRASS
GRASS:
            1 legal
            2 not legal
           .n NA
           .d DK
           .i IAP
```

---

[4] Normally, it is necessary to have at least two sampling units in each stratum in order to calculate the standard errors, and normally the GSS has at least two. In some cases, however, missing data or the analysis of a subpopulation may reduce it to one. Stata offers four options for dealing with this situation, of which **scaled** is one.

```
recode grass 1=1 2=0, gen(legmar)
lab define legmarlab 1 Supports 0 Opposes
lab val legmar legmarlab
lab var legmar "Position on legalization of marijuana"
```

We could have used a **recode** command to change the values of the original variable, but it is generally a good practice to create new variables rather than recoding an existing variable to make it easier to check for errors.

What individual characteristics might be associated with opinions about legalization of marijuana? We may wish to use age, sex, race, education, religious belief, political affiliation, and region of the country. The variables for age (age) and education (educ) are continuous and can be used as is.[5] The variables sex, race, and region are categorical variables, but we can make use of Stata's factor variable notation to include dummy variables representing them.

For religious belief, we will use the variable "relpersn," which indicates whether they consider themselves religious, taking four values: "very religious," "moderately religious," "slightly religious," and "not religious." We create a dummy variable equal to 1 for "very religious" and "moderately religious" and 0 for "slightly religious" and "not religious":

```
recode relpersn (1 2=1) (3 4=0), gen(religious)
lab def rellab 1 "Very or moderate" 0 "Slight or not"
lab val religious rellab
```

The variable "partyid" indicates political affiliation and is divided into eight categories, including two for Democrats (0 and 1), three for independents (2–4), two for Republicans (5 and 6), and one for other parties (7). We can define a new categorical variable called party taking three values: Democrat, Republican, and Other.

```
recode partyid (0 1=1) (5 6=2) (2/4 7=3), gen(party)
lab def partylab 1 Democrat 2 Republican 3 Other
lab val party partylab
```

The **logit** command is similar to the **regress** command in that we list the dependent variable followed by the independent variables and then options if any. Here is the general form:

```
logit depvar indepvar1 indepvar2 indepvar3, options
```

---

[5] The maximum age is 89, and this value is labeled "89 or older," but there are only 22 households in this group or less than 1% of the sample.

In our analysis of the GSS, we are using Stata's notation for factor variables, so that i.*varname* means that Stata should insert a set of dummy variables to represent the categorical variable *varname*. If there are *n* categories in the variable, Stata will choose one to omit and include *n* – 1 dummy variables. For example, region is a categorical variable with nine values, so i.*region* will insert eight regional dummy variables. If we want to specify which category to omit, we can use ib#.*varname*, where *b* stands for base (or omitted) category and # represents the value of the categorical variable to be omitted. In the example below, ib3.*party* means that Stata should omit the category associated with *party* = 3, which is "Other."

```
logit legmar age i.sex i.race educ ib3.party i.religious i.region
```

As a final step, we use the **svy:** prefix to indicate that the model should be estimated taking into account the characteristics of the sample design. The first line of Output 14.2 shows the command. Alternatively, we can use the menu system to run the logit model (see Dialog Box 14.1).

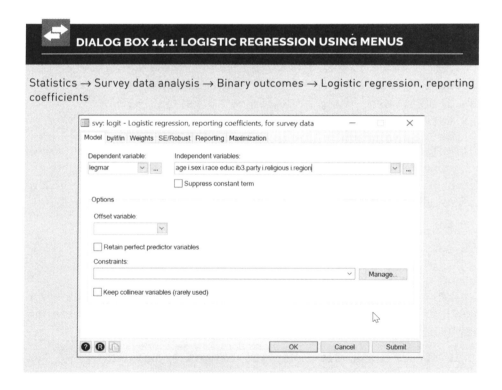

DIALOG BOX 14.1: LOGISTIC REGRESSION USING MENUS

Statistics → Survey data analysis → Binary outcomes → Logistic regression, reporting coefficients

OUTPUT 14.2: RESULTS OF LOGIT REGRESSION

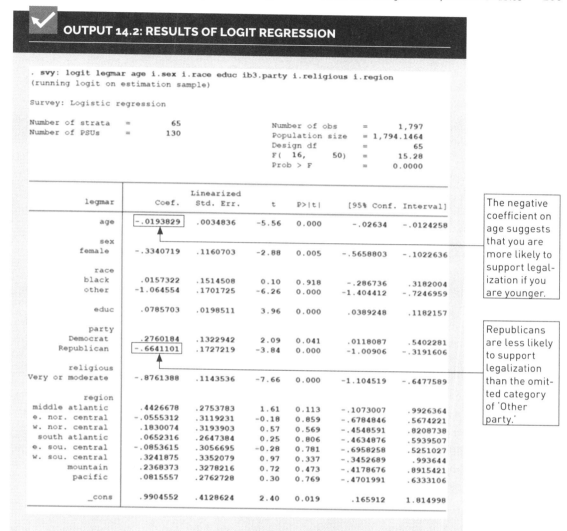

```
. svy: logit legmar age i.sex i.race educ ib3.party i.religious i.region
(running logit on estimation sample)

Survey: Logistic regression

Number of strata   =        65          Number of obs    =      1,797
Number of PSUs     =       130          Population size  =  1,794.1464
                                        Design df        =         65
                                        F( 16,      50)  =      15.28
                                        Prob > F         =     0.0000
```

legmar	Coef.	Linearized Std. Err.	t	P>|t|	[95% Conf. Interval]	
age	-.0193829	.0034836	-5.56	0.000	-.02634	-.0124258
sex						
female	-.3340719	.1160703	-2.88	0.005	-.5658803	-.1022636
race						
black	.0157322	.1514508	0.10	0.918	-.286736	.3182004
other	-1.064554	.1701725	-6.26	0.000	-1.404412	-.7246959
educ	.0785703	.0198511	3.96	0.000	.0389248	.1182157
party						
Democrat	.2760184	.1322942	2.09	0.041	.0118087	.5402281
Republican	-.6641101	.1727219	-3.84	0.000	-1.00906	-.3191606
religious						
Very or moderate	-.8761388	.1143536	-7.66	0.000	-1.104519	-.6477589
region						
middle atlantic	.4426678	.2753783	1.61	0.113	-.1073007	.9926364
e. nor. central	-.0555312	.3119231	-0.18	0.859	-.6784846	.5674221
w. nor. central	.1830074	.3193903	0.57	0.569	-.4548591	.8208738
south atlantic	.0652316	.2647384	0.25	0.806	-.4634876	.5939507
e. sou. central	-.0853615	.3056695	-0.28	0.781	-.6958258	.5251027
w. sou. central	.3241875	.3352079	0.97	0.337	-.3452689	.993644
mountain	.2368373	.3278216	0.72	0.473	-.4178676	.8915421
pacific	.0815557	.2762728	0.30	0.769	-.4701991	.6333106
_cons	.9904552	.4128624	2.40	0.019	.165912	1.814998

> The negative coefficient on age suggests that you are more likely to support legalization if you are younger.

> Republicans are less likely to support legalization than the omitted category of 'Other party.'

14.4.2 Interpreting the Results of a Logit Model

The results of the logit regression are shown in Output 14.2. In the upper right corner, the number of observations is 1,797, substantially below the full sample of 2,867. Further exploration of the data reveals that a large number of respondents did not answer the question about their views on the legalization of marijuana. The results should be interpreted with caution since it is possible that the people who did respond to the question may not be representative of the full sample. In a real study, this would merit further exploration.

The F statistic and the probability below it are a test of the null hypothesis that all the estimated coefficients are, in fact, zero. The low value (0.0000) indicates that we can reject this null hypothesis with a high level of confidence.

The **svy: logit** command does not report the "pseudo-R2" measure of goodness of fit, but this is included in the output from the ordinary **logit** command. Stata reports the McFadden pseudo-R2, one of many that have been proposed for logit models. Long and Freese (2006) warn that none of the measures of fit for logit and probit models are consistently reliable as a criterion for choosing a model. In addition, unlike the R^2 in an OLS regression, it cannot be interpreted as the share of the variance in the dependent variable that can be explained by the model.

14.4.2.1 Logit Coefficients

Logit coefficients do not have an intuitive meaning. Each coefficient (β_i) in a logit model represents the effect of a one-unit increase in the independent variable (x_i) on the log odds [$\ln(P/(1 - P))$], but this is not very helpful. However, positive and significant coefficients indicate that the independent variable is associated with greater likelihood that $y = 1$, while negative and significant coefficients imply that the variable is linked to lower probability that $y = 1$. For example, the age coefficient is negative and significant, meaning that older respondents are less likely to approve of legalizing marijuana. Other groups with negative and significant coefficients are females, "Other" race, people who consider themselves religious, and Republicans—each of these groups is significantly less likely to support legalization compared with others. The positive coefficient on education means that respondents with more education are more likely to support legalization. Similarly, Democrats are more likely to support legalization than independents (the omitted category). None of the regions shows a statistically significant difference from New England, the omitted region.

As discussed in Chapter 12, for a set of dummy variables that represent one categorical variable (e.g., region), it is better to carry out a joint test that all the coefficients are zero. We can use the **test** or **testparm** command to test the joint significance of sets of dummy variables. The **testparm** command has an advantage over **test** in allowing abbreviated variable lists. In Stata, we can describe a list of variables using the first and last variable separated by a hyphen. For example, reg_1-reg_8 would mean all the variables from reg_1 to reg_8. Or we can use the asterisk to represent any set of characters, so reg_* means any variable that starts with reg_. In addition, **testparm** allows the use of factor variable notation, such as i.*varname*, as shown in the following commands:

```
testparm i.race
testparm i.party
testparm i.region
```

The results (shown in Output 14.3) indicate that we can reject the null hypothesis that the two race dummy variables have coefficients equal to zero. In simpler terms, we can say that race has a statistically significant effect on views on legalization of marijuana, after controlling for the other independent variables. Political party identification is also a jointly significant factor in opinions on marijuana legalization. On the other hand, region is not a statistically significant factor after controlling for age, sex, race, and other characteristics.

OUTPUT 14.3: RESULTS OF JOINT HYPOTHESIS TESTS

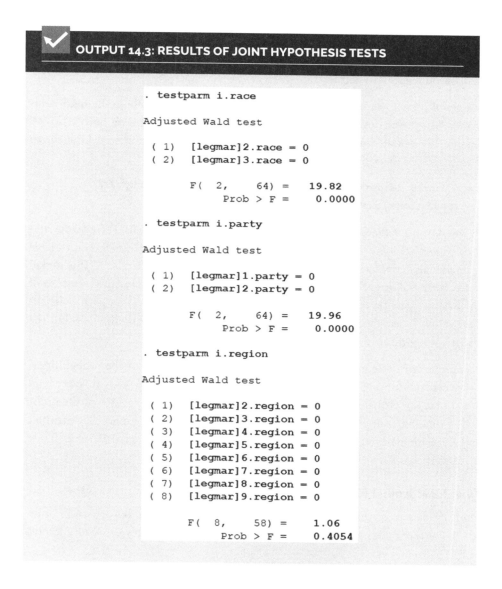

```
.  testparm i.race

Adjusted Wald test

 ( 1)    [legmar]2.race = 0
 ( 2)    [legmar]3.race = 0

        F(  2,     64) =     19.82
              Prob > F =      0.0000

.  testparm i.party

Adjusted Wald test

 ( 1)    [legmar]1.party = 0
 ( 2)    [legmar]2.party = 0

        F(  2,     64) =     19.96
              Prob > F =      0.0000

.  testparm i.region

Adjusted Wald test

 ( 1)    [legmar]2.region = 0
 ( 2)    [legmar]3.region = 0
 ( 3)    [legmar]4.region = 0
 ( 4)    [legmar]5.region = 0
 ( 5)    [legmar]6.region = 0
 ( 6)    [legmar]7.region = 0
 ( 7)    [legmar]8.region = 0
 ( 8)    [legmar]9.region = 0

        F(  8,     58) =      1.06
              Prob > F =      0.4054
```

14.4.2.2 Odds Ratios

Because of the difficulty in interpreting the coefficients (β_i) in a logit regression model, the effect of each independent variable is often expressed as an odds ratio. The odds ratio for an independent dummy variable x_i is defined as follows:

$$\text{Odds ratio} = \frac{P_i / (1 - P_i)}{P_r / (1 - P_r)} \tag{14.4}$$

where P_i is the probability that $y = 1$ for the group in question (for whom $x_i = 1$) and P_r is the probability that $y = 1$ for the reference group (for whom $x_i = 0$). For example, in our marijuana legalization model, the odds ratio for the female dummy variable is the odds that female respondents will support legalization divided by the odds that male respondents will do so.

Stata will present the results in terms of odds ratios if you combine the **logit** command with the **or** option. Alternatively, the **logistic** command gives odds ratios by default. For example, the following command estimates the same model but shows the odds ratios instead of the coefficients:

```
svy: logit legmar age i.sex i.race educ ib3.party ///
   i.religious i.region, or
```

In the output of the odds-ratio version of the model (not shown), the z scores and the p-values are identical. This means that the statistical significance of each variable is unchanged compared with the default logit output in Output 14.2. This makes sense, since the **or** option only changes the way the results are presented. Instead of coefficients, the first column of numbers consists of an odds ratio for each independent variable. The standard error and the confidence intervals are different, but the statistical significance of each variable is unchanged.

A common mistake is to interpret the odds ratio as the ratio of the probabilities. If the female dummy variable has an odds-ratio coefficient of 0.73, this does *not* mean that the probability of a female supporting legalization is 73% of the probability of a male supporting legalization. If 56.5% of females support legalization and 64% of males do, then the odds ratio would be $[0.565/(1 - 0.565)]/[0.64/(1 - 0.64)] = 0.73$.

14.4.2.3 Marginal Effects

Odds ratios are often used in research on health and nutrition, but less so in other fields. For those not used to interpreting odds ratios, it is probably easier to interpret the marginal effect of each independent variable (x_i) on the predicted probability (P). This can be calculated "by hand" using calculus:

$$\frac{\partial P}{\partial x_i} = \beta_i P(1-P) \tag{14.5}$$

This equation says that the marginal effect of independent variable x_i on P (the probability that $y = 1$) is equal to the coefficient on x_i multiplied by $P(1 - P)$. Since P varies for each respondent in the survey, we can generate a single number for the marginal effect by using the average value of P. From this equation, we know that the marginal effect is close to 0 when P is close to 0 or close to 1. The maximum value of $P(1 - P)$ is 0.25, so the largest marginal effect is $\beta_i/4$.

Alternatively (and much more easily), we can have Stata calculate the marginal effect of each independent variable on the predicted probability with the **margins** command. For example, the command shown in Output 14.4, run after the **logit** command, will give the effect of a one-unit increase in each independent variable on the predicted value of the probability. Because the marginal effect varies across observations, this command calculates the average marginal effect across all observations by default.[6] The **dydx()** option indicates that we want the marginal effects (rather than elasticities) of each variable listed in parentheses. Stata allows factor variable notation such as i.*region*. Since the region dummy variables were not statistically significant, they can be excluded. Output 14.4 shows the command and the output it generates. Alternatively, we can use the menu system (see Dialog Box 14.2).

Output 14.4 indicates that each additional year of age is associated with, on average, a 0.40 percentage point reduction in the probability of approving of legalization of marijuana. Similarly, being female reduces the probability of supporting legalization by 6.9 percentage points. Although the difference between Blacks and Whites is not statistically significant, Other races are 23 percentage points less likely to support legalization compared with Whites (the omitted category). In addition, compared with independents, Republicans are less likely to support legalization, while Democrats are more likely.

---

[6] The alternative is to have Stata calculate the marginal effects at the mean values of the independent variables.

↔ **DIALOG BOX 14.2: MARGINAL EFFECTS USING MENUS**

Statistics → Postestimation → Marginal effects of all covariates → Population averaged (average over estimation sample) → Submit

Note: Menu options do not allow marginal effects to be calculated for a subset of variables. This menu sequence will generate marginal effects of all independent variables.

✓ **OUTPUT 14.4: RESULTS OF LOGIT REGRESSION WITH MARGINAL EFFECTS COMMAND**

Each additional year of age is associated with a 0.40 percentage point reduction in the probability of supporting legalization, on average.

Republicans are 14.4 percentage points less likely to support legalization compared with independents (the omitted category).

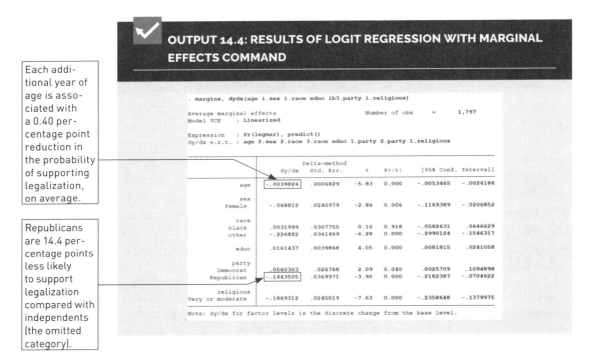

```
. margins, dydx(age i.sex i.race educ ib3.party i.religious)

Average marginal effects                     Number of obs    =    1,797
Model VCE      : Linearized

Expression     : Pr(legmar), predict()
dy/dx w.r.t.   : age 2.sex 2.race 3.race educ 1.party 2.party 1.religious

                         Delta-method
                 dy/dx     Std. Err.      t     P>|t|     [95% Conf. Interval]

         age   -.0039826   .0006829    -5.83   0.000    -.0053465    -.0026186

         sex
      female   -.068812    .0240979    -2.86   0.006    -.1169389    -.0206852

        race
       black    .0031999   .0307755     0.10   0.918    -.0582631     .0646629
       other   -.226822    .0361469    -6.28   0.000    -.2990124    -.1546317

        educ    .0161437   .0039868     4.05   0.000     .0081815     .0241058

       party
    Democrat    .0560303   .026768      2.09   0.040     .0025709     .1094898
  Republican   -.1443505   .0369971    -3.90   0.000    -.2182387    -.0704622

   religious
Very or moderate -.1869312 .0245019    -7.63   0.000    -.2358648    -.1379975

Note: dy/dx for factor levels is the discrete change from the base level.
```

14.5 LOGIT VERSUS PROBIT REGRESSION MODELS

As mentioned earlier, another option for carrying out regression analysis with a binary dependent variable is the probit model, which uses the command **probit**. It is similar to the logit model in that both describe a function that looks like an elongated "S," which never falls below $P = 0$ and never rises above $P = 1$. The probit function is different from the logit function: Instead of being based on the log odds, it is based on the cumulative normal probability function, denoted by $\Phi()$:

$$P = \Phi\left(\beta_0 + \sum_{i=1}^{k-1}\beta_i x_i\right)$$ (14.6)

Although the equations for logit and probit look quite different, in practice, the results are almost identical. Figure 14.3 combines the logit estimation from Figure 14.2 with a probit estimation using the same data. The predicted values of y (probabilities) are almost identical. As another demonstration of the similarity of results, we have run the marijuana legalization model using the **svy: probit** command, generated the predicted probabilities using the **predict** command, and then calculated the correlation between the logit and probit predictions using the **correl** command. The correlation coefficient is 0.9998. In addition, the marginal effects of the probit and logit models differ by no more than 0.003.

Because of the similarity of results, it is not worth devoting time to determining which model gives a "better" fit. The logit model used to have an advantage because it is computationally simpler, but modern computers make this difference moot. In fields that are familiar with odds ratios, such as health and nutrition, the logit function is more common. In other fields, such as economics and political science, the probit model is the default model for regression analysis with binary dependent variables.

FIGURE 14.3 ● COMPARISON OF PROBIT AND LOGIT MODELS

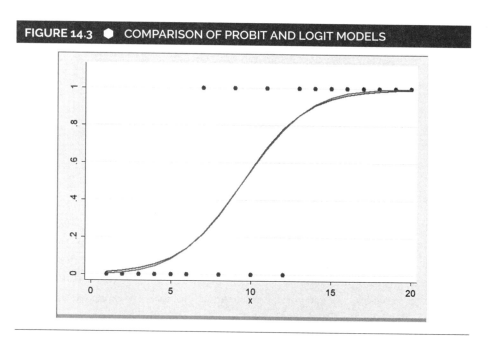

14.6 REGRESSION ANALYSIS WITH OTHER TYPES OF CATEGORICAL DEPENDENT VARIABLES

In some cases, the dependent variable is categorical with more than two possible values, so the probit and logit regression models are not suitable. An example of this might be a model to predict the marital status of adults (single, married, divorced, or widowed) or to predict the political affiliation of voters (Democrat, Republican, or other). In this situation, we can run a multinomial logit model using the **mlogit** command or a multinomial probit model using the **mproit** command.

In both cases, a base (or reference) outcome category must be identified, and the analysis will generate a set of coefficients for each of the other outcome categories. In other words, if there are n categories in the dependent variable, the results will include a set of coefficients for each of the $n-1$ categories other than the reference category.

Suppose we are developing a model to predict marital status using the 2016 GSS. The variable marital takes five values: married, widowed, divorced, separated, and never married. We want to collapse these into three categories, combining widowed, divorced, and separated into one category. The following commands create a new variable (marital3) and give it labels.

```
recode marital (1=1) (2/4=2) (5=3), gen(marital3)
lab def marital3lab 1 "Married" ///
  2 "No longer married" ///
  3 "Never married"
lab val marital3 marital3lab
lab var marital3 "Marital status"
```

The multilogit regression analysis can be implemented using the menu system (see Dialog Box 14.3) or using the **mlogit** command at the top of Output 14.5. The **svy:** prefix indicates that we want the calculations to take into account the sample design. After the **mlogit** command, we list the dependent variable (marital3) and the independent variables. The categorical independent variables are expressed using the factor variable notation. The **base(3)** option makes the third category (never married) the base or reference outcome.

The results from the multinomial logit analysis are shown in Output 14.5. The first set of coefficients show the factors that predict being married rather than never married. The positive and significant coefficients indicate that being older, female, and more educated increases the probability of being married rather than never married, holding constant other factors. At the same time, being Black decreases the chance of being married rather than never married, other factors being equal.

The second set of coefficients shows the effect of the independent variables on the likelihood of being formerly married rather than never married. Being female and older significantly increases the probability of being formerly married compared with never having been married.

Certainly, there are grounds for not taking these results too seriously. It is likely that other variables should be included in the model, such as income, which could affect the value and significance of the coefficients. In addition, there is a risk of reverse causality. For example, marital status may have an effect on the educational level. The main purpose of this exercise is to demonstrate the multinomial logit model, how to implement it in Stata, and how to interpret the results.

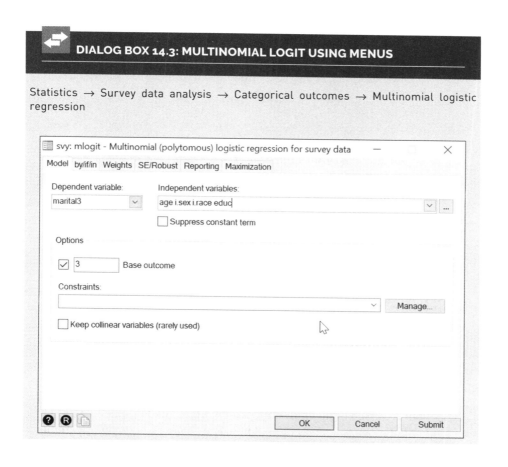

DIALOG BOX 14.3: MULTINOMIAL LOGIT USING MENUS

Statistics → Survey data analysis → Categorical outcomes → Multinomial logistic regression

OUTPUT 14.5: RESULTS FROM MULTINOMIAL LOGIT

```
. svy: mlogit marital3 age i.sex i.race educ, base(3)
(running mlogit on estimation sample)

Survey: Multinomial logistic regression

Number of strata   =        65          Number of obs     =        2,848
Number of PSUs     =       130          Population size   =    2,847.8231
                                        Design df         =           65
                                        F( 10,     56)    =        47.65
                                        Prob > F          =       0.0000
```

marital3	Coef.	Linearized Std. Err.	t	P>|t|	[95% Conf. Interval]	
Married						
age	.092523	.0057464	16.10	0.000	.0810466	.1039994
sex						
female	.2722988	.1109619	2.45	0.017	.0506926	.493905
race						
black	-1.030759	.1546168	-6.67	0.000	-1.33955	-.7219679
other	-.0816475	.1681517	-0.49	0.629	-.4174696	.2541747
educ	.0745271	.022263	3.35	0.001	.0300648	.1189894
_cons	-4.172427	.4131752	-10.10	0.000	-4.997595	-3.347259
No_longer_married						
age	.1156812	.0061337	18.86	0.000	.1034314	.127931
sex						
female	.7771531	.1199308	6.48	0.000	.5376347	1.016672
race						
black	-.2845191	.1835914	-1.55	0.126	-.6511765	.0821383
other	.2570305	.2124682	1.21	0.231	-.1672977	.6813588
educ	-.018489	.0228486	-0.81	0.421	-.0641207	.0271428
_cons	-5.389582	.3694625	-14.59	0.000	-6.127449	-4.651714
Never_married	(base outcome)					

14.7 PRESENTING THE RESULTS

As discussed in Chapter 12, the write-up should focus on not only the statistical significance of the independent variables but also the relevance of the size of the effect. It is possible to have a variable whose effect is statistically significant at the usual levels of confidence but too small to make much difference in practice. This is particularly true when working with databases with a large number of observations.

For a general audience, it is not necessary to provide a table of logit regression results. Instead, we focus on the sign of the statistically significant results, with perhaps a few examples of the marginal effects. The results of the logit model describing support for legalization of marijuana could be summarized as follows:

> What factors are linked to support for legalization of marijuana among adults in the United States? The results of the 2016 General Social Survey provide some answers. Support for legalization of marijuana is more common among younger people, men, and those with more education, holding other factors constant. At the same time, those who report being Republicans are much less likely to favor legalization than independents and Democrats. Although the difference between Blacks and Whites is negligible, other non-Whites are 23 percentage points less likely to support legalization compared with Whites. Finally, those who describe themselves as very or moderately religious are much less likely to support legalization of marijuana.

For an academic journal or a technical audience, more detail on the methods and results can be provided. For fields where odds ratios are widely used, the results can be presented in terms of odds ratios. For other fields, it may be preferable to present results in terms of the average marginal effects. After running the **logit** and **margins** commands, we can use the **outreg** command[7] to generate a table of the marginal effects and standard errors in Word format. The command is as follows:

```
outreg using "c:/Legalization model", stat(b_dfdx se_dfdx)
replace
```

The **using** portion of the command indicates the name of the Word file to create and the folder where it should be put. The **stat()** option tells Stata which statistics to include in the table, in this case the marginal effects of the coefficients and their standard errors. And the **replace** option indicates that the file should replace any file of the same name if it already exists.

The table produced by this command is shown in Output 14.6. Note that **outreg** does not make use of value labels in factor variables (e.g., i.region), so, for publication, it would be necessary to revise the first column of Output 14.6 by hand.

---

[7] As noted in Chapter 12, **outreg** is a user-defined command. Since it is not part of Stata software, it must be downloaded by typing **ssc download outreg** into the Stata command window.

OUTPUT 14.6: OUTPUT OF LOGIT REGRESSION IN WORD FORMAT

	Support for marijuana legalization
age of respondent	-0.004
	(0.001)**
1b.sex	0.000
	(0.000)
2.sex	-0.069
	(0.024)**
1b.race	0.000
	(0.000)
2.race	0.003
	(0.031)
3.race	-0.227
	(0.036)**
highest year of school completed	0.016
	(0.004)**
1.party	0.056
	(0.027)*
2.party	-0.144
	(0.037)**
3b.party	0.000
	(0.000)
0b.religious	0.000
	(0.000)
1.religious	-0.187
	(0.025)**
1b.region	0.000
	(0.000)
2.region	0.090
	(0.057)
3.region	-0.012
	(0.066)
4.region	0.038
	(0.066)
5.region	0.014
	(0.055)
6.region	-0.018
	(0.064)
7.region	0.066
	(0.068)
8.region	0.049
	(0.068)
9.region	0.017
	(0.058)
N	1,797

$* p<0.05; ** p<0.01$

The description of the results for a technical audience can be more detailed, as shown below:

> Data from the 2016 General Social Survey were used to explore the socioeconomic characteristics associated with support for legalization of marijuana. A logit model was used to analyze the 1,797 respondents who answered the legalization question. Standard errors were adjusted to take into account clustering and other characteristics of the sample design. The results indicate that opinions on legalization of marijuana vary significantly by age, gender, race, education, political party affiliation, and self-reported intensity of religious belief. The results are presented in terms of the average marginal effect of each independent variable on the probability of supporting legalization. Each additional year of age is associated with a 0.398 percentage point reduction in the probability of supporting legalization, with a confidence interval (CI) of 0.262 to 0.535 percentage points. Other things being equal, support among women is 6.88 percentage points lower (CI 2.06, 11.7) than among men. The difference in support between Blacks and Whites is not statistically significant, but support among other non-Whites is 22.7 percentage points lower (CI 15.5, 29.9) than among Whites. Each additional year of education is associated with a 1.61 percentage point increase (CI 0.818, 2.41) in the probability of favoring the legalization of marijuana. Support for legalization among Democrats is 5.60 percentage points higher than among independents (CI 0.257, 19.95), while support among Republicans is 14.4 percentage points lower (CI 7.04, 21.8) than among independents, holding constant other factors. Finally, those who describe themselves as very or moderately religious are 18.8 percentage points (CI 13.8, 23.6) less likely to support legalization of marijuana. After controlling for other factors, we find no regional differences in the support for legalization of marijuana.

14.8 SUMMARY OF COMMANDS USED IN THIS CHAPTER

As described in Chapter 4, this last section of each chapter summarizes all of the Stata code used in the chapter. In addition, all Stata code used throughout the book is summarized in Appendix 1.

Scatterplot of a binary dependent variable

```
twoway (scatter y x) (lfit y x), legend(off) yscale(range(0 1.5))
```

Describe all variables

```
des
```

List of all value labels for one variable

```
label list GRASS
```

Generate a new variable and apply labels

```
recode grass 1=1 2=0, gen(legmar)
lab define legmarlab 1 Supports 0 Opposes
lab val legmar legmarlab
lab var legmar "Position on legalization of marijuana"
recode partyid (0 1=1) (5 6=2) (2/4 7=3), gen(party)
lab def partylab 1 Democrat 2 Republican 3 Other
lab val party partylab
recode relpersn (1 2=1) (3 4=0), gen(religious)
lab def rellab 1 "Very or moderate" 0 "Slight or not"
lab val religious rellab
```

Logit regression command

```
logit legmar age i.sex i.race educ ib3.party i.religious i. ///
    region
```

Logit regression command with adjustments for sample design

```
svy: logit legmar age i.sex i.race educ ib3.party i.religious i. ///
   region
```

Logit regression command with adjustment for sample design and presenting odds ratio

```
svy: logit legmar age i.sex i.race educ ib3.party i.religious i. ///
   region, or
```

Testing joint significance

```
testparm i.race
testparm i.party
testparm i.region
```

Calculating the marginal effects of selected variables after a nonlinear regression model

```
margin, dydx(age i.sex i.race educ ib3.party i.religious)
```

Multinomial logit model

```
recode marital (1=1) (2/4=2) (5=3), gen(marital3)
lab def marital3lab 1 "Married" 2 "No longer married" ///
   3 "Never married"
lab val marital3 marital3lab
svy: mlogit marital3 age i.sex i.race educ, base(2)
```

Generate a table of logit results in Word format

```
outreg using "c://Legalization model", stat(b_dfdx se_dfdx) ///
   replace
```

EXERCISES

1. As the cost of college tuition rises, many politicians have called for tuition assistance for low-income students to level the playing field. Others have recommended that all community colleges should be free for anyone who wants to attend. On the flip side, some politicians argue against free college and have even called for a tax on tuition waivers and a reduction in state funding of public colleges. Using the 2016 GSS, we can explore the characteristics of those who support financial aid for college students.

   a. In the GSS2016 data set, one question is, "The government should assist low-income college students." There were four possible responses: definitely should, probably should, probably should not, and definitely should not. Begin by recoding this variable (aidcol) into two categories. Combine those who think the government definitely should and probably should into one category. Combine those who think they probably shouldn't and definitely shouldn't into a second category.

   b. Run a logistic regression with your new variable from Part "a" as the dependent variable. The independent variables should include income (realrinc), age (age), sex (sex), and someone's political affiliation. For the sex variable, generate a new variable whereby 1 is female and 0 is male. For the political affiliation variable (partyid), generate a new variable that has three categories: Democrat, Republican, and other. The Democrats would include strong Democrat and not strong Democrat. Republicans would include strong Republican and not strong Republican. The third category, independent, would include independent, independent near Democrat, independent near Republican, and other party. Be sure to examine the numeric codes before you make the new variable.

   c. Use the **margins, dydx(*)** command immediately after running your logistic regression in Part "b."

   d. Write a paragraph for a scholarly journal that would describe the results.

2. In the 2016 GSS, respondents were asked whether they would favor or oppose a law that would require a person to obtain a police permit before he or she could buy a gun (gunlaw). Run a logit regression to examine the characteristics of people who favor or oppose the gun permit law. You can use any variables in the data set that you think would be relevant to whether or not someone would oppose or favor the gun permit law. Then, write a brief report summarizing your findings. This should be four to five paragraphs: An introduction, two to three paragraphs that make up your key points, and a concluding paragraph. You can assume that you are writing this as a short article in *Newsweek* or *The Economist*.

   Hint: To quickly find variables that may be of interest, open the variable manager. In the space in the upper left corner, it says, "enter filter text here." You can type in anything you are looking for, and it will show you all variables that have those words in the description.

REFERENCES

De Pinto, J., Backus, F., Khanna, K., & Salvanto, A. (2017). *Marijuana legalization support at all-time high*. Retrieved from www.cbsnews.com/news/support-for-marijuana-legalization-at-all-time-high/

Greene, W. H. (2018). *Econometric analysis*. New York, NY: Pearson.

Long, J. S., & Freese, J. (2006). *Regression models for categorical dependent variables using Stata*. College Station, TX: Stata Press.

Peduzzi, P., Concato, J., Kemper, E., Holford, T. R., & Feinstein, A. R. (1996). A simulation study of the number of events per variable in logistic regression analysis. *Journal of Clinical Epidemiology, 49*(12), 1373–1379.

WRITING A RESEARCH PAPER

PART FIVE

WRITING A RESEARCH PAPER

Chapter Preview

1. Introduction to the research paper
   a. Describe the general topic
   b. What research has been done and what are the gaps in this literature?
   c. Define your specific question and how it relates to the gaps or contributes to the literature
   d. How will you answer your question (method)?
   e. Overview of results
   f. Outline of paper
2. Literature review
   a. Identify key themes in literature related to the research question
   b. Summarize significant sources within each theme
   c. Identify remaining gaps in literature that you intend to address
3. Theory, data, and methods
   a. Sample size, selection method, time period
   b. Type of analysis
   c. Expected outcomes based on theory
   d. Measurement of variables
4. Results
   a. Restate research questions
   b. Results related to each research question

5. Discussion

   a. Do results agree or disagree with literature?

   b. Recommendations based on the results

   c. Limitations of the study

   d. Areas for future research

6. Conclusions

   a. Summarize the key findings

   b. Why are the results important?

15.1 INTRODUCTION

As described in Chapter 1, the research process begins with reading the literature, identifying gaps in the literature, and defining your research question. Once you have defined your research question, there are six parts to a typical research paper. This may vary depending on the journal or type of publication, but in general, all of the components listed above will be included in a research paper. We will review each of these six parts.

15.2 INTRODUCTION SECTION OF A RESEARCH PAPER

The introduction to a journal article or research paper should begin by defining the general topic. In other words, what is the big picture? Why is this research important or why should the reader be interested? Using a paper by Minot and Goletti (1998), "Export Liberalization and Household Welfare: The Case of Rice in Vietnam," we will illustrate each part of the introduction. Their opening paragraph is as follows:

> Many of the policy reforms undertaken in **developing countries over the last fifteen years**, including devaluation, price decontrol, and export liberalization, can result in **high food prices**. This is a **matter of concern** because the price of staple foods is an important determinant of the well-being of poor families in low-income countries. Higher food prices **reduce the real income** of urban households, particularly **poor urban households** since they tend to spend a relatively large share of their budgets on food. It is **difficult to generalize about the overall effect of higher food prices** on the poor, however, because the rural poor are both producers and consumers. (p. 738)

The bold and italicized parts of the text are used to illustrate that the authors first identify the problem (high food prices), where it is taking place (developing countries), and over what time period (the past 15 years). They then tell us why this is a concern (it reduces real income of poor urban households). In the last sentence, they identify the problem they hope to address (how to determine the overall effect of high food prices on the poor).

The second part of the introduction is to illustrate in brief what has already been written about this topic. This is not the full literature review, but only a selection of literature that will support your rationale for choosing the topic. It will also begin to identify gaps in the literature. Minot and Goletti (1998) do this in three paragraphs that are shown below:

> Mellor noted that the direct welfare effect of higher food prices depends on the net sales position of the household: net sellers, such as commercial farmers, gain, while net buyers, such as urban consumers and landless rural households, lose. His data from India revealed that only the poorest quintile of rural households were net buyers. Weber et al. reviewed the results from five studies in sub-Saharan Africa showing that 15% to 73% of farm households are net buyers, depending on the crop and the country. Other studies have estimated that net buyers of rice account for 49% of the farmers in Madagascar (Barrett and Dorosh) and for 84% of the rural households in Sri Lanka (Sahn).

> A number of studies have quantified the welfare impact of food price changes. Computable general equilibrium models have been widely used to examine the impact of policy on different household groups (for example, see Bourguignon, de Melo, and Morrrison). *Although these models capture the indirect effects of policy reforms on labor markets and nonagricultural sectors, they generally have just four to eight household types, limiting the degree of detail that can be provided regarding the distributional impact of policy.*

> Other studies combine household data and hypothesized price changes. Deaton studied the distributional effect of high rice prices that would result from export liberalization in Thailand. He used nonparametric regression methods to examine the relationship between per capita household expenditure and the net benefit ratio (NBR), defined as the value of net sales as a proportion of income. The NBR for a commodity can be interpreted as the short-term elasticity of real income with respect to the price of that commodity. Similar methods were adopted in studies of the distributional

effect of higher food prices in Cote d'Ivoire (Budd) and in Madagascar (Barrett and Dorosh). (p. 738)

In these three paragraphs, Minot and Goletti (1998) describe different methods used in various studies to determine the impact of higher food prices on the urban poor. They also begin to identify gaps or limitations in the studies, as illustrated in the italicized sentence.

Once it has been established that there are gaps in the literature, the next step is to define your own research question and determine how it fits into the literature and how it addresses the gaps. This is demonstrated in Minot and Goletti's (1998) paper as follows:

> ***This study examines the effect of the higher rice prices*** associated with export liberalization on income distribution and poverty in Vietnam. Our approach ***expands on the studies mentioned above in several ways. First,*** we use a national household sample, allowing us to consider the trade-off between gains to surplus farmers and losses to urban consumers and other net buyers. ***Second,*** in addition to calculation of the impact on average income, we also estimate the effect of price changes on various poverty measures. ***Third,*** we use a welfare measure that distinguishes between farmgate and retail prices and that incorporates household responses to price changes. And ***fourth,*** we simulate the price changes at the regional level using a spatial-equilibrium multimarket model, rather than assuming a uniform price change for all regions within the country. (pp. 738–739)

Notice that Minot and Goletti (1998) first state the purpose of their paper. Next, they explicitly identify four ways in which their paper expands on the existing literature.

After identifying your research question, the next section of the introduction typically describes the method used to answer the study. It may also be included as part of the explanation of how you expand on the literature, as done by Minot and Goletti (1998). The method may include a variety of techniques used to do your research. These include case studies, benefit–cost analyses, regression analyses, surveys, meta-analyses, and forecasting. Some studies are simply an exhaustive literature review. If your study is a literature review, you should not describe the method as "I used primary and secondary sources." Instead, you should be specific about how you used the sources or what you looked for in the sources. In their abstract below, Allgood, Walstad, and Siegfried (2015) provide an excellent example of how to describe their method that uses a literature review of research on teaching economics to undergraduates:

> This survey summarizes the main research findings about teaching economics to undergraduates. After briefly reviewing the history of research on

undergraduate economic education, it discusses the status of the economics major-numbers and trends, goals, coursework, outcomes, and the principles courses. Some economic theory is used to explain the likely effects of pedagogical decisions of faculty and the learning choices that students make. Major results from empirical research are reviewed from the professor's perspective on such topics as teaching methods, online technology, class size, and textbooks. Studies of student learning are discussed in relation to study time, grades, attendance, math aptitude, and cheating. The last section discusses changes in the composition of faculty who teach undergraduate economics and effects from changes in instructional technology and then presents findings from the research about measuring teaching effectiveness and the value of teacher training. (p. 285)

Following a description of the method, one paragraph is typically used to describe the results or key highlights of the paper. Below is the example from Minot and Goletti (1998):

The results indicate that less than one-third of the Vietnamese households have net sales of rice. Furthermore, the higher rice prices associated with export liberalization exacerbate inequality among regions and within urban and rural areas. At the same time, the gains outweigh the losses, the average income of the poor rises, and somewhat surprisingly, the incidence of poverty declines slightly. We examine several explanations for these apparently paradoxical results. (p. 739)

Finally, the last paragraph of the introduction to a journal article or report is often used to indicate what will be included in each section of the paper. This is not essential, and it is not always included in a short journal article. Longer papers or reports, however, typically do have this paragraph. Below is an example from the Allgood et al. (2015) paper on teaching economics to undergraduates:

The article is divided into eight sections that include this short introduction and a conclusion. In the second section, we briefly review the history of research on teaching college economics to acquaint instructors with the major developments and sources of information on the subject since its origins in the 1960s. In the third section, we survey the landscape of undergraduate economics to describe enrollments, the typical curriculum of courses for undergraduate economics students, and outcomes from the economics major. In the fourth section, we use economic theory to explain the likely effects of decisions that economics professors can make either in structuring or teaching their courses, and also students' decisions about enrolling and participating in economics courses. The purpose of this theory section is to increase the understanding of empirical findings about faculty teaching decisions and selected student behaviors and decisions that are the subjects of the fifth and sixth sections. The seventh section briefly discusses how changes in the characteristics of faculty and changes in technology are likely to affect undergraduate economics instruction in the future, before turning to the issue of teaching effectiveness and examining research on the assessment of instruction from student and faculty perspectives. (p. 286)

15.3 LITERATURE REVIEW

As noted in the previous section, part of the literature review appears in the introduction. It may also be woven into other parts of the paper. For example, results from empirical studies are sometimes compared with the previous literature in the results or discussion section of the paper. The data and methods section may also review methods used in previous studies. In many papers, however, there is a separate section devoted to the literature review. We offer guidelines about this section below.

The purpose of a literature review is to summarize the most significant sources related to a research question. Rather than describing each article or source in its own paragraph like an annotated bibliography, the sources are woven into paragraphs based on themes or main points. The literature review should identify where the sources agree or disagree and how they relate to the research question of the paper. Overall, like the introduction to the paper, the literature review should convince the reader that your topic is interesting, is important, and fills a gap in the literature.

Students often ask how many sources they should include in the literature review. There is no magic number. If the research question is well-defined, it will help narrow your search. If the question is too broad, then there could be thousands of articles on a topic. Once you have refined your question, you should include significant sources specifically related to your question. "Significant sources" would generally refer to articles that appear in peer-reviewed journals and are cited frequently by other articles or papers. Obviously, if articles are very recent, they won't have a large number of citations. These should be reviewed to determine if they are relevant to your question.

In the example of a literature review below, Enfield (2013) conducts a study in which he "flips the classroom." He first reviews the literature related to the benefits and drawbacks of flipping the classroom and then describes the results of his own experiment.

Flipping the classroom involves providing instructional resources for students to use outside of class so that class time is freed up for other instructional activities. The Flipped Classroom Model is described and defended by Mull (2012). While not all of the principles Mull describes are utilized by all teachers who flip their classroom, all implementations include the idea that, "Students prepare for class by watching video, listening to podcasts, reading articles, or contemplating questions that access their prior knowledge." (para. 3)

Milman (2012) explains "the idea is that rather than taking up valuable class time for an instructor to introduce a concept (often via lecture), the instructor can create a video lecture, screencast, or podcast that teaches students the concept, freeing up valuable class time for more engaging (and often collaborative) activities typically facilitated by the instructor" (p. 85). Milman goes on to note that formative and summative assessment should be incorporated as well as meaningful face-to-face learning activities.

Proponents of a Flipped Classroom provide many arguments for engaging students in the content outside of the class to free up time in class for other instructional activities. Milman (2012) identifies what could be considered the primary advantage: increased class time for more engaging instruction. Millard (2012) describes advantages such as increased student engagement, strengthening of team-based skills, personalized student guidance, focused classroom discussion, and creative freedom of faculty while maintaining a standardized curriculum. Fulton (2012) notes that Flipped Classrooms allow students to move at their own pace, access instruction at any time, access expertise from multiple people, benefit from better used classroom time and more.

While many educators who have flipped their classrooms tout the benefits they experienced, there are critics to this approach. Nielsen (2012) discusses concerns with accessibility to instructional resources being provided online, the growing move towards no homework, increased time requirements without improved pedagogy, lack of adapting the classroom environment to reflect the flipped classroom's ability to support student-centered learning (allowing students to learn at their own pace), and use of lectures to provide instruction with disregard to individual student learning styles. Mull (2012) addresses several of the common concerns which, in addition to some previously mentioned, include teachers' concerns that their role will be diminished, the students' experience with the out-of-class instruction will not be interactive, a lack of accountability for students to complete the out-of-class instruction, and the restrictive cost and time needed to produce instructional materials. Milman (2012) also notes several concerns with the Flipped Classroom approach, including poor quality video production, conditions in which the students view the video, inability to monitor comprehension and provide just-in-time information when needed, and use with second language learners or students with learning disabilities.

Given all of the benefits and drawbacks of the approach, it appears that there is a place for the Flipped Classroom Model for at least some instructional contexts. "Although there are many limitations to the flipped classroom strategy and no empirical research exists to substantiate its use, anecdotal reports by many instructors maintain that it can be used as a valuable strategy at any level, depending on one's learners, resources, and time" (Milman, 2012, p. 86). Milman notes that while the Flipped Classroom approach lends itself well to learning of procedural knowledge, it can also be used for the learning of factual, conceptual, and metacognitive learning. (Enfield, 2013, pp. 14–15)

Overall, Enfield reviews five sources in his literature review. Rather than writing about each of the five articles in separate paragraphs, he weaves them into paragraphs based on the main argument or theme of each paragraph. Note the same authors can appear in multiple paragraphs and on both sides of the argument. Overall, the structure is as follows:

Paragraph 1: Introduces the idea of a flipped classroom as presented by Mull

Paragraph 2: Discusses the benefits of a flipped classroom as presented by Milman

Paragraph 3: Lists other benefits identified by three authors, Milman, Millard, and Fulton

Paragraph 4: Identifies criticisms of a flipped classroom by three authors, Nielsen, Mull, and Milman

Paragraph 5: Acknowledges that there are benefits and drawbacks based on the literature review. Identifies the gap—no empirical research on the effectiveness of the flipped classroom

Another key question when conducting a literature review is when to use a direct quote from the literature and when to paraphrase. Direct quotes are typically used when the original passage is so unique or well stated that it can't be easily paraphrased. They are also used if they offer a definition for an unusual word or concept. Paraphrasing, on the other hand, is used to summarize or simplify other research. Generally, direct quotes should be limited, while paraphrasing is much more common.[1]

15.4 THEORY, DATA, AND METHODS

The method used in a research paper is typically described briefly in the introduction as discussed earlier. If the paper is based on some type of empirical research (analysis of data), then the data and methods section will go into much greater detail. It is considered the most important part of the paper since it establishes the validity of the paper. In other words, it allows the audience to judge if the results are valid, how they fit into known theories, and if they can be applied to the general population. Because of its importance, this section should be clear, precise, and detailed enough that the same study could be replicated.

For the type of study that we describe in this book (collecting data and using statistical techniques to analyze the data), the following information would be included in the data and methods section:

Data information

- When and where the data were collected

- Who collected the data (which organization)

- The sampling method and sample size

- Limitations or problems with the data

- Adjustments to the data and weighting procedures

Method information

- Type of analysis (regression, descriptive statistics, hypothesis testing—t tests, ANOVA, chi-squared tests, case studies, forecasting, etc.)

- Expected outcomes or signs of variables (based on theory and hypotheses)

- Measurement of variables used in the analysis

Although theory is often woven into the introduction and the literature review, it often appears in the methods section to position the research approach within a school of thought or to indicate the expected outcome of the research based on theory.

---

[1] For a nice summary of when to quote and when to paraphrase, see Jerman (2012).

Below is an example of a description of the data collection method from an article on the use of prescription stimulants among undergraduate students (Teter, McCabe, Cranford, Boyd, & Guthrie, 2005):

> The Institutional Review Board at the University of Michigan approved the protocol for the present study and all participating students gave informed consent. The study was conducted during a 1-month period in March and April of 2003, drawing on a total undergraduate population of 21,294 full-time students (10,860 women and 10,434 men). Two drug-related surveys were being conducted at the same time and we did not want to burden undergraduate students with taking 2 similar surveys. Therefore, we surveyed the entire population but this study was based on a random sample of 19,278 students and the other study used the remaining students. We sent the sample group an e-mail message describing the study and inviting them to self-administer the Student Life Survey (SLS) by using a unique password and clicking on a link to access the Web survey. The Web survey was maintained on an Internet site running under the secure socket layer protocol to ensure privacy and security. We sent 3 reminder e-mails to non-respondents. By participating in the survey, students became eligible for a sweepstakes of 13 cash prizes ranging from $100 to $1,000. The final response rate was 47%, which is consistent with other college-based AOD studies. (pp. 253–254)

This same article then has additional subsections describing the questionnaire, measures used for different variables, and procedures used in data analysis. For example, in the "Measures" subsection, the authors provide the exact wording used on the questionnaire to determine how often students used illicit drugs over the past year and over their lifetime.

15.5 RESULTS

The purpose of the results section is to identify the most relevant results needed to answer the research question(s). In addition, however, summary statistics related to the variables used in the analysis are also given, such as a table showing the mean and standard deviation of each key variable.

In some journals, the results section includes an interpretation of the results and possible policy implications. In other journals, however, the results section is used strictly to state the results. Interpretation and analysis then follow in a "Discussion" or "Comment" section. Some guidelines for the results section are offered below.

15.5.1 Logical Sequence

The results section often follows the order of the research questions or hypotheses stated in the introduction and then reports on the tests related to each question or hypothesis. Typically, broader results are reported first followed by detailed analyses of each research question. For example, in the Teter et al. (2005) paper on the use of stimulant drugs among undergraduates, they state two primary objectives or questions in their introduction: (1) What is the prevalence and motive for use of stimulant drugs? (2) Is there a link between the motives for use of stimulants and the use of alcohol and other drugs? Their results section is then divided into two sections that answer these questions as follows:

Prevalence Rates and Motives for Use

More than 8.1% of the undergraduate student sample ($n = 689$) reported the illicit use of prescription stimulants in their lifetime, and 5.4% ($n = 458$) reported illicit use in the past year; undergraduate men reported significantly higher lifetime rates than did undergraduate women (9.3% vs 7.2%, $p < 0.001$). Lifetime rates were higher for White (9.5%) and Hispanic (8.9%) students than for African-American (2.7%), Asian (4.9%), or other racial student groups (5.8%), $\chi^2(4, N = 8{,}460) = 55.08$, $p < 0.001$.

The primary motives that students gave for using prescription stimulants illicitly were (1) to help with concentration, (2) to increase alertness, and (3) to get high. We observed no gender differences in motives for illicit use. The frequencies for each motive and the index describing the number of motives endorsed are presented in Table 3. Approximately half the students who endorsed the illicit use of prescription stimulants gave more than 1 motive for this behavior. On average, students reported 1.65 ± 0.91 motives (range 0–5, mode 1.0) for the illicit use of prescription stimulants. Of the 689 students who endorsed the lifetime illicit use of prescription stimulants, 31 did not provide a motive for their behavior, 19 students chose the "Refused" category, and 12 students did not provide any motive.

The proportion of each motive within a given frequency range was relatively consistent (see Figure 1). For example, using prescription stimulants "to help concentrate" accounted for approximately 30% of the motives, regardless of the number of occasions of illicit stimulant use. However, the distribution in the actual frequency range of illicit prescription stimulant use was skewed, with a steady decrease in the number of students reporting more frequent use. For example, a total of 254 students reported the illicit use of prescription stimulants on 1 to 2 occasions, compared with 45 who reported 40 or more occasions. The data in Figure 1 do not represent those 31 students who did not provide a motive and therefore consist of 658 students.

Approximately 14% ($n = 97$) of the illicit prescription stimulant users also reported being prescribed stimulant medication in their lifetime. We found no differences in any of the motivations endorsed by those illicit users who were also prescribed stimulants in their lifetime compared with the illicit users who had never been prescribed stimulants. For example, approximately 40% of those who endorsed the illicit use of prescription stimulants provided "to get high" as a motive, regardless of whether they had also been legitimately prescribed stimulant medications.

Alcohol and Other Drug Use Behaviors

Chi-square analysis revealed significantly higher rates of AOD use for those students who reported the illicit use of prescription stimulants, compared with nonstimulant users (see Table 4). Furthermore, regardless of the motive or motives for the illicit use of prescription stimulants, the 689 students who endorsed these behaviors also reported significantly higher rates of AOD use in the recent past. For example, only 1.6% of those who reported no illicit prescription stimulant use had used cocaine in the past year, whereas those who reported the illicit use of prescription stimulants to help them concentrate, increase alertness, or get high had past-year cocaine prevalence rates of 28.6%, 31.1%, and 35.4%, respectively. Data in Table 4 also show that the "counteracts the effects of other drugs" and the "to get high" motives were strongly associated with cocaine and amphetamine use. Finally, AOD use was positively related to the number of motives given for the illicit use of prescription stimulants, particularly for cocaine, ecstasy, and amphetamine use (See Table 5). (Teter et al., 2015, pp. 256–257)

Notice in the first paragraph that Teter et al. (2015) begin with the larger picture— what percentage of students report stimulant drug use over their lifetime. The paragraph then continues with the results that are more detailed, including drug use in the past year, drug use by men and women, and finally drug use broken down by racial and ethnic background.

15.5.2 Tables, Figures, and Numbers

Tables and figures, which include graphs and pictures, are used in the results section to display and summarize data. They should be numbered consecutively with one set of numbers for tables and a second set for figures. When referring to a specific table or figure, the word "Table" or "Figure" is always capitalized. References to specific tables or figures appear within sentences or in parentheses as illustrated in the results section of the Teter et al. (2005) paper:

"The frequencies for each motive … are presented in Table 3."

"The proportion of each motive … was relatively consistent (see Figure 1)."

"The data in Figure 1 do not represent …"

"Chi-square analysis revealed significantly higher … (see Table 4)."

"Data in Table 4 also show that …"

"Finally, AOD use was positively related to the number of motives … (See Table 5).

When referring to information from tables and figures, you should not repeat the numbers in the tables or figures since the reader can see them. Instead, you should focus on identifying patterns or highlighting the most relevant results. As one example from the Teter et al. (2005) paper, Table 3 shows the exact number of students (not percentages) who gave zero, one, two, and three or more motives for using stimulant drugs. Instead of repeating each of these numbers in the text, they write, "approximately half the students who endorsed the illicit use of prescription stimulants gave more than 1 motive for this behavior."

All tables and figures should have complete titles and labels so that the reader can understand the table without having to read the additional text. A good rule of thumb is that if a table or figure falls out of a book and someone picks it up, they should be able to understand it fully.

Finally, there are rules for writing out numbers in academic documents. The *Publication Manual of the American Psychological Association*, which is used by the social sciences and is referred to as APA style, suggests that numbers one through nine should be spelled out and that numbers 10 and above should be written as numerals (American Psychological Association, 2009).[2] There are exceptions to these rules such as references to tables or figures, numbers that are grouped for comparison and include numbers above and below 10, and numbers that represent time, dates, and age. Numbers that begin sentences should always be written out as well.

---

[2] The humanities field and often social science fields use the *Chicago Manual of Style*, which suggests spelling out numbers 1 through 99 and using numerals for all higher numbers (University of Chicago Press, 2010).

15.5.3 Reporting Results From Statistical Tests

As described in earlier chapters, the method of reporting results from statistical tests will vary depending on the publication source of the article and/or the audience. If you are writing a report for a newspaper with a wide audience, you would indicate if there was a "statistically significant difference" when comparing means or percentages. In a scholarly journal, however, you would need to include more details about the tests and the results. The APA style offers specific guidelines on reporting of statistics. These rules are shown below followed by examples of each of the statistical tests we have covered in this textbook.

15.5.3.1 APA Style Rules for Reporting the Results of Statistical Tests

- Report the descriptive statistics, including means and standard deviations.

- Include the test statistic, degrees of freedom, and obtained value of the test.

- Round test statistics and p-values to two decimal places.

- Italicize all statistical symbols (excluding Greek letters)—*N, n, M, SD, p, t,* and so on.

- Report the p-value (the probability of observing the result or a more extreme value) in one of two ways:

    - Report the exact level ($t(40) = 2.5$, $p = 0.02$). If the p-value were less than 0.001, rather than rounding this to two decimal places, you would write $p < 0.001$.

    - Use the alpha level ($t(40) = 2.5$, $p < 0.05$), assuming that your alpha level is 0.05.

15.5.3.2 Examples

Reporting a significant difference in a sample mean compared with the population mean

Students who listened to Beethoven for 1 hour before taking the Scholastic Aptitude Test scored higher ($M = 1,642$, $SD = 18$) than the national average, $t(50) = 2.47$, $p = 0.02$.

Reporting a significant difference in two means

Students who multitasked while studying for an exam scored lower ($M = 82$, $SD = 10$) than students who did not multitask ($M = 88$, $SD = 12$), $t(56) = 2.10$, $p = 0.04$.

Reporting a significant difference in more than two means

A one-way analysis of variance was conducted to examine the effect of car ownership type on behavior toward bicyclists on the road. Drivers were divided into three groups based on the cost of a new vehicle of the type that they were driving. The space between the passing car and bicyclist was then measured on a 1-mile length of road in a suburban area. There was a statistically significant difference in the average distance between the bicyclist and car among the three categories $F(2, 87) = 4.42$, $p = 0.02$. Drivers with the most expensive cars allowed 2 feet of space on average between their car and bicyclists ($SD = 1.3$) compared with 2.5 feet among drivers of midrange cars ($SD = 1.2$) and 3 feet among the drivers in the least expensive car group ($SD = 1.3$).

Reporting a significant difference in percentages

A higher percentage of people in the age-group 20 to 40 reported that they supported gay marriage (65%) compared with those in the 41 to 60 age-group (38%), $\chi^2(1, n = 200) = 14.6$, $p < 0.001$.

Reporting a significant correlation

Examining different regions of the world, a recent study showed a positive correlation between greater air pollution and deaths caused by respiratory disease ($r = 0.57$, $n = 42$, $p = 0.05$).

15.5.4 Active Versus Passive Voice and the Use of First-Person Pronouns

It is important to use the active voice in writing whenever possible. One example is below:

Passive voice: It was shown that students who listen to Beethoven before an exam earn higher scores.

Active voice: Our results showed that students who listen to Beethoven before an exam earn higher scores.

Regarding the first-person pronouns such as I or we, notice that in the active voice example, the sentence begins with "our results" instead of "the results." Generally, the first person is preferred when describing tasks performed by the authors. In addition, a single author will often use "we" instead of "I." For example, "we find that many students …" This is sometimes thought of as the "collective we," in which you are including the audience in the plural pronoun. In other words, "we (as a group) can see that the results are interesting."

15.6 DISCUSSION

The purpose of the discussion section is to interpret your results and place them within the context of the literature. Do your results agree or disagree with the literature or with theory? What are the possible explanations for this? Even if your results are unexpected or not significant, it is still important to discuss the implications. Generally, this section will not include any new statistics or even refer to tables or figures from the results section. Instead, it highlights the major findings and offers explanations.

In addition to interpreting and highlighting the results, the discussion section is also used to offer recommendations, identify limitations, and suggest areas for future research. The recommendations should come strictly from the results of your study and are often related to policy implications. In the paper by Minot and Goletti (1998), for example, they write as follows:

> Another implication is that it is important to capture regional differences when examining the distributional effect of policy, particularly in large countries, countries with poor transportation networks, or countries with regions that are self-sufficient in the relevant commodity. (p. 746)

Regarding limitations, all studies have them. They may arise from sampling, measurement of key variables, or a fault in the questionnaire, for example. It is important to list them clearly so that the readers can more accurately determine the quality of your work and its implications. If there are limitations that you have not listed, but the reader can identify them, they may then assume that you are not aware of these limitations and therefore question your entire paper. Or they may assume that you are aware of them and are trying to hide the limitations. Overall, all papers should list their limitations without hesitation. Below is an example of a list of limitations from the Teter et al. (2005) paper.

> We should note several limitations in this study before readers assess the implications of our findings. Our sample consists of students from a single campus, which limits the generalizability of our results. In addition, our study sample was drawn from a predominantly White student population attending a large public university. Therefore, our findings need to be compared with more diverse samples (both of students attending college and young adults who are not college students). Nonresponse may have introduced potential bias in the present study; however, these concerns were somewhat reduced because the demographic characteristics in the

final obtained sample closely resembled the overall student population. In addition, the rates of drug use in the present study were comparable to rates found in other national substance use surveys of college students. We did not survey students about the quantity of prescription stimulants they used illicitly per occasion. Also, we did not collect information on the route of administration (i.e., intranasal or injection), which would have an important impact on the long-term morbidity and mortality as well as the abuse potential of stimulant medication. (p. 260)

Finally, almost all papers will suggest areas for future research. Some of these may come from the list of limitations. For example, in the Teter et al. (2005) paper, they identify one of their limitations as choosing a sample from one campus that is predominantly White. They suggest further research "in various populations, such as urban residents, those not attending college, and those with diverse racial backgrounds" (p. 261).

15.7 CONCLUSIONS

Conclusions are sometimes included as part of the discussion section of a paper, and at other times they are presented as the final section of the paper. Regardless of their location, conclusions are always brief and frequently just one or two paragraphs. Rather than repeating information from the discussion section, the conclusion section is used to summarize the main findings of the paper, relate them back to the big ideas presented in the introduction, and emphasize their importance. An example from the Teter et al. (2005) paper is as follows:

College students use prescription stimulants illicitly for many reasons. Our findings highlight the importance of assessing the motives for the illicit use of prescription stimulants and suggest that these motivations may be associated with greater use of alcohol and other drugs, especially if the student reports the illicit use of such stimulants to counteract the effect of other drugs or is using them to get high. In addition, those students who provide multiple motives for the illicit use of prescription stimulants may also be using excessive amounts of AODs. Although the long-term morbidity and mortality from these behaviors remain unknown, the problem of prescription stimulant abuse exists in the college population and should be addressed both clinically and experimentally. (p. 261)

Overall, this chapter on writing a research paper is a snapshot of the research process and an overview of each section of a research paper. There are many excellent sources that go into much greater detail about the research process and each part of the final paper. One excellent source for further reading is *The Craft of Research* by Booth, Colomb, Williams, Bizup, and Fitzgerald (2016). For a concise set of rules related to writing, Weingast (2010) offers the *Caltech Rules for Writing Papers*.

EXERCISES

1. Find a newspaper or magazine article about the results of a recent study that used data. It can be in any field such as health, economics, sociology, psychology, and so on. Then find the primary source of the study in the scholarly journal where it was first published. Take one of the findings and copy exactly how it was reported in each of the two sources. Then point out the differences in the language used to report that finding.

2. Find two articles in a scholarly journal in your area of interest that include a literature review section. Write an outline of each of the two literature reviews where each bullet in your outline is the topic of one paragraph. How similar or different are the two literature reviews in their structure?

3. Using the same two articles from Question 2, write an outline of their data and/or methods section. How do they differ and how are they similar?

4. Using the same two articles from Question 2, summarize what the authors have identified as the limitations of each study and the areas of future research.

REFERENCES

Allgood, S., Walstad, W. B., & Siegfried, J. J. (2015). Research on teaching economics to undergraduates. *Journal of Economic Literature, 53*(2), 285–325. doi:10.1257/jel53.2.285

American Psychological Association. (2009). *Publication manual of the American Psychological Association* (6th ed.). Washington, DC: Author.

Booth, W. C., Colomb, G. G., Williams, J. M., Bizup, J., & Fitzgerald, W. T. (2016). *The craft of research* (4th ed.). Chicago, IL: University of Chicago Press.

Enfield, J. (2013). Looking at the impact of the flipped classroom model of instruction on undergraduate multimedia students at CSUN. *Tech Trends, 57*(6), 14–27.

Jerman, B. (2012, June). *When to quote and when to paraphrase*. Retrieved from writingcommons.org/open-text/research-methods-methodologies/integreat-evidence/summarize-paraphrase-sources/692-when-to-quote-and-when-to-paraphase

Minot, N., & Goletti, F. (1998). Export liberalization and household welfare: The case of rice in Vietnam. *American Journal of Agricultural Economics, 80,* 738–749.

Teter, C. J., McCabe, S. E., Cranford, J., Boyd, C., & Guthrie, S. (2005). Prevalence and motives for illicit use of prescription stimulants in an undergraduate student sample. *Journal of American College Health, 53*(6), 253–262.

University of Chicago Press. (2010). *Chicago manual of style* (16th ed.). Chicago, IL: Author.

Weingast, B. R. (2010). *Caltech rules for writing papers: How to structure your paper and write an introduction.* Retrieved from https://web.stanford.edu/group/mcnollgast/cgi-bin/wordpress/wp-content/uploads/2013/10/CALTECH.RUL_.pdf

APPENDIX 1: QUICK REFERENCE GUIDE TO STATA COMMANDS

All Stata commands must be in lowercase. General commands are found above each output and use the following abbreviations:

contvar = continuous variable

catvar = categorical variable

varname = can be either continuous or categorical

GRAPHS

Pie Chart

```
graph pie, over(catvar) plabel(_all percent)

graph pie, over(Sector3) plabel(_all percent)
```

FIGURE 6.4 ⬡ PIE CHART OF COLLEGE TYPES

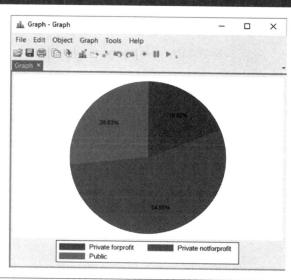

Histogram

```
hist contvar, bin(1) frequency

hist TotalPriceInStateOnCampus, bin(10) frequency
```

(*Note:* The **bin** command is not essential since Stata will try to choose the optimal number of bins.)

FIGURE 6.3 ● HISTOGRAM OF TUITION OF COLLEGES IN THE UNITED STATES

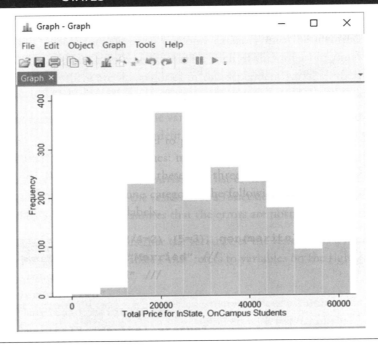

Bar Chart With Continuous Variable Summarized Over a Categorical Variable

```
graph bar(mean) contvar, over(catvar)
```

```
graph bar(mean) TotalPriceInStateOnCampus, over(Sector3)
```

FIGURE 6.1 ⬡ BAR GRAPH OF AVERAGE TUITION BY TYPE OF COLLEGE

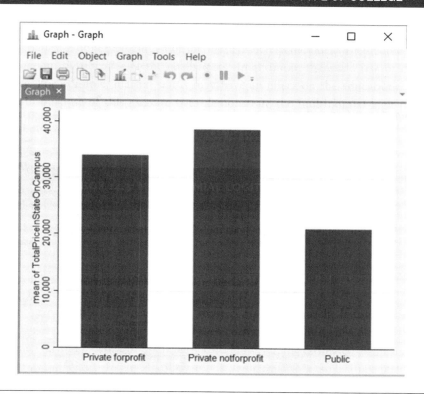

Bar Chart With Continuous Variable Summarized Over Two Categorical Variables

```
graph bar (mean)contvar, over(catvar1) over (catvar2)
```

```
graph bar (mean)coninc, over(sex) over (degree)
```

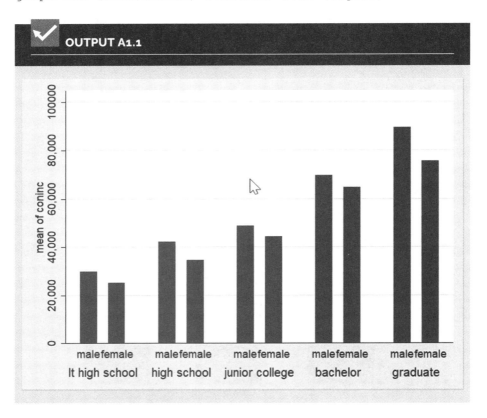

Box Plot

```
graph box contvar, over(catvar)
```

```
graph box TotalPriceInStateOnCampus, over(Sector3)
```

FIGURE 6.2 ●   BOX PLOT OF AVERAGE TUITION BY TYPE OF INSTITUTION

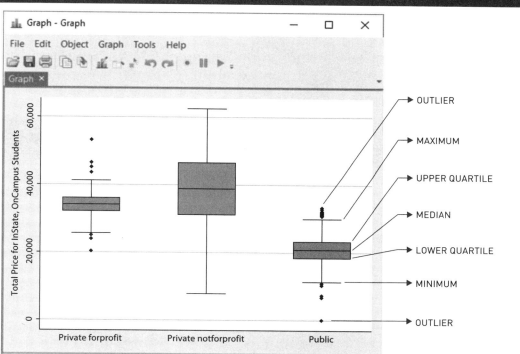

FREQUENCIES AND CROSS TABULATIONS (PERCENTAGES)

Frequency Table

The commands **table** and **tabulate** are not the same. Table is never abbreviated.

Tabulate can be abbreviated to "**tab**."

Tabulate produces frequency tables, whereas **table** generates other statistics.

To generate several frequency tables in a row, use "**tab1** var1 var2 var3," and so on.

```
tab varname
```

OUTPUT 4.1: FREQUENCY TABLE OF INSTAGRAM USE

```
. tab instagrm

        use
   instagrm        Freq.       Percent         Cum.

        yes          423         30.83        30.83
         no          949         69.17       100.00

      Total        1,372        100.00
```

Crosstab With Two Categorical Variables: Row Percentages

The variable with more categories should appear first since the table will be more likely to fit on a page.

When deciding on whether to generate row or column percentages, always add up over the independent variable.

```
tab catvar1 catvar2, row
```

OUTPUT 6.7: COMBINING TWO CATEGORICAL VARIABLES USING THE TABULATE COMMAND

`. tab Sector3 atsp, row`

Key
frequency
row percentage

Sector	Admissions Test Scores Policy			Total
	Neither	Recommend	Required	
Private forprofit	104	72	9	185
	56.22	38.92	4.86	100.00
Private notforprofit	153	145	772	1,070
	14.30	13.55	72.15	100.00
Public	5	48	481	534
	0.94	8.99	90.07	100.00
Total	262	265	1,262	1,789
	14.65	14.81	70.54	100.00

MEANS AND SUMMARY STATISTICS

Summarize a Variable

`sum varname`

OUTPUT 6.4: MEAN OF COLLEGE SIZE

`. sum Size`

Variable	Obs	Mean	Std. Dev.	Min	Max
Size	2,264	3782.575	7246.969	3	208742

Summarize a Variable With More Detail

sum varname, detail

OUTPUT 6.3: PERCENTILES AND MEDIAN

```
. sum Size, detail
```

Size (Undergrad FTE)

	Percentiles	Smallest		
1%	36	3		
5%	118	3		
10%	225	10	Obs	2,264
25%	598.5	17	Sum of Wgt.	2,264
50%	1538.5		Mean	3782.575
		Largest	Std. Dev.	7246.969
75%	3877.5	41520		
90%	9976	53091	Variance	5.25e+07
95%	17162	69351	Skewness	11.73627
99%	28179	208742	Kurtosis	291.0279

25% of all colleges have less than or equal to 598.5 students.

Table With Selected Statistics and Formatting

table catvar, c(mean contvar median contvar) format(%6.0fc)

OUTPUT 6.5: MEANS AND MEDIANS FOR SUBCATEGORIES

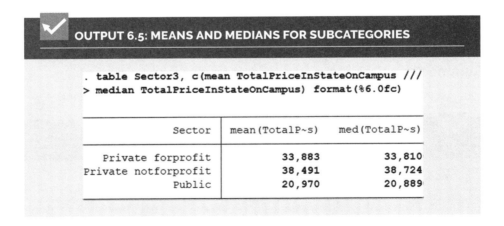

```
. table Sector3, c(mean TotalPriceInStateOnCampus ///
> median TotalPriceInStateOnCampus) format(%6.0fc)
```

Sector	mean(TotalP~s)	med(TotalP~s)
Private forprofit	33,883	33,810
Private notforprofit	38,491	38,724
Public	20,970	20,889

Table With Two Categories and the Mean of a Continuous Variable

```
table catvar1 catvar2, c(mean contvar) format(%5.0f)
```

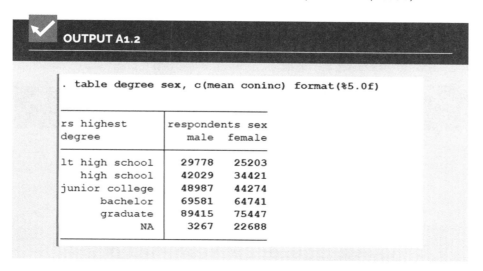

OUTPUT A1.2

```
. table degree sex, c(mean coninc) format(%5.0f)

rs highest        respondents sex
degree               male   female

lt high school      29778    25203
   high school      42029    34421
junior college      48987    44274
      bachelor      69581    64741
      graduate      89415    75447
            NA       3267    22688
```

TESTING HYPOTHESES

One-Sample *t* Test

```
ttest contvar==# (where # could be any number that you are
testing)
```

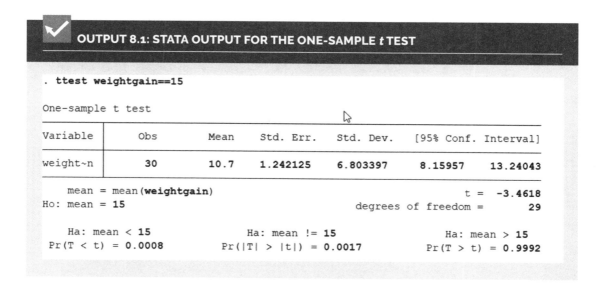

OUTPUT 8.1: STATA OUTPUT FOR THE ONE-SAMPLE *t* TEST

```
. ttest weightgain==15

One-sample t test
```

Variable	Obs	Mean	Std. Err.	Std. Dev.	[95% Conf. Interval]	
weight~n	30	10.7	1.242125	6.803397	8.15957	13.24043

```
    mean = mean(weightgain)                                    t =  -3.4618
Ho: mean = 15                                degrees of freedom =        29

    Ha: mean < 15              Ha: mean != 15              Ha: mean > 15
 Pr(T < t) = 0.0008        Pr(|T| > |t|) = 0.0017        Pr(T > t) = 0.9992
```

Two Independent-Samples *t* Test

```
robvar contvar, by(catvar)

ttest contvar, by(catvar)

esize twosample contvar, by(catvar) cohensd unequal (or
leave out unequal if variances are equal)
```

 OUTPUT 9.2: STATA OUTPUT FOR VARIANCE RATIO TEST

```
. robvar rhhwork, by(sex)
```

Sex	Summary of how many hours a week does r spend on hh work		
	Mean	Std. Dev.	Freq.
Male	8.3207547	9.4333454	583
Female	11.861472	12.702049	693
Total	10.24373	11.458679	1,276

```
W0  =  31.424330    df(1, 1274)     Pr > F = 0.00000003

W50 =  21.521522    df(1, 1274)     Pr > F = 0.00000386

W10 =  23.090941    df(1, 1274)     Pr > F = 0.00000173
```

 OUTPUT 9.3: STATA OUTPUT FOR TWO-SAMPLE *t* TEST WITH UNEQUAL VARIANCES

```
. ttest rhhwork, by(sex) unequal
```

Two-sample t test with unequal variances

Group	Obs	Mean	Std. Err.	Std. Dev.	[95% Conf. Interval]	
Male	583	8.320755	.3906892	9.433345	7.553422	9.088087
Female	693	11.86147	.4825109	12.70205	10.91411	12.80883
combined	1,276	10.24373	.3207814	11.45868	9.614413	10.87305
diff		-3.540717	.6208501		-4.758735	-2.322699

```
    diff = mean(Male) - mean(Female)                          t =  -5.7030
Ho: diff = 0                   Satterthwaite's degrees of freedom =  1255.28

   Ha: diff < 0                  Ha: diff != 0                  Ha: diff > 0
 Pr(T < t) = 0.0000      Pr(|T| > |t|) = 0.0000         Pr(T > t) = 1.0000
```

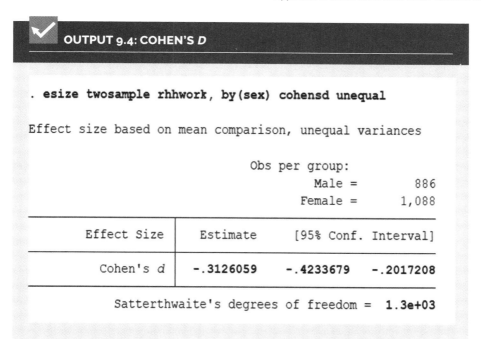

OUTPUT 9.4: COHEN'S *D*

```
. esize twosample rhhwork, by(sex) cohensd unequal

Effect size based on mean comparison, unequal variances

                              Obs per group:
                                    Male =          886
                                  Female =        1,088
```

Effect Size	Estimate	[95% Conf. Interval]	
Cohen's *d*	-.3126059	-.4233679	-.2017208

```
            Satterthwaite's degrees of freedom =  1.3e+03
```

One-Way Analysis of Variance

oneway contvar catvar

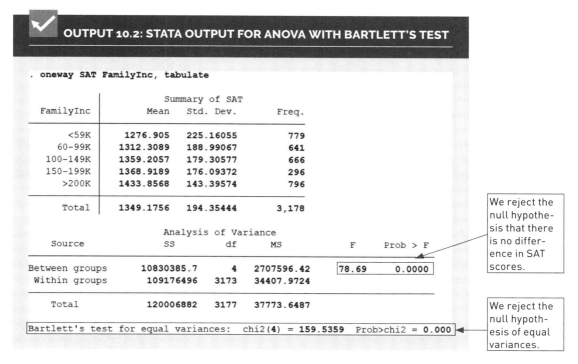

OUTPUT 10.2: STATA OUTPUT FOR ANOVA WITH BARTLETT'S TEST

```
. oneway SAT FamilyInc, tabulate
```

	Summary of SAT		
FamilyInc	Mean	Std. Dev.	Freq.
<59K	1276.905	225.16055	779
60–99K	1312.3089	188.99067	641
100–149K	1359.2057	179.30577	666
150–199K	1368.9189	176.09372	296
>200K	1433.8568	143.39574	796
Total	1349.1756	194.35444	3,178

	Analysis of Variance				
Source	SS	df	MS	F	Prob > F
Between groups	10830385.7	4	2707596.42	78.69	0.0000
Within groups	109176496	3173	34407.9724		
Total	120006882	3177	37773.6487		

```
Bartlett's test for equal variances:  chi2(4) = 159.5359  Prob>chi2 = 0.000
```

> We reject the null hypothesis that there is no difference in SAT scores.

> We reject the null hypothesis of equal variances.

Comparing Two or More Percentages in a Cross Tabulation

```
tab catvar1 catvar2, row V chi2
```

OUTPUT 11.2: STATA OUTPUT FOR THE PEARSON CHI-SQUARED TEST

The chi-squared statistic is slightly different compared with the previous section (χ^2 =12.36) due to rounding.

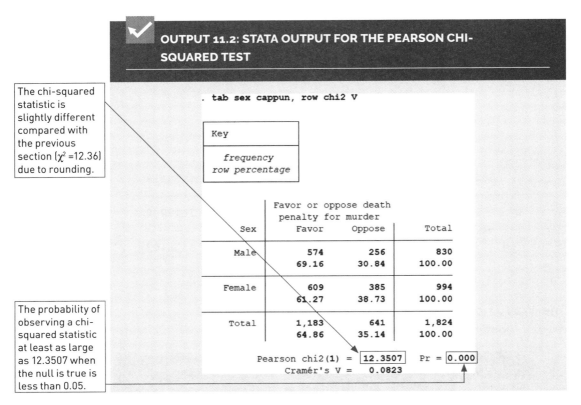

```
. tab sex cappun, row chi2 V

+------------------+
| Key              |
|                  |
|    frequency     |
|  row percentage  |
+------------------+

                 |  Favor or oppose death
                 |   penalty for murder
           Sex   |    Favor      Oppose   |    Total
-----------------+------------------------+----------
          Male   |      574         256   |      830
                 |    69.16       30.84   |   100.00
-----------------+------------------------+----------
        Female   |      609         385   |      994
                 |    61.27       38.73   |   100.00
-----------------+------------------------+----------
         Total   |    1,183         641   |    1,824
                 |    64.86       35.14   |   100.00

        Pearson chi2(1) =   12.3507   Pr = 0.000
            Cramér's V =    0.0823
```

The probability of observing a chi-squared statistic at least as large as 12.3507 when the null is true is less than 0.05.

Correlation Between Two Variables

```
pwcorr contvar1 contvar2, sig
```

OUTPUT 12.1: PEARSON CORRELATION COEFFICIENT

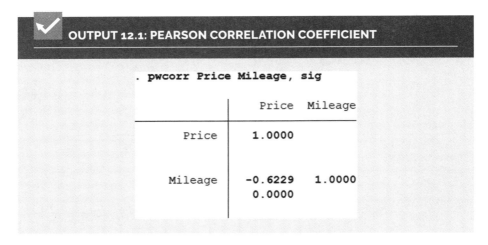

```
. pwcorr Price Mileage, sig

             |    Price   Mileage
-------------+------------------
       Price |   1.0000
             |
             |
     Mileage |  -0.6229    1.0000
             |   0.0000
```

Regression

```
regress dependentvar var1 var2 var3
```

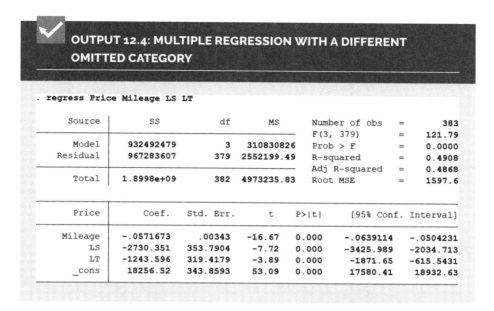

OUTPUT 12.4: MULTIPLE REGRESSION WITH A DIFFERENT OMITTED CATEGORY

```
. regress Price Mileage LS LT
```

Source	SS	df	MS		
Model	932492479	3	310830826		
Residual	967283607	379	2552199.49		
Total	1.8998e+09	382	4973235.83		

Number of obs = 383
F(3, 379) = 121.79
Prob > F = 0.0000
R-squared = 0.4908
Adj R-squared = 0.4868
Root MSE = 1597.6

Price	Coef.	Std. Err.	t	P>|t|	[95% Conf. Interval]	
Mileage	-.0571673	.00343	-16.67	0.000	-.0639114	-.0504231
LS	-2730.351	353.7904	-7.72	0.000	-3425.989	-2034.713
LT	-1243.596	319.4179	-3.89	0.000	-1871.65	-615.5431
_cons	18256.52	343.8593	53.09	0.000	17580.41	18932.63

```
svy: logit dependentvar var1 var2 i.catvar1 i.catvar2
```

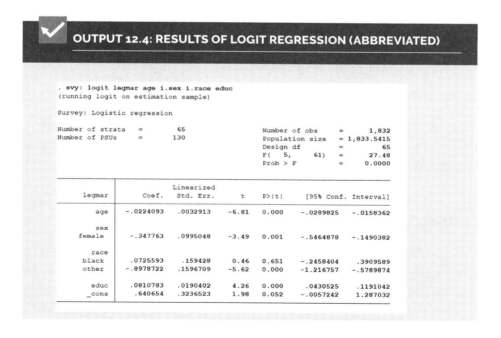

OUTPUT 12.4: RESULTS OF LOGIT REGRESSION (ABBREVIATED)

```
. svy: logit legmar age i.sex i.race educ
(running logit on estimation sample)

Survey: Logistic regression
```

Number of strata = 65
Number of PSUs = 130

Number of obs = 1,832
Population size = 1,833.5415
Design df = 65
F(5, 61) = 27.48
Prob > F = 0.0000

legmar	Coef.	Linearized Std. Err.	t	P>|t|	[95% Conf. Interval]	
age	-.0224093	.0032913	-6.81	0.000	-.0289825	-.0158362
sex						
female	-.347763	.0995048	-3.49	0.001	-.5464878	-.1490382
race						
black	.0725593	.159428	0.46	0.651	-.2458404	.3909589
other	-.8978722	.1596709	-5.62	0.000	-1.216757	-.5789874
educ	.0810783	.0190402	4.26	0.000	.0430525	.1191042
_cons	.640654	.3236523	1.98	0.052	-.0057242	1.287032

TRANSFORMING AND DEFINING VARIABLES AND VALUES PLUS GENERAL COMMANDS

Open a File

```
use "C:\file location\filename"
```

Rename a Variable

```
rename originalvarname newvarname
```

```
rename var1 gender
```

Create a Variable Label

label variable **varname** "Any description you like of any length"

```
label variable sex "Gender of respondent"
```

Create Value Labels

```
label def sexlabel 1 "Female" 2 "Male"
```

```
label val sex sexlabel
```

Add New Value Labels

```
label def sexlabel 3 "Other", add
```

```
label val sex sexlabel
```

Add New Value Labels and Change Existing Ones

```
label def sexlabel 1 "Male" 2 "Female" 3 "Other", modify
```

(*Note:* Quotation marks are only necessary in labels if there is a space in the label names.)

List Values for All Observations of Selected Variables

```
list varname1 varname2
```

Destring: Changing Format From String Variable to Numeric

```
destring varname, gen(numvar) ignore(",")
```

(Use the ignore command if there are commas separating numbers such as 1,000.)

Recode Variables

```
recode catvar(1 2=1) (3 4=2), gen(newcatvar)
```

```
recode catvar (1/5 = 1) (6/10=2), gen(newcatvar)
```

```
recode varname .=0, gen(newvar)
```
(when you want to change missing values to zeros)

Generate Dummy Variables

If you have a categorical variable (catvar) with three or more categories, you can generate a dummy variable for each category with these commands. You can substitute any letter for "g" in parentheses.

```
tab catvar, gen(g)
```

If you allowed a respondent to choose more than one category, each category will appear as its own variable. To change each of these to a dummy or 0/1 variable, use this:

```
recode catvar1 .=0
```

```
recode catvar2 .=0
```

Using Only Certain Responses in Your Analysis

If you want to keep certain responses, you can use the **keep if** command. This command will remove the observations for all remaining analyses until you use the **clear** command. The next time you open the file, all observations will be there unless you saved the data file after using "keep if."

```
keep if varname <=21
```

Combining Multiple Response Question Into One Variable

If you allowed respondents to choose more than one option, each option will appear as a separate variable such as q5_1, q5_2, and q5_3. To make up one new variable with three categories plus a fourth category that indicates that the respondent chose more than one, you would use the following code:

```
recode q5 _ 1 .=0
```

```
recode q5 _ 2 .=0
```

```
recode q5 _ 3 .=0
```

```
gen newvar = q5 _ 1 + q5 _ 2 + q5 _ 3

gen newvar2 = newvar

replace newvar2 = 1 if q5 _ 1 == 1

replace newvar2 = 2 if q5 _ 2 == 1

replace newvar2 = 3 if q5 _ 3 == 1

replace newvar2 = 4 if newvar > 1
```

APPENDIX 2: SUMMARY OF STATISTICAL TESTS BY CHAPTER

Chapter	Chapter Title	Null Hypothesis	Test	Info Known/Type of Variables	Procedures/Interpretation
7	The Normal Distribution	There is no difference in SAT scores among those students who took a preparatory course and those who did not.	Z score or standard score	Single sample; Know population mean; Know population standard deviation	1. Standard error of mean = $(\sigma / \sqrt{n})$ 2. Standard score $(|\bar{X} - \mu|/$ Standard error of mean) 3. Look up percentages for standard score using normal distribution When the null hypothesis is true, the probability of observing a z score greater than +1.41 or less than –1.41 is less than 0.16. Do not reject the null hypothesis.
8	Testing a Hypothesis About a Single Mean	College students gain 15 pounds on average in the first year.	One-sample t test	Single sample; Know population mean; Don't know population standard deviation	1. Standard error of mean = $(s / \sqrt{n})$ 2. Standard score $(|\bar{X} - \mu|/$ Standard error of mean) 3. Look up area for t statistic When the null hypothesis is true, the probability of observing a t value greater than 3.46 or less than –3.46 is less than 0.0017. Reject the null hypothesis.
9	Testing a Hypothesis About Two Independent Means	There is no difference in the hours of housework done by men and women in the United States.	Two independent-samples t test	Two samples; Two populations	1. Standard error of the mean difference = $\sqrt{\dfrac{s_1^2}{n_1} + \dfrac{s_2^2}{n_2}}$ 2. Calculate t statistic = $\dfrac{\bar{X}_1 - \bar{X}_2}{\sqrt{\dfrac{s_1^2}{n_1} + \dfrac{s_2^2}{n_2}}}$ 3. Look up area for t statistic When the null hypothesis is true, the probability of observing a t value greater than 5.7 or less than –5.7 is less than 0.01. Reject the null hypothesis.
		Variances of the two populations are equal.	Levene's test of equality of variances		1. Use F test from output When the null hypothesis is true, the probability of observing an F value at least as large as 31.42 is less than 0.05. Reject the null hypothesis.

Chapter	Chapter Title	Null Hypothesis	Test	Info Known/Type of Variables	Procedures/ Interpretation
10	One-Way Analysis of Variance	There is no difference in SAT scores among college students from families with different levels of income.	One-way ANOVA	One categorical variable and more than two means	1. Calculate the *F* ratio by running the ANOVA to test When the null hypothesis is true, the probability of observing an *F* ratio at least as large as 78.69 is less than 0.05. Reject the null hypothesis.
		Variances of the groups are equal.	Bartlett's test for equal variances		1. Use the Bartlett's test from the output When the null hypothesis is true, the probability of observing a chi-square at least as large as 159.54 is less than 0.05. Reject the null hypothesis.
11	Cross Tabulation and the Chi-Square Statistic	There is no difference in the percentage of men and women who oppose the death penalty.	Chi-square statistic	Two categorical variables Comparing percentages, not means	1. Calculate the chi-square statistic by running the Pearson chi-squared test When the null hypothesis is true, the probability of observing a chi-square statistic at least as large as 12.35 is less than 0.05. Reject the null hypothesis.

Chapter	Chapter Title	Null Hypothesis	Test	Info Known/Type of Variables	Procedures/Interpretation
12	Linear Regression Analysis				
	Correlation	There is no correlation between Car Prices and Mileage.	Pearson correlation	Two continuous variables	1. Run Pearson or Spearman −1 to +1 for perfect negative or positive relationship Must be significant to claim correlation Between −0.5 and +0.5 is weakly correlated when significant When the null hypothesis is true, the probability of observing a Pearson's R at least as large as −0.62 is less than 0.05.
	Multiple Regression	There is no linear relationship between price and the independent variables.	F test	One continuous variable that is the dependent variable Several variables (both categorical and continuous) that affect the dependent variables	When the null hypothesis is true, the probability of observing an F value at least as large as 121.79 is less than 0.05.
		The population partial regression coefficient for each variable is 0.	t test		When the null hypothesis is true, the probability of observing a t value greater than 16.67 or less than −16.67 is less than 0.05. (Do this for each independent variable.)

Chapter	Chapter Title	Null Hypothesis	Test	Info Known/Type of Variables	Procedures/ Interpretation
13	Regression Diagnostics	There are no omitted variables that are powers of y or x.	Ramsey omitted variable test	Used after running regression model to check for specification error	Run **estat ovtest**. If p-value is less than 0.05, reject null hypothesis of no omitted variables. If null hypothesis is rejected, try adding new variables to model, including quadratic terms and interaction terms.
		The variance of the error terms is homoscedastic.	Breusch–Pagan/ Cook–Weisberg test of heteroscedasticity	Used after running regression model to check for heteroscedasticity	Run **estat hettest**. If p-value is less than 0.05, reject null hypothesis of homoscedasticity. If null hypothesis is rejected, add **vce(robust)** option to **regress** command or implement generalized least squares.
		Residuals are normally distributed.	D'Agostino skewness–kurtosis test	Used after running regression model to check normality in residuals	Run **sktest** on residual. If p-value is less than 0.05, reject null hypothesis of normally distributed residual. Options include transforming dependent variable (e.g., log[y]) or adopt higher standard for significance of coefficients. If sample is large, coefficient estimates will be normal even if residuals are not.

Chapter	Chapter Title	Null Hypothesis	Test	Info Known/Type of Variables	Procedures/ Interpretation
14	Regression Analysis With Categorical Dependent Variables	Age and education have no effect on views on legalization of marijuana.	t test of coefficients using logit regression	Dependent variable is dichotomous. Includes several independent variables (both categorical and continuous) that affect the dependent variable	Using margin analysis, interpretation is as follows: Each additional year of age is associated with a 0.4 percentage point reduction in the probability of supporting legalization. Support among other non-Whites is 22.7 percentage points lower than among Whites.

Note: SAT = Scholastic Aptitude Test; ANOVA = analysis of variance.

APPENDIX 3: DECISION TREE FOR CHOOSING THE RIGHT STATISTIC

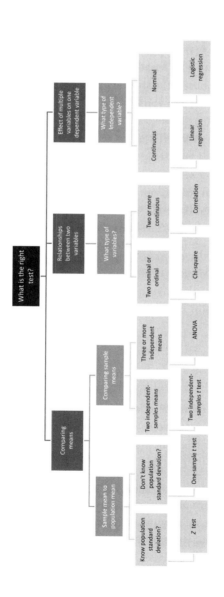

APPENDIX 4: DECISION RULES FOR STATISTICAL SIGNIFICANCE

Null Hypothesis (H_0)

- Hypothesis about the population
- No difference among groups
- It is never accepted or proved
- It is rejected or not rejected
- Example:

$$H_0: \mu_1 = \mu_2$$

Alternative Hypothesis (H_1 or H_a)

- Opposite of the null hypothesis
- Example

$$H_1: \mu_1 \neq \mu_2$$

p-Value or p (Calculated)

- The probability of rejecting the null hypothesis when it is true (Type I error)
- The probability of obtaining a result equal to or more extreme than what was observed when the null hypothesis is true
- Derived from sample results

α Level or p (Critical)

- Predetermined upper limit of the probability of making a Type I error
- Significance level
- Typically set at 0.05

Decision Rule

- Select α

- If $p \leq \alpha$, reject the null hypothesis

- If $p > \alpha$, do not reject the null hypothesis

APPENDIX 5: AREAS UNDER THE NORMAL CURVE (Z SCORES)

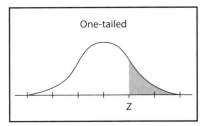
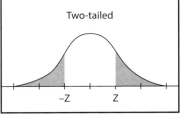

Z Scores	Probability	
	One-tailed	Two-tailed
0	0.50000	1.00000
0.1	0.46017	0.92034
0.2	0.42074	0.84148
0.3	0.38209	0.76418
0.4	0.34458	0.68916
0.5	0.30854	0.61708
0.6	0.27425	0.54851
0.7	0.24196	0.48393
0.8	0.21186	0.42371
0.9	0.18406	0.36812
1	0.15866	0.31731
1.1	0.13567	0.27133
1.2	0.11507	0.23014
1.3	0.09680	0.19360

Z Scores	Probability	
	One-tailed	Two-tailed
1.4	0.08076	0.16151
1.5	0.06681	0.13361
1.6	0.05480	0.10960
1.7	0.04457	0.08913
1.8	0.03593	0.07186
1.9	0.02872	0.05743
2	0.02275	0.04550
2.1	0.01786	0.03573
2.2	0.01390	0.02781
2.3	0.01072	0.02145
2.4	0.00820	0.01640
2.5	0.00621	0.01242
2.6	0.00466	0.00932
2.7	0.00347	0.00693
2.8	0.00256	0.00511
2.9	0.00187	0.00373
3	0.00135	0.00270
3.1	0.00097	0.00194
3.2	0.00069	0.00137
3.3	0.00048	0.00097
3.4	0.00034	0.00067
3.5	0.00023	0.00047
3.6	0.00016	0.00032
3.7	0.00011	0.00022
3.8	0.00007	0.00014
3.9	0.00005	0.00010

Note: All values are computed by the authors using Excel.

APPENDIX 6: CRITICAL VALUES OF THE *t* DISTRIBUTION

df	Two-Tailed Test	
	$\alpha = 0.05$	$\alpha = 0.01$
1	12.71	63.66
2	4.3	9.92
3	3.18	5.84
4	2.78	4.6
5	2.57	4.03
6	2.45	3.71
7	2.36	3.5
8	2.31	3.36
9	2.26	3.25
10	2.23	3.17
11	2.2	3.11
12	2.18	3.05
13	2.16	3.01
14	2.14	2.98
15	2.13	2.95
16	2.12	2.92
17	2.11	2.9
18	2.1	2.88
19	2.09	2.86
20	2.09	2.85
21	2.08	2.83

df	Two-Tailed Test	
	α = 0.05	α = 0.01
22	2.07	2.82
23	2.07	2.81
24	2.06	2.8
25	2.06	2.79
26	2.06	2.78
27	2.05	2.77
28	2.05	2.76
29	2.05	2.76
30	2.04	2.75
35	2.03	2.72
40	2.02	2.7
∞(Z)	1.96	

Note: All values are computed by the authors using Excel.

Example:

If *n* = 30 so that the degrees of freedom are 29, the positive and negative *t* values that would represent 5% of the area under the tails is +2.05 and −2.05 as illustrated below.

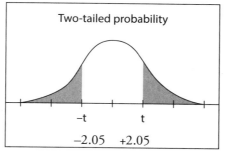

APPENDIX 7: STATA CODE FOR RANDOM SAMPLING

This appendix provides Stata code to carry out different types of sampling. It is meant to accompany the discussion of sampling methods in Chapter 2. However, we have put this material in an appendix because it contains somewhat more advanced Stata code that will only be needed by students carrying out multistage random sample surveys.

In this appendix, we start with simple random sampling and proceed to discuss more complex types of sampling such as multistage sampling and stratification.

SIMPLE RANDOM SAMPLING IN STATA

We can use Stata or any spreadsheet software to randomly select the sample. Table A7.1 shows some useful functions in Stata.

In this section, we work with the Stata file called "UScounties.dta" with a list of 3,142 counties in the United States. Initially, we wish to draw a simple random sample of 100 of them. The probability of selection for each county is 100/3,142 or roughly 0.0318. We can select 100 counties randomly using the Stata code shown in Figure A7.1.

TABLE A7.1 ⬡ USEFUL FUNCTIONS IN STATA FOR SAMPLING		
Stata Function	**Description**	**Examples**
=runiform()	Creates a random number between 0 and 0.99999	**gen x=runiform()**
=runiform(a,b)	Creates a random number between *a* and *b* (including nonintegers)	**gen y=runiform(0.5,10.5)**
=runiformint(a,b)	Creates a random integer between *a* and *b*	**gen z=runiformint(1,150)**

FIGURE A7.1 ⬧ SIMPLE RANDOM SAMPLE

```
* Simple random sample
set seed 1234              // sets seed to ensure same sample each time
clear                      // clears data from memory
use "c:/UScounties.dta"    // opens file with list of counties
local n = 100              // defines desired sample size
gen sorter = runiform()    // defines "sorter" to be random over 0-1
sort sorter                // sort by random number
gen select=0               // create dummy indicating selected units
replace select=1 if _n<=`n'  // selects first `n' units randomly
list if select==1          // show list of selected counties
```

The function "**runiform()**" creates a random number uniformly distributed between 0 and 1 for each observation, that is, for each county. A uniform random number is a random number with equal probability throughout the range. The variable "_N" is a Stata variable equal to the number of observations in the database.

The do-file in Figure A7.1 gives every county a random number between 0 and 1, then sorts by this number, so that the counties are now in random order. To pick a random sample of 100, the code just selects the first 100 on the newly sorted list.[1]

SYSTEMATIC RANDOM SAMPLING IN STATA

The systematic random sample can be implemented easily in Stata. We need to calculate a starting point, which identifies the first unit to be selected, and an interval, which determines the gap between subsequent units. If the population is N and the desired sample is n, then the interval between selected units is N/n, and the starting point is a random number between 1 and N/n.

Suppose we are working with the same list of 3,142 counties and wish to select 100 of them. The Stata code in Figure A7.2 will select a systematic random sample.

In this case, the interval is 3,142/100 or 31.42. This means that each county (after the first one) will be 31 or 32 counties down the list from the previous one.

We identify the first unit to be selected with local macro "start." We need to use a local macro because we want just one random number for the start value. Note that,

---

[1] Thanks to Bill Rising from Stata Corporation for suggesting this approach, as well as for improvements in the other do-files in this appendix.

FIGURE A7.2 ⬡ SINGLE-STAGE SYSTEMATIC RANDOM SAMPLE

```
* Systematic random sample
set seed 1234                              // sets seed to ensure same sample each time
clear                                      // clears data from memory
use "c:/UScounties.dta"                    // opens file with list of counties
local n = 100                              // defines desired sample size
local interval = _N/`n'                    // defines interval between selected units
local start = runiform(0,`interval')   /   // defines random starting point
gen select = mod(_n-`start',`interval')<1  // selects `n' counties systematically
list if select==1                          // shows list of selected counties
```

when referring to local macros, the name needs to be placed inside left and right single quotation marks (' ').

The next line defines the "select" variable to be 1 if the inequality is true and 0 if it is false. The **mod(x,y)** function calculates the modulus, defined as the difference between x and the largest multiple of y that is less than x (it can also be calculated as **x-y*int(x/y)**). The expression _n is a Stata variable indicating the observation number. Whenever the modulus is less than 1, the expression (_n - start) has passed another multiple of the interval and it is time to select the county.

Earlier, we said that if the sampling frame is sorted by a variable, a systematic random sample spreads out the sample across the values of that variable. In this case, the sampling frame is sorted by state, from Alabama to Wyoming. A systematic random sample ensures (roughly) proportional representation of each state. For example, Alabama has 67 counties, 2.1% of the counties in the country. With an interval of 31.42, a systematic random sample will always include 2 or possibly 3 counties from Alabama, corresponding to 2% or 3% of the sample. In contrast, a simple random sample might exclude all the counties in Alabama or it might conceivably include all 67 of them. Systematic random sampling is widely used in surveys because of this advantage and because it is only slightly more complex than simple random sampling.

MULTISTAGE SAMPLING IN STATA

To demonstrate how to carry out multistage sampling in Stata, we will use the code for systematic sampling for each stage. Figure A7.3 shows a set of Stata commands that selects 20 states and then selects five counties in each state, using systematic random sampling in each level.

FIGURE A7.3 ● MULTISTAGE SAMPLING WITH STATA

```
* Multi-stage systematic sampling
* Select n1 states
set seed 1234                          // sets seed to ensure same sample each time
clear                                  // clear data from memory
use "c:/UScounties.dta"                // opens file with list of counties
local n1 = 20                          // set number of states to select
local n2 = 5                           // set number of counties/state to select
drop if state==9                       // drop DC (only 1 county)
collapse (sum) population, by(state)   // collapse to state level
local interval1 = _N/`n1'              // calculate interval between selected states
local start1 = runiform(0,`interval1') // generate random number for first state
gen select1 = mod(_n-`start1',`interval1')<1  // selects states
keep if select1==1                     // keep only selected states
list                                   // list selected states
gen statenbr = _n                      // create state counter for later
save "c:/SelectedStates", replace      // save list of selected states for later
* Select n2 counties in each state
clear
use "c:/UScounties.dta"                // opens file with list of counties
drop if state==9                       // drop DC
merge m:1 state using "c:/SelectedStates" // merge counties with selected states
keep if select1==1                     // keep only counties in selected states
gen interval = .                       // define interval variable
gen select2 = .                        // define county selection variable
forvalues s = 1/`n1' {                 // loop through s=1 to n1 states
    preserve                           // save data in memory to be restored later
    keep if statenbr==`s'              // keep only the state numbered `s'
    local interval2 = _N/`n2'          // calculate interval between counties
    local start2 = runiform(0,`interval2')    // generate random number for first county
    replace select2 = mod(_n-`start2',`interval2')<1 // select counties
    list state county if select2==1          // list state & selected counties
    restore                            // restore data in memory (all selected states)}
}
```

The first section of the do-file selects the 20 states. It starts with the file containing the list of counties and then collapses to the state level. In other words, in the original file, each observation is a county, but after the collapse, each observation is a state. After the **collapse** command, the state selection is similar to the county selection in Figure A7.2. The do-file specifies the desired number of states, calculates the interval between states, generates a random starting point, and then uses the **mod(x,y)** function to select the states.

The second section of the code selects five counties in each of the 20 selected states. We use the **merge** command to combine the list of selected states and the full list of counties. Then we drop the counties that are in states that were not selected. The loop goes through the 20 states, carrying out a systematic random selection of five counties in each. The **preserve** command stores the data in memory, just before deleting the data for all but one of the states. After selecting and displaying the five counties in that state, the **restore** command brings back the data for all 20 states and the loop goes on to the next state.

In the end, the result is a list of 100 counties, composed of five counties from each of 20 states. Note that Delaware has only three counties, so if it were one of the selected states, the do-file would select a total of 98 counties.

STRATIFIED SAMPLING IN STATA

How do we draw a stratified sample using Stata? To keep it simple, we will consider a single-stage sampling with two strata. Suppose we decide that we want to oversample counties with large populations, either because we are particularly interested in those counties or because we believe that large counties are more diverse, so our variables of interest have greater variance in large counties. As shown in Figure A7.4, the first step is to define large counties. We generate a new variable "size," equal to 0 if the population is less than 500,000 and 1 if the population is greater than or equal to 500,000. We use "preserve" to store a copy of the data (with the "size" variable). Next, large counties are removed from the data, and 60 small counties are selected by systematic random sampling using the commands in Figure A7.2. After restoring the full set of counties, we remove the small counties and repeat the process, selecting 40 of the large counties.

There are only 134 large counties, 4.26% of the total. Because we stratified and oversampled large counties, they represent 40% of the sample. In contrast, small counties account for 95.74% of all counties but just 60% of the sample.

FIGURE A7.4 ● STRATIFIED RANDOM SAMPLING WITH STATA

```
* Stratification
set seed 1234                          // sets seed to ensure same sample each time
clear                                  // clears data from memory
use "c:/UScounties.dta"                // opens file with list of counties
gen size = (population>=500000)        // define "size" as 0 if <500k, 1 if >=500k
local n1 = 60                          // defines sample for small counties
local n2 = 40                          // defines sample for large counties
* Small counties
preserve                               // save copy of data
keep if size==0                        // keep only small counties
local interval1 = _N/`n1'              // defines interval between selected units
local start1 = runiform(0,`interval1') // defines numbers used to start selection
gen select = mod(_n-`start1',`interval1')<1   // selects small counties
list state county population if select==1   // lists names of selected small counties
restore                                // restore data to point of preserve
* Large counties
keep if size==1                        // keep only large counties
local interval2 = _N/`n2'              // defines interval between selected units
local start2 = runiform(0,`interval2') // defines rand nbrs to start selection
gen select = mod(_n-`start2',`interval2')<1   // selects large counties
list state county population if select==1   // lists names of selected large counties
```

APPENDIX 8: EXAMPLES OF NONLINEAR FUNCTIONS

In Chapter 13, we discuss different ways to estimate nonlinear relationships using linear regression by transforming the dependent variable (y) and/or the independent variables (x_i). To illustrate the shape of these nonlinear functions, we provide graphs of each type, along with the Stata code to generate the graphs.

QUADRATIC FUNCTIONS

One common way to estimate a nonlinear relationship between y and x is to add powers of x, such as x^2 and x^3, to the regression equation as independent variables. Here, we consider the case of a quadratic equation, which takes the following form:

$$y = \beta_0 + \beta_1 x + \beta_2 x^2$$

How do we graph this function using Stata? First, we generate a Stata data set with the variable x that runs from 1 to 100. The **set obs #** command (where # is a number) creates an empty data file with # observations. We then use the special Stata variable _n, which represents the row number, to create values of x from 1 to 100. Next, we define the y variable, choosing values for the three coefficients β_0, β_1, and β_2. After defining the y variable, we graph x and y as a line graph.[1] A quadratic function with a positive value for β_2 creates a U-shaped graph, as shown in Figure A8.1.

```
clear
set obs 100
gen x = _n
gen y1 = 1000 - 50*x + x²
twoway (line y1 x)
```

---

[1] Stata also offers a way to generate graphs directly from the **twoway** command. The above quadratic function can be graphed with the command: **twoway function y1 = 1000 − 50*x + x^2, range(0 100)**. This approach is more concise but somewhat less transparent to the new Stata user.

FIGURE A8.1 ⬡ QUADRATIC FUNCTION WITH POSITIVE QUADRATIC COEFFICIENT

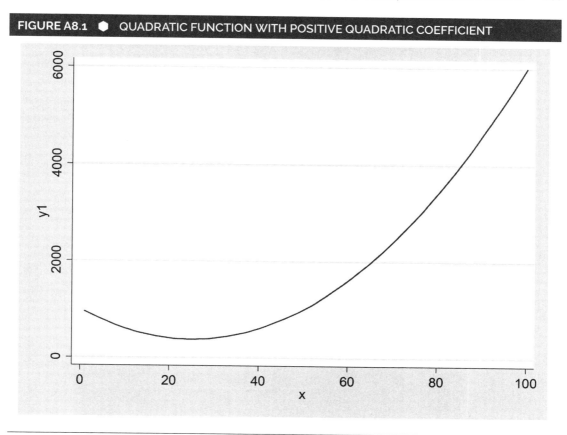

If β_2 (the quadratic coefficient) is negative, as shown in the **generate** command below, the result is an inverse U shape, as shown in Figure A8.2.

```
gen y2 = 400 + 100*x - 0.8*x²
twoway (line y2 x)
```

We are often interested in the marginal effect of x on y. In other words, what is the effect of a one-unit change in x on y. Graphically, this is the slope of the graph of y on the vertical axis and x on the horizontal axis. In a linear function, the marginal effect is simply the coefficient on the x variable, and it is constant. But in a nonlinear relationship, the marginal effect of x on y changes over the ranges of x. We can calculate the marginal effect using calculus. In the case of a quadratic equation with one independent variable,

FIGURE A8.2 ⬡ QUADRATIC FUNCTION WITH NEGATIVE QUADRATIC COEFFICIENT

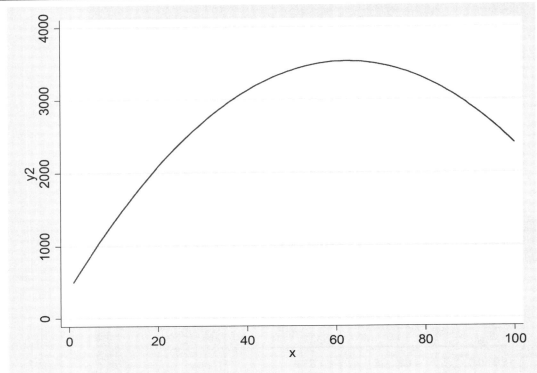

$$y = \beta_0 + \beta_1 x + \beta_2 x^2$$

and the marginal effect is expressed as

$$\frac{\partial y}{\partial x} = \beta_1 + 2\beta_2 x$$

This means the marginal effect is partly a function of the value of x. If $\beta_2 > 0$, then the marginal effect (or slope) rises as x increases, and the graph of y against x has a U shape. On the other hand, if $\beta_2 < 0$, the slope falls as x increases and the graph has an inverted U shape ($\cap$). We can calculate the "turning point" where the slope is horizontal by setting the marginal effect to 0 and solving for x.

$$\frac{\partial y}{\partial x} = \beta_1 + 2\beta_2 x = 0$$

$$x = \frac{-\beta_1}{2\beta_2}$$

For example, the estimated equation for the data shown in Figure A8.2 is as follows:

$$y = 400 + 100x - 0.8x^2$$

This means that β_0 = 400, β_1 = 100, β_2 = −0.8. Using the equation for the marginal effect,

$$\frac{\partial y}{\partial x} = \beta_1 + 2\beta_2 x = 100 + (2)(-0.8)x = 100 - 1.6x$$

The turning point is where $x = -\beta_1/2\beta_2$ = −100/((2)(-0.8)) = 62.5. The turning point is consistent with the curve shown in Figure A8.2.

SEMILOG FUNCTIONS

Another way to estimate a nonlinear function with linear regression is to transform the dependent variable by taking its natural logarithm. Here is the general form:

$$\log(y) = \beta_0 + \beta_1 x$$

Taking the exponential function of both sides, we can isolate y, as follows:

$$y = \exp(\beta_0 + \beta_1 x)$$

If β_1, the coefficient on x, is positive, the relationship will be rising at an increasing rate, as shown in Figure A8.3.

```
gen y3 = exp(1 + 0.05*x)
twoway (line y3 x)
```

FIGURE A8.3 ● SEMILOG FUNCTION USING LOG(Y) AND POSITIVE COEFFICIENT

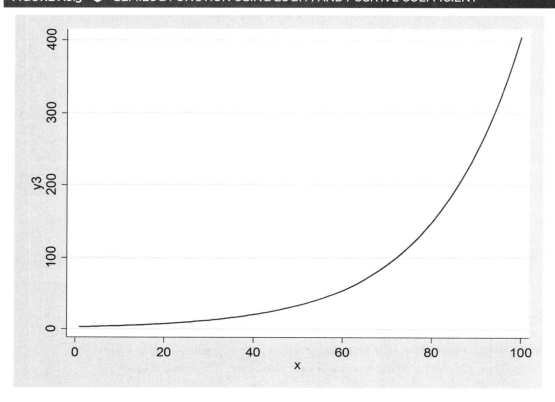

If we use the same functional form, but the β_1 coefficient is negative, the graph slopes down but never crosses the horizontal (x) axis (see Figure A8.4). To be more precise, for each one-unit increase in x, y declines by a fixed proportion.

```
gen y4 = exp(5 - 0.02*x)
twoway (line y4 x)
```

What is the marginal effect of this type of semilog function? If the function is

$$\log(y) = \beta_0 + \beta_1 x$$

then the marginal effect is

$$\frac{\partial y}{\partial x} = \beta_1 y$$

FIGURE A8.4 ●   SEMILOG FUNCTION USING LOG(*Y*) AND NEGATIVE COEFFICIENT

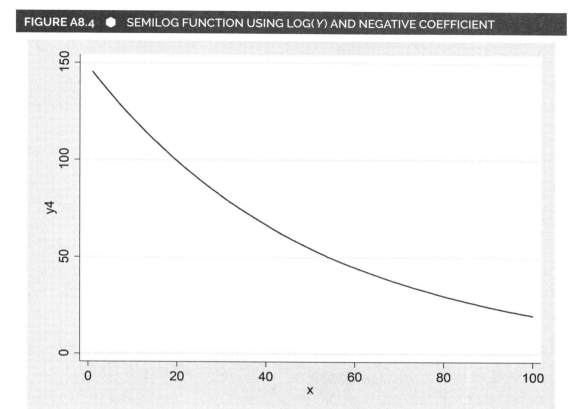

In other words, for each unit increase in x, the value of y increases or decreases by a constant proportion, which is determined by β_1. In the example above, $\beta_1 = -0.02$, so y declines by about 2% for each one-unit increase in x.[2]

Another nonlinear function can be created by having the logarithm of x on the right side. With a positive coefficient on log(x), the curve takes the form shown in Figure A8.5. The value of y rises indefinitely, never reaching a maximum.

```
gen y5 = 1.5 + 4*log(x)
twoway (line y5 x)
```

---

[2] Because of compounding, the decline is actually about 1.98% per unit. In other words, as x changes from (say) 50 to 51, the value of y decreases, which in turn lowers the rate of change in y.

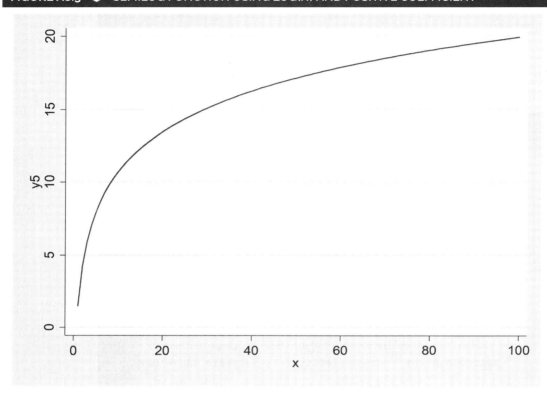

FIGURE A8.5 ● SEMILOG FUNCTION USING LOG(X) AND POSITIVE COEFFICIENT

Alternatively, if the coefficient is negative, the curve slopes down, as shown in Figure A8.6.

```
gen y6 = 10 - 1.5*log(x)
twoway (line y6 x)
```

The marginal effect of this type of semilog function can be calculated as follows:

$$\frac{\partial y}{\partial x} = \frac{\beta_1}{x}$$

In the example above, $\beta_1 = -1.5$, so the marginal effect is $-1.5/x$. If $x = 30$, then the marginal effect is -0.05.

FIGURE A8.6 ● SEMILOG FUNCTION USING LOG(X) AND NEGATIVE COEFFICIENT

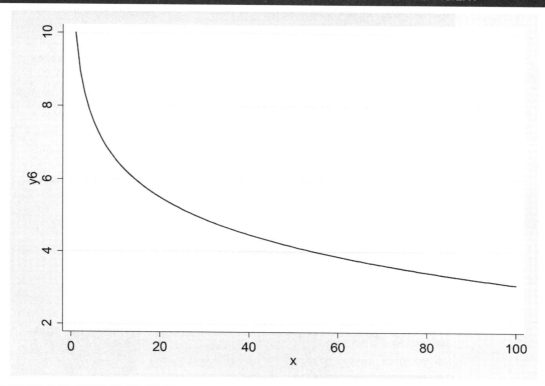

DOUBLE-LOG FUNCTIONS

Another functional form is the double-log function, in which both y and x are transformed into logarithms:

$$\log(y) = \beta_0 + \beta_1 \log(x)$$

As described above, we need to take the exponential function of both sides in order to express the equation in terms of y.

$$y = \exp(\beta_0 + \beta_1 \log(x)) = \exp(\beta_0)x^{\beta_1} = \alpha x^{\beta_1}$$

where $\alpha = \exp(\beta_0)$. If the coefficient β_1 is greater than 1, the function will rise at an increasing rate, as shown in Figure A8.7.

```
gen y7 = exp(3 + 1.5*log(x))
twoway (line y7 x)
```

FIGURE A8.7 ● DOUBLE-LOG FUNCTION WITH POSITIVE COEFFICIENT GREATER THAN 1

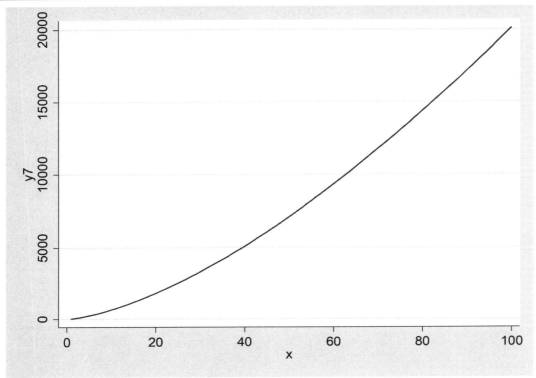

If the coefficient is positive, but less than 1, the function rises but at a decreasing rate, as shown in Figure A8.8.

```
gen y8 = exp(3 + 0.5*log(x))
twoway (line y8 x)
```

FIGURE A8.8 ● DOUBLE-LOG FUNCTION WITH POSITIVE COEFFICIENT LESS THAN 1

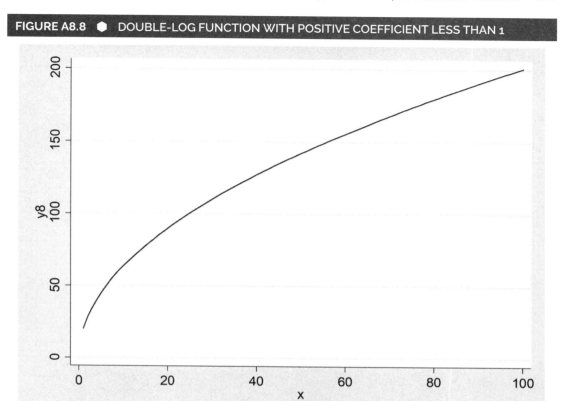

On the other hand, if the coefficient is negative, then the function declines but never crosses the horizontal (x) axis, as shown in Figure A8.9.

```
gen y9 = exp(5 - 0.5*log(x))
twoway (line y9 x)
```

FIGURE A8.9 ● DOUBLE-LOG FUNCTION WITH NEGATIVE COEFFICIENT

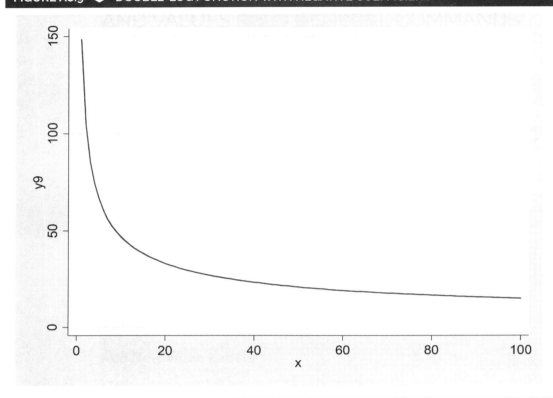

The marginal effect of the double-log functional form can be calculated as follows:

$$\frac{\partial y}{\partial x} = \beta_1 \frac{y}{x}$$

This can be rewritten as follows:

$$\beta_1 = \frac{\partial y / y}{\partial x / x}$$

This means that the coefficient represents the ratio of the proportional change in y divided by the proportional change in x, also called the elasticity of y with respect to x. In other words, one of the characteristics of the double-log functional form is that the elasticity is constant. In the example above, $\beta_1 = -0.5$. This means that if x increases by 1%, y will decrease by 0.5%, and this relationship holds throughout the range of x.

Table A8.1 summarizes the nonlinear functions discussed here and, for each one, the expression for calculating marginal effect of x on y. In each case, the marginal effect varies with different values of x.

TABLE A8.1 ⬡ COMMON NONLINEAR FUNCTIONS AND THE MARGINAL EFFECTS OF EACH		
Name of Functional Form	**Functional Form**	**Marginal Effect**
Quadratic	$y = \beta_0 + \beta_1 x + \beta_2 x^2$	$\dfrac{\partial y}{\partial x} = \beta_1 + 2\beta_2 x$
Linear with interaction of two variables	$y = \beta_0 + \beta_1 x + \beta_2 x_2 + \beta_3 x_3$	$\dfrac{\partial y}{\partial x_1} = \beta_1 + \beta_3 x_2$
Semilog (log y)	$\log(y) = \beta_0 + \beta_1 x$	$\dfrac{\partial y}{\partial x} = \beta_1 y$
Semilog (log x)	$y = \beta_0 + \beta_1 \log(x)$	$\dfrac{\partial y}{\partial x} = \dfrac{\beta_1}{x}$
Double-log	$\log(y) = \beta_0 + \beta_1 \log(x)$	$\dfrac{\partial y}{\partial x} = \beta_1 \dfrac{y}{x}$

APPENDIX 9: ESTIMATING THE MINIMUM SAMPLE SIZE

In Chapter 2, we discussed the factors that influence the necessary sample size. In this appendix, we show how to calculate the minimum sample size needed to achieve the desired level of precision in the results. These are called power calculations.

In that chapter, we used the example of a survey of recent college graduates designed to see whether there is a difference in salaries between men and women. Table A9.1 describes five factors that help determine the minimum sample size needed. On the left side, we repeat the description of the factors influencing the sample size from Chapter 2 in terms of the study of gender differences in salaries. On the right side, we present the more technical description of the five factors.

According to the National Association of Colleges and Employers (2018), the average salary of a student who graduated in 2017 was $51,022. Suppose we expect our sample of graduates to be close to the national average in salaries and want to be able to detect a gender gap of at least 5% or (roughly) $2,500.

TABLE A9.1 ⬢ FACTORS INFLUENCING THE MINIMUM SAMPLE SIZE

Intuitive Explanation	Technical Explanation
How small a difference in salaries do we want to be able measure?	Minimum detectable effect size
How much variation is there in salaries?	Standard deviation of the variable of interest
How small should the probability be of incorrectly concluding that there *is* a difference between men and women?	Alpha is the maximum probability of Type I error that we are willing to accept.
How small should the probability be of making a mistake when we state that there is *no* difference between men and women?	Beta is the maximum Type II error that we are willing to accept. The power of the test is $1 - \beta$.
How was the sample selected?	Design effect

The standard deviation of the salaries of college graduates must be obtained from secondary data. Suppose we find that the standard deviation of these salaries is $11,000.

Type I error is to reject the null hypothesis (no gender difference) when it is true. In this case, Type I error would be to reject the equality of male and female wages when in fact they are equal. The maximum acceptable probability of a Type I error is labeled alpha or α. The convention in the social sciences is to set $\alpha = 0.05$, that is, to reject the null hypothesis only if the risk of being wrong is less than 0.05.

Type II error is the risk of accepting the null hypothesis when it is false. In our case, it is the risk of concluding that there is no gender difference in salaries when in fact there is one. The maximum allowable probability of Type II error is labeled beta or β. Researchers often set β at 0.20, although it depends on the "cost" of being wrong. It is worth noting that the power of the test is $1 - \beta$, or 0.80 in this case.

The design effect is an adjustment for the sampling design, which may increase or reduce the precision of estimates relative to a simple random sample. In this case, we will assume that we are able to draw a simple random sample of recent graduates, so we do not need to take into account the design effect.

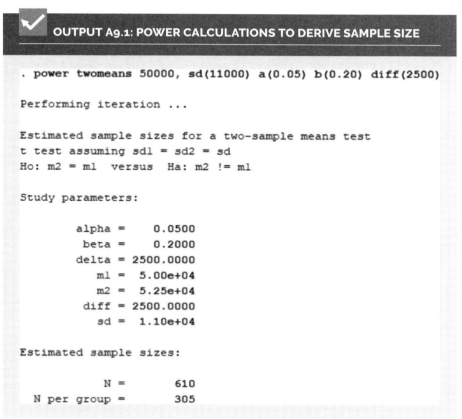

OUTPUT A9.1: POWER CALCULATIONS TO DERIVE SAMPLE SIZE

```
. power twomeans 50000, sd(11000) a(0.05) b(0.20) diff(2500)

Performing iteration ...

Estimated sample sizes for a two-sample means test
t test assuming sd1 = sd2 = sd
Ho: m2 = m1   versus   Ha: m2 != m1

Study parameters:

         alpha =     0.0500
          beta =     0.2000
         delta = 2500.0000
            m1 =   5.00e+04
            m2 =   5.25e+04
          diff = 2500.0000
            sd =   1.10e+04

 Estimated sample sizes:

             N =        610
 N per group =        305
```

The command in Stata for carrying out power calculations is **power**. It can be used to estimate the sample size based on the size effect, standard error, and levels of alpha and beta. Output A9.1 shows the command and the resulting output. Translating into English, the command says, "What is the sample size needed to detect a difference of $2,500 if the mean salary is $50,000, the standard deviation is $11,000, the maximum acceptable probability of Type I error is 0.05, and the maximum acceptable probability of Type II error is 0.20, assuming a simple random sample?"

The output repeats the values of the parameters being used to calculate the sample size. The result is shown at the bottom: We need a sample size of 610 graduates, including 305 men and 305 women. Note that we did not actually need to include the options **a(0.05)** and **b(0.20)** because these are the defaults. If we leave out these options, Stata will adopt $\alpha = 0.05$ and $\beta = 0.20$.

Stata allows us to carry out multiple power calculations with one command by inserting number lists in **a()**, **b()**, **sd()**, and **diff()**. A number list can be a series of numbers, such as "10 20 30 40 50," or it can be a range with step value such as "10(10)50," which means from 10 to 50 in increments of 10. Furthermore, if number lists are put into multiple options, Stata will carry out the calculations for all combinations. In the example below,

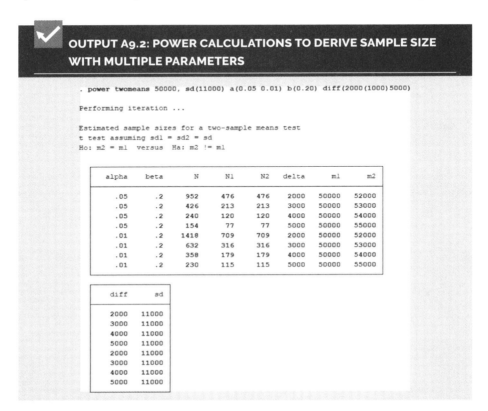

OUTPUT A9.2: POWER CALCULATIONS TO DERIVE SAMPLE SIZE WITH MULTIPLE PARAMETERS

```
. power twomeans 50000, sd(11000) a(0.05 0.01) b(0.20) diff(2000(1000)5000)

Performing iteration ...

Estimated sample sizes for a two-sample means test
t test assuming sd1 = sd2 = sd
Ho: m2 = m1  versus  Ha: m2 != m1
```

alpha	beta	N	N1	N2	delta	m1	m2
.05	.2	952	476	476	2000	50000	52000
.05	.2	426	213	213	3000	50000	53000
.05	.2	240	120	120	4000	50000	54000
.05	.2	154	77	77	5000	50000	55000
.01	.2	1418	709	709	2000	50000	52000
.01	.2	632	316	316	3000	50000	53000
.01	.2	358	179	179	4000	50000	54000
.01	.2	230	115	115	5000	50000	55000

diff	sd
2000	11000
3000	11000
4000	11000
5000	11000
2000	11000
3000	11000
4000	11000
5000	11000

we check four different size effects and two levels of alpha. The output is eight sample sizes, one for each combination of the four effect sizes and the two levels of alpha.

The column "N" indicates the sample size needed for each value of delta (the effect size) and alpha. For example, if we want to detect salary differences down to $2,000 at the 1% confidence level, we would need a sample of 1,418 graduates. At the other extreme, if we only need to detect a salary difference of $5,000 or more at the 5% confidence level, then a sample of just 154 graduates would suffice.

In this case, the power calculations were carried out to compare two sample means, hence the **twomeans** option. However, the **power** command will also carry out power calculations for other types of statistical tests:

- **onemean**—Comparison of a sample mean with a fixed number. Example: Is the average salary for graduates from this college greater than $50,000?

- **oneprop**—Comparison of a sample mean with a fixed proportion. Example: Is the unemployment rate for graduates from this college greater than 5%?

- **twoprop**—Comparison of two sample proportions. Example: Is the unemployment rate different for male and female graduates?

The **power** command is quite flexible and can be used in many other ways. For example,

- It can generate graphs or tables giving the sample size required for different values of alpha, beta, or the standard deviation.

- It will also calculate the minimum detectable size effect based on the sample size, the standard deviation, and alpha and beta.

- It will also calculate the power of the test (defined as $1 - \beta$) based on the size effect, the standard deviation, and alpha.

- Starting with Stata 15, it is possible to incorporate the sampling design into the power calculations, taking into account the design effect, that is, the effect of clustering and stratification on the relationship between precision, risk of Types I and II error, and sample size.

In summary, the **power** command is a useful tool in the design of surveys for examining the relationship between sample size and level of precision estimating parameters and carrying out statistical tests.

REFERENCES

National Association of Colleges and Employers. (2018). *Compensation*. Retrieved from www.naceweb.org/job-market/compensation/

GLOSSARY

Alpha level: The maximum acceptable probability of a Type I error (rejecting the null hypothesis when it is true), set by the researcher before starting the analysis. In social science research, alpha (α) is often 0.05, which corresponds to a 95% confidence interval.

Alternative hypothesis: The alternative of the null hypothesis. Often, the alternative hypothesis (denoted H_1 or H_a) is that a pattern observed in data is the result of a nonrandom effect. For example, the null hypothesis is that there is no change, and the alternative hypothesis is that there is a change.

Analysis of variance (ANOVA): A statistical method that tests for significant differences among two or more means.

Bar graph: A graph that uses rectangles, where the height or length of the rectangles represents the numerical values of different groups. For example, two bars could be used to represent the average wage of male and female workers.

Bartlett's test: A test used to determine if the variances of several samples are equal.

Binary variable (also called a dichotomous or dummy variable): A type of variable that has a value of either 0 or 1. For example, 0 = male and 1 = female.

Bonferroni test: A method of adjusting p-values when multiple tests are carried out to take into account the fact that the likelihood of getting a false positive (Type I error) rises with multiple tests.

Breusch–Pagan/Cook–Weisburg test: A test for heteroscedasticity in a linear regression model.

Categorical responses: Answers to a question that are limited to a fixed number of options, each one defined by a group or label. The alternative is continuous responses.

Categorical variable: A variable that allows a limited number of values, each of which represents a group and has no units (e.g., dollars or kilograms). Examples include gender, political affiliation, and religion. The alternative is continuous variables.

Chi-square distribution: The probability distribution of the sum of squared variables, each of which has a standard normal distribution. It has one parameter, k, which describes the number of random variables. It is often denoted by χ^2 or $\chi^2(k)$.

Chi-square statistic: A statistic that tests for a relationship between two categorical variables.

Cleaning data: The process of examining data for errors and inconsistencies and then correcting or dropping errors.

Closed-ended questions: Questions that allow only predefined categorical responses or numerical responses. The alternative is open-ended responses, which allow unlimited numerical and text responses.

Coefficient β: In linear regression analysis, a measure of the effect of a one-unit increase in an independent variable on the dependent variable, holding constant other independent variables.

Coefficient of determination: A statistic that measures the strength of the relationship between two continuous variables. Denoted by R^2, the coefficient of determination varies between 0 (no relationship) and 1 (perfect correlation).

Coefficient of variation: The ratio of the standard deviation of a variable to the mean of the variable. It is a unit-less measure of variability and is abbreviated as CV.

Cohen's d: A measure of the size of the difference between two variables relative to their standard deviations. It is usually used in conjunction with measures of the statistical significance of the difference.

Confidence interval: A pair of numbers that indicate the level of precision in measuring a number. For example, the 95% confidence interval is a range such that there is a 95% probability that the true value lies in that range.

Confidence level: The probability that the true value of a parameter lies within a specified range.

Continuous responses: Answers to a question that represent a numerical count, usually involving units such as hours, kilometers, or kilograms. The alternative is categorical responses.

Continuous variable: A variable whose values represent a measurement of some quantity, usually involving units such as hours, kilometers, or kilograms. The alternative is a categorical variable.

Correlation coefficient: A measure of strength of the relationship between two continuous variables. Denoted by r, it ranges from -1 (a perfect negative relationship) to 1 (a perfect positive relationship).

Cramér's V: A measure of the strength of the relationship between two categorical variables. It is used in conjunction with tests of statistical significance such as the chi-squared test.

Critical value: A threshold number that is compared with a test statistic to determine whether to reject the null hypothesis. The critical value is based on the alpha level, the type of probability distribution, and whether a one-tailed or two-tailed test is being used.

Cross tabulation: A table that shows the number or percentage of observations in each combination of two categorical variables.

Data analysis: The process of converting raw data into usable results such as tables, graphs, statistical tests, and regression analysis.

Data files: Files that contain values of one or more variables for each of one or more observations. In Stata, data files have the extension .dta.

Degrees of freedom: The number of independent observations in a sample minus the number of parameters that must be estimated from sample data.

Dependent variable: In regression analysis, the variable of interest that is being explained by the independent variable(s). *See* independent variable.

Descriptive statistics: Basic statistics that summarize a set of variables such as frequency tables for categorical variables and the mean, standard deviation, minimum, and maximum of continuous variables.

Do-file: A type of file in Stata that contains a series of commands to be carried out. Do-files have the file extension .do.

Enumerator: A person responsible for carrying out interviews and recording responses as part of a survey.

Error: In regression analysis, it is the difference between an observation and the true relationship between the dependent variable and the independent variables. It is denoted by ε.

Estimate: In statistics, an approximation of a population parameter calculated from sample data. It may be a point estimate (the most likely value) or an interval estimate (the confidence interval around the point estimate).

Estimation: A statistical procedure for generating one or more estimates, usually with confidence interval(s). This term is also used more narrowly to refer to generating a result that describes a population based on a sample.

Estimator: A method for calculating the value of an estimate.

Eta-square: A measure of the size of the relationship in an ANOVA.

Exhaustive responses: A set of answers that covers all possible responses to a question. This is a goal in the design of a questionnaire.

Expected value: In probability, the average result across all possible outcomes. It is calculated as the weighted average of different values of the variable, where the weights are the probabilities of getting each value.

F distribution: A probability distribution that describes the ratio of two variables, each of which has a chi-square distribution. The F distribution has two parameters, defining the degrees of freedom of each chi-square distribution. It is often denoted as $F(d_1, d_2)$.

Frequency table: A table that shows the number and/ or percentage of observations for each value of a categorical variable.

F test: A statistical test for a variable that has an *F* distribution under the null hypothesis. For example, *F* tests can be used to compare the means of two normally distributed variables with the same variance.

General Social Survey: A sociological survey of adults in the United States conducted regularly since 1972 by the University of Chicago.

Heteroscedasticity: A condition in which the variance of a variable differs across the range of observations. If the error term in a regression model is heteroscedastic, this violates the assumptions behind ordinary least squares regression analysis. The alternative is homoscedasticity.

Histogram: A graph showing the distribution of one variable, where the values of the variable are on the horizontal axis and the frequency of observations is on the vertical axis.

Homoscedasticity: A condition in which the variance of a variable is constant across observations. It is one of the assumptions behind ordinary least squares. The alternative is heteroscedasticity.

Hypothesis: An educated guess regarding the outcome of a test or experiment, which will be tested using data.

Hypothesis test: A formal procedure to decide whether to reject a null hypothesis using sample data.

Imputation: The practice of replacing missing values of a variable with estimates based on values of the same variable and/or other variables. A simple example would be replacing missing values with the mean of the variable.

Independence of observations: The condition where each observation has no effect on other observations.

Independent variable: A variable that causes or predicts the dependent variable. Also called the explanatory variable. *See* dependent variable.

Intercept: In a graph, the value of *Y* when *X* = 0. In a regression equation, it is also called the constant.

Interval scale: A type of measurement scale in which the difference between values is meaningful (based on measured units) but the zero is arbitrary. Examples include temperature in Fahrenheit or Celsius and year. *See also* nominal scale, ordinal scale, ratio scale.

Kurtosis: A measure of the "thickness" of the tails in a probability distribution. The kurtosis of a normal distribution is 3.

Leading question: A question that is phrased in a way that prompts or encourages a particular response. Leading questions should be avoided in research questionnaires.

Levene's test: A test of the null hypothesis that the variance in two or more groups is the same.

Likert scale: A set of responses designed to capture the strength of agreement with a statement or an evaluation of an object or experience. Typically, a Likert scale uses five responses, with the middle one being neutral.

Linear regression: A statistical method that identifies a linear equation that best fits the relationship between one dependent variable and one or more independent (or explanatory) variables, subject to some assumptions.

Literature: A set of scholarly papers that describe the results of research on a topic.

Log file: A type of file that contains both commands and the output from those commands. In Stata, log files have one of two possible extensions: .log or .smcl.

Logit regression: A statistical method for identifying the nonlinear equation that best fits the relationship between a binary dependent variable and one or more independent (or explanatory) variables, subject to some assumptions. Also called logistic regression. It is similar to a probit regression but uses a different function.

Macro: In Stata, a temporary variable that can be used in loops and other programming. Stata has local and global macros.

Margin of error: The maximum expected difference between the true value and a sample estimate of a parameter due to sampling for a given probability. The margin of error may be expressed at different confidence levels, most commonly 95%.

Mean: The average value of a set of numbers or the expected value of a probability distribution.

Measurement error: The difference between a measured value of an observation and its true value.

Median: The middle value of a set of numbers, such that there are equal numbers of observations greater and less than this value. It is equivalent to the 50th percentile.

Multicollinearity: In regression analysis, a condition in which two or more independent variables are closely correlated with one another. Multicollinearity reduces the precision of coefficient estimates, but does not make them biased.

Multiple regression analysis: A statistical method for estimating the relationship between a dependent variable and two or more independent variables. *See also* regression analysis, simple regression analysis.

Nominal scale: A scale for categorical variables in which each value describes a category or label with no natural order. The values are not measured, so the interval between values is not meaningful. Examples include sex (male and female) and region (north, center, south). *See also* interval scale, ordinal scale, ratio scale.

Nonnormality: A condition in which a variable is not normally distributed. In regression, it refers to the situation where the error terms are not normally distributed.

Nontechnical audience: A type of reader or listener who does not have advanced training in a topic. In the context of this book, it refers to those who do not have a background in statistical methods.

Normal distribution: A probability distribution that occurs frequently in statistics, having two parameters: the mean and the standard deviation. The normal distribution has a symmetric bell shape with infinite tails on either side.

Null hypothesis: The null hypothesis is a testable statement indicating that there is no significant difference in a set of observations. For example, in comparing two means, the null hypothesis is that there is no difference. In regression analysis, the null hypothesis is usually that the coefficients are zero.

Observation: One element of a variable or a set of variables. Each observation is usually represented as a row in a database. *See* unit of observation.

One-sample *t* test: A statistical test that compares a sample mean with a fixed (nonrandom) number.

One-tailed test: A test of a null hypothesis in which the alternative hypothesis is expressed as an inequality (greater than or less than).

Open-ended questions: Questions that leave room for respondents to answer in their own words. *See* closed-ended questions.

Ordinal scale: A scale for categorical variables in which each value describes a category or label with a natural order, but they are not measured, so the interval between values is not meaningful. Examples include quality (good, better, best) and military rank. *See also* interval scale, nominal scale, ratio scale.

Outlier: An observation that lies extremely far from the mean or median. It is sometimes defined in terms of the number of standard deviations from the mean.

Parameter: A measurable characteristic of a population, such as the mean or the standard deviation. In contrast, a statistic is a characteristic of a sample.

Pearson's chi-square: A statistical test applied to sets of categorical data to test the null hypothesis that there are no differences between the sets. It could be used to test whether there is a gender difference in political party affiliation (two categorical variables).

Percentile: The percentage of observations of a variable that are below a given value. For example, 100 is the 30th percentile if 30% of the observations are below 100.

Pie graph: A circular graph divided into slices, where each slice represents a category and the size of the slice represents the percentage of observations in this category. Also called a pie chart.

Population: The complete set of observations that can be made. For example, the population of car dealers in the United States is the full list of all car dealers.

Predicted value: In regression analysis, the value of the dependent variable that is expected for each observation based on the values of the independent variables and the estimated coefficients.

Probit regression: A statistical method for identifying the nonlinear equation that best fits the relationship between a binary dependent variable and one or more independent (or explanatory) variables, subject to some assumptions. It is similar to a logit regression but uses a different function.

Purposive sampling: A method of selecting a sample that does not rely on random selection.

***p*-Value:** The probability that a test statistic is larger than the observed value if the null hypothesis is true and if the assumptions behind the test are valid. A low *p*-value (often <0.05) is interpreted as a rejection of the null hypothesis.

Questionnaire: A set of questions and rules for coding the responses that is used to guide an interview and collect data for a study.

Random sampling: A group of methods for selecting a subset of the population where the selection is made using random numbers. Types of random sampling include simple random sampling, stratified random sampling, and multistage random sampling.

Ratio scale: A type of measurement scale for continuous variables in which the interval is meaningful (based on measured units) and there is a natural zero. Examples include income, weight, and length. *See also* interval scale, nominal scale, ordinal scale.

Regression analysis: A statistical method for estimating the relationship between a dependent variable and one or more independent variables. *See also* multiple regression analysis, simple regression analysis.

Research question: The query that a researcher attempts to answer in a study.

Residual: In regression analysis, the difference between the predicted value of the dependent variable and the observed value. It is often denoted by *e*.

Respondent fatigue: The tendency of survey respondents to become tired or impatient with long interviews, affecting data quality.

Sample: A subset of observations selected from a population to make inferences about the population. For example, a sample of 1,000 voters may be selected to make inferences about the popularity of a candidate.

Sampling distribution: The distribution of all possible values of a statistic.

Sampling weights: Numbers used to compensate for the under- and oversampling caused by the sampling design so that the weighted sample statistics are unbiased estimates of population parameters. The weights are calculated as the inverse of the probability of selection.

Significance level: The probability of committing a Type I error, meaning rejecting the null hypothesis when it is actually true.

Simple random sample: A sampling method in which the researcher starts with a full list of the population and selects a sample with each unit having an equal probability of selection.

Simple regression analysis: A statistical method for estimating the relationship between a dependent variable and one independent variable. *See also* multiple regression analysis, regression analysis.

Skewness: A characteristic of a probability distribution that is often used to assess the level of asymmetry. A symmetric distribution has a skewness of zero, though the reverse is not always true.

Skip patterns: In questionnaire design, the rules for skipping over questions based on the responses to earlier questions. For example, if the respondent is single, the skip patterns indicate that one should skip over questions about his or her spouse.

Standard deviation: A statistic that measures the degree of dispersion around the mean. The standard deviation is the square root of the variance.

Standard error of the mean: The standard deviation of the means of all possible samples from a population. An estimate of this parameter can be calculated as the standard deviation of the sample divided by the square root of the sample size.

Statistic: A measurable characteristic of a sample, such as the sample mean or the sample standard deviation. In contrast, parameters are characteristics of the population.

Statistically significant: A condition in which the probability of Type I error (rejecting the null hypothesis when it is true) is below the value of alpha (the highest acceptable level of Type I error). In practice, it is often defined as when the *p*-value is less than 0.05, indicating that the 95% confidence interval does not include zero.

Strata: In sampling, groups within a population, each with their own sampling design. The singular is stratum.

Stratification: In sampling, the process of dividing the population into groups (or strata) and having a different sampling design for each one. For example, a population may be stratified by region or by income group.

Systematic random sample: A random sampling of units characterized by an equal interval between selected units. It is used to ensure that the sample is dispersed across the population in the dimension in which they are sorted.

t **Distribution:** A probability distribution that results from estimating the mean from a normal distribution with a small sample.

Technical audience: Readers or listeners who have some training in scientific methods and statistics. The type of audience influences the appropriate writing style.

Two independent-samples *t* test: Compares the means of two independent groups to determine whether there is statistical evidence that the population means are different from each other.

Type I error: The error of rejecting the null hypothesis when it is true.

Type II error: The error of accepting the null hypothesis when it is false.

Unit of observation: An object about which information is collected. For example, in survey data, the unit of observation may be people, households, companies, or some other category of objects. *See* observation.

Variable: A quantified characteristic or attribute of each observation that varies across observations. In a database, each variable is usually represented by a column of numbers.

Variance: A parameter used to indicate the degree of dispersion in a variable. It is the square of the standard deviation.

Z **score:** The value of an observation minus the mean, divided by the standard deviation. In other words, it measures how many standard deviations above or below the mean an observation is.

ABOUT THE AUTHORS

Lisa Daniels is the Hodson Trust Professor of Economics at Washington College in Chestertown, Maryland. She specializes in development in Africa, where she worked for 10 years, beginning as a Peace Corps volunteer. During her time in Africa, she studied agricultural markets, market information systems, poverty trends, and micro- and small-scale enterprises. As part of her research on micro- and small-scale enterprises, she directed national surveys of 7,000 to 56,000 households and businesses in Bangladesh, Botswana, Kenya, Malawi, and Zimbabwe funded by the U.S. Agency for International Development. In each survey, she was responsible for the questionnaire design, sample selection, data collection and analysis, and report preparation. Her work from these surveys and other research in Africa and Asia appears in consulting reports and in peer-reviewed journals. In addition to research and fieldwork, she has taught a range of courses over the past 22 years, including a research methods course and a data analysis course that she has taught 16 times. She has also presented her work related to teaching at more than a dozen workshops.

Nicholas Minot is a Senior Research Fellow at the International Food Policy Research Institute (IFPRI) in Washington, D.C. Since joining IFPRI in 1997, he has carried out research on agricultural market reform, income diversification, spatial patterns in policy, and food price volatility in developing countries. This research often involves carrying out surveys of farmers, cooperatives, traders, and consumers to better understand changes in food marketing systems. In addition to research, he is involved in outreach and capacity-building activities, including offering short courses on the use of Stata for survey data analysis. Before joining IFPRI, he taught at the University of Illinois in Urbana–Champaign, served as a policy adviser in Zimbabwe, and analyzed survey data in Rwanda. Overall, he has worked in more than two dozen countries in Latin America, sub-Saharan Africa, North Africa, and Asia.

The authors are married, live in Annapolis, Maryland, and have two children—Andrea (20) and Alex (17)—and one cat, Dusty (12).

NAME INDEX

SUBJECT INDEX

Active voice, 298

Adjusted R^2, 199

Admitted Student Questionnaire (ASQ) dataset, 58, 68, 162

Alpha level (α), 124–125, 166, 295, 348–353, 357

Alternative hypothesis, 163, 166, 326

American Psychological Association (APA) style, 296–298

Analysis of variance (ANOVA). *See* One-way analysis of variance

APA style, 296–298

append command, 53

Areas under the normal curve, 117–118t, 123, 126, 328–329t. *See also* Standard scores

Assumptions
  for chi-square, 178
  for logit regression, 260
  for one-way ANOVA, 163–165
  for regression analysis. *See* Regression diagnostics
  for two independent-samples t test, 147–148, 151

Asterisks in Stata® do-files, 49

Autocorrelation, 219n

Average. *See* Mean

Bar graphs, 96, 97f, 305–306

Bartlett's test for homogeneity of variances, 165

base(3) option, 272

Bell curve. *See* Normal distribution

Belmont Report, 38

Best linear unbiased estimates (BLUE), 218–219, 244, 249

Between-group variability estimation, 160

Biases
  in nonprobability sampling, 15
  in questionnaires, 33

Bimodal distribution, 126

Binary variables, 203, 254
  linear probability model, 257
  as dependent variable, 256–258
  as independent variable, 203–209, 235
  See also Dummy variables

bin() command, 100, 304

Biomedical research ethics, 38

Bonferroni test, 166

Box plots, 96, 98–100, 307

Breusch-Pagan/Cook-Weisberg test, 240, 250

browse command, 222–223

Capital punishment, 173–174

Categorical variables, 45, 75–77
  coding for logit regression analysis, 262
  descriptive statistics for, 91–94
  dummy variables in regression analysis, 203–209, 235
  survey responses, 35–36
  See also Regression analysis with categorical dependent variables

Causal relationships, 195, 242

Censuses, 13, 75

Central limit theorem, 126, 244

Chicago Manual of Style, 296n

Chi-square distribution, 175

Chi-squared test, 172, 321t
  assumptions, 178
  calculating, 175–177
  conducting, 177–178
  interpreting output, 179–181
  presenting results, 181–182
  summary of commands used in chapter, 182
  when to use, 174–175t

clear command, 261, 317

Closed-ended questions, 28, 34, 35–36

Cluster sampling (multistage sampling), 19

codebook command, 60, 66

Coefficient of determination (R^2), 194, 199

Coefficient of variation (CV), 88–90

Cohen's d, 152

collapse command, 335

College freshmen weight gain, 132–133

Command Window, 44, 46

Comparing two means. *See* Two independent-samples t test

Computer-assisted personal interview (CAPI) methods, 29

Conclusions section of a research report, 300–301

Confidence intervals, 15, 125
  interpreting t-test results, 139–140, 152
  regression analysis output, 201
  reporting results, 212

Confidentiality, 38

Confounding factors, 242

Consent, 38

Continuous variables, 76
  descriptive statistics for, 83–90
  survey responses, 34–35
  using cross-tabulation, 94

gen or **generate** command, 63–64, 203–204, 208, 213, 214, 233, 250, 251, 318, 339, 341–347
Google Doc, 96
Google Scholar, 5
graph command, 101–103, 105, 303, 305–307
Graphs, 96
    bar graphs, 96, 97*f*, 305–306
    box plots, 96, 98–100, 307
    histograms, 100, 112, 304
    pie charts, 101–103, 303
    quick reference guide, 303–307
    scatter plots, 190, 227

help command, 54, 119, 128
Help in Stata®, 54–55
Heteroscedasticity, 219, 225, 238–241, 250, 260
Histograms, 100, 112, 304
hist or **histogram command**, 100, 105, 112, 128, 245, 252, 304
Homogeneity of variances assumptions, 148, 151, 164, 165
Housework, 143 (article), 144
Hypothesis development, 6–7
Hypothesis testing, 122–123
    confidence intervals, 125
    decision rules for statistical significance, 326–327
    decision tree for choosing right statistic, 134*f*, 325
    interpreting results, 125
    null hypothesis, 122
    presenting results, 127–128
    rejecting or not rejecting null hypothesis, 124–125
    Stata quick reference guide, 311–315
    summary of commands used in chapter, 128
    summary of statistical tests, 320–324*t*
    testing for statistical significance, 122–123
Hypothesis testing about a single mean. *See* One-sample *t* test
Hypothesis testing about two independent means. *See* Two independent-samples *t* test
Hypothesis testing using regression. *See* Regression analysis

if command, 64
Imperfect multicollinearity, 235
Imputation, 69
Independence of observations assumption, 147, 163, 178
Independent variables, 93, 230–232
    best linear unbiased estimates (BLUE), 218–219
    diagnosing regression assumption issues. *See* Regression diagnostics
    dummy variables in regression analysis, 203–209
    endogeneity, 196, 219, 242–244
    error term correlation, 242

    exogenous, 195, 242
    interaction effects, 226–227
    measurement error, 219–224
    multicollinearity, 217
    multiple regression analysis, 203
    presenting regression analysis results, 211
    regression analysis, 188, 195, 203*n*
Indicator variables, 203
Informed consent, 38
Institutional review boards (IRBs), 38–39
Instrumental variables, 243
Interaction effects, 226–227
Interquartile range, 83
Interval scales, 76–77
    descriptive statistics for, 81–83
Introduction section of a research report, 285–289
Inverse probability sampling weights (IPSW), 22
ivregress command, 243

kdensity command, 248
keep if command, 317
Kurtosis, 246–249

label define command, 49, 50, 55, 71
label list, 262
label values command, 49, 55, 71
lab or **label** command, 245, 263, 272, 278–279, 316
Leading questions, 32–33
Likert-type scales, 77
Limitations of studies, discussing in a research paper, 299–300
Linear probability model (LPM), 257
Linear regression analysis, 186, 195–201, 322*t*
    best linear unbiased estimates (BLUE), 218–219, 244, 249
    linear probability model for binary dependent variables, 257
    presenting results, 211–213
    summary of commands used in chapter, 213–214
    See also Regression analysis; Regression diagnostics
Linear regression analysis, testing assumptions and remedying violations. *See* Regression diagnostics
list command, 316
Listwise deletion, 69
Literature review, 4–6, 289–292
Logarithmic transformations for regression models, 232, 248
    double-log functions, 345–348
    semilog functions, 341–344
log close command, 53
log command, 51
Log files in Stata®, 51–54